The Business of Crime

The Business of Crime

A Documentary Study of Organized Crime in the American Economy

EDITED AND WITH AN INTRODUCTION BY

Alan A. Block

Westview Press

BOULDER • SAN FRANCISCO • OXFORD

Copyright © 1991 by Westview Press, Inc.

Published in 1991 in the United States of America by Westview Press, Inc., 5500 Central Avenue, Boulder, Colorado 80301, and in the United Kingdom by Westview Press, 36 Lonsdale Road, Summertown, Oxford OX2 7EW

Library of Congress Cataloging-in-Publication Data
Block, Alan A.
    The business of crime : a documentary study of organized crime in the American economy / Alan A. Block.
    p. cm.
Includes index.
ISBN 0-8133-7942-3 — ISBN 0-8133-7943-1 (PB)
    1. Organized crime—Economic aspects—United States. 2. Business—United States—Corrupt practices. I. Title.
HV6448.B55 1991
364.1′06′0973—dc20   90-43498
                                                                              CIP

Printed and bound in the United States of America

The paper used in this publication meets the requirements of the American National Standard for Permanence of Paper for Printed Library Materials Z39.48-1984.

10   9   8   7   6   5   4   3   2   1

Contents

Acknowledgments

The idea for this book came while I was teaching a graduate seminar on organized crime, part of my department's new graduate program in the administration of justice. I was determined to find a work that would both summarize relevant material on the organization of crime as well as introduce students to various kinds of readily available data dealing with organized crime, particularly its entrepreneurial expressions. The task stymied me. There are, of course, numerous excellent monographs on different aspects of organized crime but none that explicitly fulfill my dual purposes. That frustration and the sympathetic ear of Spencer Carr, senior editor at Westview Press, led to this book.

In all my work at The Pennsylvania State University, I have received ample support from Daniel Maier-Katkin, chair of the Department of Administration of Justice. It is he who supplied the critical material necessary for contemporary scholarship and created the environment essential for reflection and writing. My debt to Daniel grows year by year; it is starting to worry me. The department's senior secretary as well as my friend, Melody Lane, typed the manuscript with her usual skill and breakneck speed. Her dependability at meeting even the harshest deadlines is unsurpassed.

Because of the genesis and purpose behind *The Business of Crime*, I would like to dedicate it to that first class of graduate students, especially the indefatigable Lisa Vardzel.

Alan A. Block

1

Introduction: The Business of Organized Crime

The presence of organized crime in the U.S. industrial economy is undeniable. This book presents primary evidence of this association through an assortment of government documents generated in the past three decades. These edited records form the heart of this work, and I intend to let them speak mostly for themselves. By doing so, I hope to introduce students to the rich cache of material on organized crime available in the government (state and federal) documents section of research libraries, in the libraries and archives of state capitals, and in easily available court documents. Although two complementary purposes--intellectual and pedagogical--are sufficient to warrant this book, I also wish to advance some propositions concerning the interplay of organized crime and U.S. economic institutions in order to provide a context for the documents I've chosen.[1]

I have always believed--along with many others--that organized crime is completely enmeshed within the U.S. industrial economy. It is not some sort of peripheral aberration but exerts a force within the many layers of industry. Apocryphal statements attributed to racketeers, such as "We are bigger than General Motors," signify a giant, cohesive organized-crime conspiracy. In fact, leaving aside for the moment the questions of size and overall influence, it has been shown that organized criminals did work closely with one American car giant. This was the Ford Motor Company, whose contact with the underworld was engineered by Ford's security chief, Harry Bennett. Always acting with Henry Ford's blessing, Bennett "positively revelled in making personal contact with the underworld, [his] memoirs are a boastful catalogue of the murderers, racketeers, and extortionists whose friendship he purchased with the funds and influence of the Ford Motor Company."[2] Among the friends he cultivated was Chester LaMare, a bootlegger and killer who led an important Italian-American gang in Detroit. Bennett gave Crescent Motor Sales, a Ford agency, to LaMare and also granted the racketeer an exclusive franchise to supply fruit to the lunch stands and canteens in Ford plants.

1

Bennett was certainly bold, once inviting a gangster known as Black Leo (Leonard Cellura) to a luncheon attended by the governor of Michigan. In the East, Bennett contacted New York mobsters Joe Adonis, Sr., and Tony D'Anna and gave them lucrative "franchises to truck Ford cars to dealers on the eastern seaboard.[3] Ford biographer Robert Lacey comments, "By the middle of the 1930s, Harry Bennett had woven the Ford Motor Company into a network of underworld connections with hoodlums of largely Italian origin, and the unholy alliance came into its own in the battle which Ford fought against the unions with increasing ferocity as the decade went by."[4] Mobster control of Ford agencies and distributorships long outlived the violent union-management battles of the 1930s. Professional criminals seek economic opportunities in the same arenas as do many others. Moreover, their typical lack of restraint may be their most appealing quality to those, like Ford and Bennett, who were helped by their violence against unions and were also excited by it.

The involvement of organized criminals in businesses large and small has been noted time and again.[5] For instance, an investigation into organized crime in New York that began in 1930 inventoried the types of businesses "pervaded" by racketeers: bead, cinder, cloth shrinking, clothing, construction, flower shops, Fulton fish market, funeral, fur dressing, grap, hod carriers, ice, kosher butchers, laundry, leather, live poultry, master barbers, milk, millinery, musical, night patrol, neckwear, newsstands, operating engineers, overall, paper box, paper hangers, shirt makers, taxicabs, waterfront workers, and window cleaners.[6] New York's economy was overrun by organized crime. Garment manufacturing, one of New York's premier industries, provides a clear example. Key parts of the manufacturing process were gangster controlled, in addition to those mentioned above. Organized criminals regulated the trucking of garments in and out of New York and heavily influenced the industry's trade and labor associations. In 1910, 47 percent of Manhattan's factories manufactured clothing and 46 percent of the city's industrial labor force was employed in that industry.[7] Add to garment manufacturing the construction and waterfront industries, food distribution, and at least one form of public transportation, to judge just how fully integrated organized crime and the city's economy had become.

If New York in 1930 seems too far removed from the present, then regard the data provided in the fall of 1963 by the Senate's Permanent Subcommittee on Investigations, in the full flush of its "Mafia" counting following the supposed revelations of mob informant Joseph Valachi. The appendix to the hearing record on <u>Organized Crime and Illicit Traffic in Narcotics</u> lists infiltrated firms in finance, waste disposal, food, construction, insurance, liquor, vending, jukeboxes, and several others.[8] More elaborate information on criminal infiltration into Detroit businesses was provided in Exhibit No. 36, a chart entitled "Some Legitimate Businesses Owned, Infiltrated or Influenced by the Mafia." Bars, restaurants, real estate companies, bakeries, motels, a barber college, construction firms, metal finishers, tool and die companies, cleaners, food wholesalers, farms, insurance agencies, race tracks, truck companies, warehouses, paving and steel firms, car washes, office buildings, and many other types of enterprises were catalogued from information gathered by the Criminal Information Bureau of the Detroit Police Department.

On the New York waterfront, organized crime's control of the port was manifested through its control of the International Longshoremen's Association (the nation's primary waterfront labor union), several score private businesses, and the major shipping and stevedore companies. For instance, in the 1950s, organized crime chieftain Vito Genovese bought a 49 percent interest for $245 in the waterfront firm Erb Strapping, "which straps cargo, that is, the placing of steel straps traveling aboard ship, a service incidental to the movement of waterborne freight."[9] Subsequently, Erb Strapping became a million dollar business, and by the late 1960s it was the "dominant company in the Port of New York in the areas of strapping, coopering and inspection of meats."[10]

In the mid-1960s, Erb Strapping's insurance business was turned over to a new company owned by the son of a prominent mobster very closely associated with Genovese. Further investigations by the Waterfront Commission (itself created to combat the racketeers' domination of the port) revealed that a Genovese partner, Peter DeFeo, apparently controlled the house trucker at Pier 13, East River, New York City, and at Port Newark. This outfit had a "monopoly in the trucking of bananas imported into New York City and consigned to jobbers within a 50 mile radius of New York City and somewhat farther on Long Island."[11]

Other less well known organized crime figures also attempted to mask their activities in legitimate businesses or used firms to squeeze illegal monies from others. The Chet Maintenance Corporation, owned by a former New York police officer and his partner (who was convicted for grand larceny and robbery), is a case in point. It provided jobs for racketeers such as Harold Bell and John Keefe and consistently overbilled shipping companies for phantom employees. Keefe had actually been barred from the New York waterfront years earlier, so notorious were his racketeering activities. That prohibition meant little, however, as Keefe was simply put on the books of the company's affiliate in Baltimore, Maryland.[12]

In the early 1970s, one of the more surprising discussions about the association of organized crime and legitimate businesses occurred when a sports conglomerate known as Emprise Corporation came under scrutiny. Details about Emprise and its subsidiaries, including a firm named Sportservice Corporation, were provided by Congressman Sam Steiger of Arizona and Nevada's Attorney General Lee Johnson. According to the two men, Emprise had a greater hold upon American professional sports than any other entity and was also joined to organized crime in a variety of ways. In 1970, Congressman Steiger noted that Emprise "controls or owns completely over 450 separate corporate entities in at least 23 states, the District of Columbia, Canada, Puerto Rico, and England."[13] Emprise developed from "a concessionaire for the Detroit Tigers in 1927 to a present day structure holding concession rights for seven major league baseball clubs, eight professional football teams, four hockey teams, plus concessions at fifty horse and dog tracks throughout the United States."[14] Emprise or its subsidiaries also operated as the concessionaires at approximately three hundred theaters, and at bowling alleys, drive-in theaters, airport restaurants, and air-catering services. In addition, they owned outright a professional basketball team and had obtained an interest in the Montreal Expos.

The Nevada attorney general's investigators noted that Emprise (Sportservice) was a financial "laundromat" for organized crime, providing phony loans to racketeers: "Organized crime . . . is faced with one major consistent problem, that is how to invest its 'bad' or 'black' money in legitimate enterprises. . . . It [is] necessary for these men to hide their interest behind 'loans' ostensibly made to them, which they in turn invest."[15] The investigators uncovered loans and other business arrangements between Emprise and organized crime figures from Detroit, Cleveland, St. Louis, Chicago, Wheeling (West Virginia), Las Vegas, Los Angeles, and New York.

Organized criminal activities are overwhelmingly embedded in enterprises. They mix legitimate and illegitimate interests to wash money, to secure the economic edge this mix provides, and to confuse law enforcement. Even illicit endeavors such as policy (numbers gambling) that may at first glance seem only to need secrecy are commercially covered. In 1944, New York City's Department of Investigation, in a communication to Mayor Fiorello H. LaGuardia that dealt with one of the reportedly largest policy banks operating in the Harlem area, noted that the principals shielded the operation behind their "check cashing business known as Harlem Check Cashing Corp."[16] The corporation was used "as a reservoir" to aid the racketeers in syphoning part of the funds from their policy racket into an outwardly legitimate business.[17]

Sophisticated drug smuggling is also conducted through a variety of companies--freight forwarders, import-export firms, travel agencies, and several types of ethnic food businesses. A significant portion of Sicilian-based heroin smuggling in the 1970s was covered in the United States by chains of pizza parlors, including the M. Piancone Pizzerias.[18] The Piancone Pizzerias (primarily in the Northeast, though Piancone was also expanding in and around San Diego shortly before federal agents wrapped up his operations) were also used to facilitate the smuggling of Sicilian gangsters into the United States. In 1978, the Drug Enforcement Administration claimed to have apprehended "over 30 aliens in Piancone owned or franchised establishments" and claimed that "aliens sponsored by PIANCONE are known to have become involved with arson, mob assassination attempts and large scale narcotic smuggling."[19]

Organized Criminals and Violence

The success of organized criminals is contingent upon many factors. The primary one may be their reputation for violence. An important extortion trial in Michigan in the early 1980s confirmed this commonly held belief. Vincent Meli, whose official position was head of public relations for a Detroit steel hauling firm that was central to the racketeering conspiracy, had a reputation of being a member of the Mafia. Testimony about this connection was admitted in evidence in order to allow jurors to evaluate the victims' state of mind. Meli, who was convicted, charged on appeal that the "Mafia" discussion was prejudicial and thus should not have been allowed. The Sixth Circuit Court of Appeals affirmed the conviction by finding reputational evidence admissible.[20] As this extortion case illustrated, a person's reputation for violence among clients, associates, and victims can have an affect and can be considered as evidence.

A reputation for violence is naturally not the same as actual violence, and there are some who argue that the reputations of organized criminals for violence are often inflated. In a discussion of loansharking in New York, for instance, Peter Reuter and Jonathan Rubinstein recognized, "violence and . . . threats are generally believed to be the essential and critical operating features of the successful loanshark."[21] But according to their research, the probability of "intimidation and threat . . . as a central part of the collection procedure for many loansharks" was not very high. Significantly, Reuter and Rubinstein determined that many (perhaps most) loansharks were not organized criminals in the traditional sense, that is, they did not belong to a government-recognized crime syndicate or family. Their sample included "unconnected" criminal lenders with modest ambitions, who did not look to cause trouble, and did not wish to initiate violent methods of collection should borrowers be unreliable. Debtors who did not meet their payments would simply be denied future access to funds.

Reuter and Rubinstein critiqued the more-or-less official characterization of loansharking as an inherently violent, mob-dominated activity. Besides questions raised about formal organized crime involvement, there were other reasons, they reckoned, for misunderstanding the relationship of loansharking and violence. One was the nature of police data. They had no discernible complaint with the material in police intelligence files, only with the clumsy way others drew conclusions based on this information. Reuter and Rubinstein determined that most investigations of loansharking began with a customer complaint that naturally followed some sort of threat: "The police, therefore, dealt mainly with those loansharks who are prepared to resort to physical violence."[22] They contended that people who rely on police data incorporate an important bias concerning loansharks and their activities.

Even this careful work, however, seems to contradict its own interesting premise. When Reuter and Rubinstein finally proposed a definition of loansharking, they listed four basic stipulations. According to one, "threats or violence in the event of the failure of a loanshark borrower to make repayment on time, <u>while not anticipated by the borrower, are certainly understood by him to be a possible consequence of the type of agreement into which he has entered</u>" (emphasis added).[23] This waffling over the issue of violence undercuts their point. Indeed, if borrowers believe the lenders may use violence, then the conclusions drawn from police reports may not be so off the mark as Reuter and Rubinstein suggest. Possibly those borrowers who do not complain have not been threatened only because they are already motivated by the implicit threat always present in these types of agreements. The value of a bad reputation (which Reuter later cogently discussed in <u>Disorganized Crime</u>) operates in these transactions as part of the subscript.[24]

A more interesting question is how loansharks have gained such helpful bad reputations, if so many are in fact not violent. One answer might lie in comparative data that compare violent encounters in loanshark transactions and in other illicit enterprises. Reuter and Rubinstein's appraisal then could be correct but not very relevant. There may actually be more than enough attendant violence within the loanshark environment to color all of its participants--even the more-or-less nonviolent. The threat of violence is symbolic in any case. Surely, frequent assaults on a significantly large percentage of borrowers would discourage them from participating. It is clear, nevertheless, that there must be enough violent loansharks and mayhem stemming from late payments to create an effective symbol. There are many examples of violent loansharks to support the image.

Let us consider what borrowers contemplating the illicit market might have concluded from a 1984 New York case centering on a leasing firm called Cooper Funding. The U.S. District Court in New York's Southern District charged Cooper Funding's president and fifteen others with racketeering and loansharking.[25] It involved figures identified by the government as well-known La Cosa Nostra (LCN) members, such as Vincent Joseph Rotondo. The most important principals, however, were non-Italian racketeers Melvin Cooper, the head of Cooper Funding, Cooper Equities, Etna Leasing Services, and, eventually, Resource Capital; Jesse David Hyman, a dentist with a clinic in Buffalo; and Chaim Gerlitz, a cantor associated with Temple Israel, Great Neck, Long Island, New York. Among the victims of this loanshark group were dress firms, discos, restaurants, and trucking businesses in New York, as well as garbage businesses located across the nation. The trucking scam worked as follows: Cooper Funding leased trucks at very high interest rates to individuals who were coerced into forming their own trucking businesses. Cooper's trucks "would be of poor mechanical quality and when the individuals leasing the trucks would be unable to perform enough work to keep up with the payments, the trucks would be repossessed and again leased out in a similar manner."[26] The supply of reluctant customers was provided by the bosses of the East Coast Truckers Association, Roadmasters Incorporated, and Independent Truckers.[27]

Violence was this group's stock in trade. Of particular importance was Hyman whose criminal activities, like the rest of those charged in this case, were extremely widespread. Hyman's primary dental practice was a clinic that handled the needs of Local 210 of the Laborers International Union of North America in Buffalo, New York. There was a kickback scheme between Hyman and union officers, some of whom were represented by Buffalo-area organized criminals. Buffalo, though, was not the only area to receive Human's dental attention. The New Jersey Commission of Investigation in an inquiry titled "Organized Crime Infiltration of Dental Care Plan Organizations," stated that Hyman moved money from organized crime gangs in Cleveland, Buffalo, Boston, and New York City into New Jersey dental clinics that were under contract with Teamster locals. Profits, it was found, were "siphoned back to these criminals."[28]

Hyman and Cooper were convicted of a staggering array of criminal activities. From government wiretaps and electronic bugs, evidence was gathered on the following crimes: "loansharking, advance fee schemes, bank frauds, ERISA [union pension fund] frauds and embezzlements, Taft-Hartley Act violations, money laundering, counterfeit videotapes, narcotics conspiracy, petty larcenies, grand larcenies, bribery, usury, tax frauds, illegal gambling, SBA [Small Business Administration] frauds, perjury, and obstruction of justice."[29] To say the least, this was serious organized crime, in which both actual and potential brutality was at the center of affairs.

Two major players in the Buffalo scheme were murdered in 1980 after a government investigation began probing the clinic's affairs. One was killed "shortly after he received immunity to testify before a Federal Grand Jury in the case," the other because he was thought to be an informer.[30] In the Cooper Funding/Resource Capital trial, mention was made of yet another homicide. In 1979, during an investigation of Cooper's business activities, Cooper Funding employee Richard Stone, a government informant, was shot several times, stabbed in the chest, and stuffed in the trunk of a cadillac registered to a Cooper company. According to the court transcriptions, violence was so much a part of this complex loanshark group that the government's argument for anonymous jury selection was based on the defendants' record of past violence, including the three murders.[31] The court was also told that Cooper borrowers were both threatened and beaten. Concerned for the jury's safety, prosecutors asserted that three of the Cooper Funding defendants, who were also associated with another organized crime group, had been charged in a different case with bribing a juror and witnesses and more ominously, with assassinating two potential witnesses.[32] The Cooper defendants had a penchant for mayhem; five of them had past arrests for assault, arson, armed robbery, and battery.

Criminal Conspiracy and Instability

Constant scheming is one of the least "appreciated" characteristics of organized criminals, who exist in a world of daily criminal opportunities. At the most fundamental level, the endless weaving of criminal conspiracies is the meaning of organized crime. Belonging to a crime family or syndicate, or what the government styles La Cosa Nostra, suggests an organizational restraint upon the activities of professional criminals that appears quite unlikely. This does not mean that there are no recognizable hierarchies among organized criminals or that there are no boundaries to particular activities. There are some, but they are challenged more often than not; territories and organizations are honored only in the breach. A great deal of criminal opportunity undermines the stability of hierarchies, which leads to ceaseless disputes over rackets and territories. In turn, this competitiveness is often characterized by immoderate instances of murderous treachery, which further frustrates organizational security and permanence.

The life histories of racketeers reveal much violent instability; thus a great deal of anxiety characterizes the environment within which these unbridled capitalists exist. The life and violent death of Gabriel "Gabe" San Felice provides a good example.[33] At the time of his murder in 1978, the 42-year-old San Felice was the secretary-agent of Sano Carting, a garbage company incorporated in March 1966 that operated in Hoboken, Elizabeth, Jersey City, Bayonne, Union City, and Kearny, New Jersey. His wife, Frances, was the company's president. Her relatives were also in private carting businesses and were allegedly close to major organized crime figures who acted as controllers in the region's carting industry. San Felice came to New Jersey by way of Brooklyn, New York, where he had had a fairly heavy criminal record. His application for a private carter's license from the New Jersey Public Utilities Commission discloses San Felice had been convicted of assault and battery in Brooklyn in 1957, 1962, and twice more in 1963. Despite all of these convictions his combined prison time came to only eight months.

The problems for San Felice began in 1972 when Sano Carting moved into areas controlled by other garbage firms that were affiliated with organized crime. Although denied entry to at least one landfill near his new routes, San

Felice continued his expansion. He was subsequently pressured in several ways. Some of his trucks were vandalized, and racketeer leaders of Teamster Local 945 threatened to organize Sano's workers. In response, San Felice contacted Frank Caruso, a personal friend, and important member of the Genovese crime syndicate. Caruso arranged a emoting between San Felice and Ernie Palmeri, the mob leader of Local 945. A deal was worked out, although there was almost immediate cheating. This necessitated another mob meeting, at which Caruso threatened Palmeri.

The situation seemed under control until 1975, when Sano's competitive moves aroused anger once again. In the interim, San Felice's protector, Caruso, had died. Many of Caruso's interests were taken over by Vinnie Mauro, another important Genovese syndicate gangster who had major investments in loansharking and narcotics. San Felice began to pay Mauro a small monthly sum for protection. The change from Caruso to Mauro was not very beneficial. At a subsequent meeting, representatives from competing garbage firms and Palmeri threatened San Felice. At one point, Palmeri pointed at him and told him he was a "dead man."[34] San Felice retorted that Palmeri had better watch his own back. The word was soon out that Mauro was advised "to walk away from Gabe San Felice" by another gangster.[35] Still, there was no gunplay, possibly because San Felice had not yet run out of organized crime contacts.

This time he turned to Philip "Brother" Moscato, a friend of his wife's family for many years. Moscato, in turn, called on two other New Jersey mobsters to calm the situation. The new players were the notorious Tino Fiumara and John DiGilio. Fiumara, who was placed in charge of peacemaking, told San Felice to return several carting contracts to another carter and to report to racketeer Carmine Franco if he had further problems. For a short while, things did calm down. But then Sano Carting ran into new difficulties.

The Internal Revenue Service claimed San Felice owed over $25,000 in back taxes. Other, far more pressing, financial problems also surfaced. San Felice was so broke that he stopped paying loanshark Peter Palazotto from Brooklyn. The payments were for a 1972 loan of $20,000 that turned out to total around $190,000 in the end. When Sano Carting fell on hard times, San Felice was so broke that he told Palazotto he couldn't pay him any more and then threw him out of his office. San Felice then contacted Moscato again asking for assistance.

A few days after his call, Moscato and Vincent Ravo appeared at the Sano office. Ravo reportedly worked for Moscato as chief enforcer in Mosscato's own major loansharking operation. Moscato decided that Ravo would be San Felice's bill collector and would help with any other problems. It was quickly apparent that Ravo was only a temporary solution. Moscato's actual solution came in the spring of 1978, when he offered to buy Sano Carting for what amounted to peanuts. In effect, Moscato would take over the business, paying

San Felice and his wife modest salaries to continue working for the time being. The ungenerous offer was flatly turned down. Angered, Moscato turned away. Shortly afterward, San Felice was shot twice in the head at the Global Landfill in New Jersey.

The Police investigation into the San Felice killing turned up several organized crime figures lining up on different sides of the many disputes, often threatening one another with violence. Interestingly enough, they were primarily members of the Genovese syndicate. This should give pause to those who think organized crime syndicates are unique because they inhibit intra-syndicate violence.

The Historical Background of Organized Crime

Organized Crime is a peculiar variant of corporate or business crime and has a long developmental history in the United States. Observers have tried to discern a pattern in this, with some degree of success. Crime consultant Ralph Salerno, for example, worked out an interesting approach in 1967.[36] He believes there is a "classic pattern of organized crime," which reveals itself through an analysis of "two different kinds of violations of law." The first type, "Strategic and Tactical Crimes," does not have an "immediate economic gain." These consist of arson, assault, blackmail, bribery, corruption, coercion, extortion, monopoly, and murder. Such crimes are necessary preparation for organized criminals to then "enter into, dominate and sometimes control to a very considerable degree, illegal businesses and activities" the second type of violations. Among these are cigarette smuggling, counterfeiting, frauds (arson and bankruptcy), gambling, hijacked alcohol distribution, loansharking, narcotics, prostitution, protection rackets, and fencing.

According to Salerno's classic pattern, organized criminals merge the two types of crime in their operations of "legitimate" businesses. They use strategic and tactical methods to obtain "peculiar advantages which the racketeer[s] will enjoy over [their] competitors, and therefore bring a greater profit to [themselves], ILLEGALLY!" Through their expertise, organized criminals reduce free competition, restrain trade, and establish illegal monopolies whenever they can. Typical businesses are auto dealerships, factoring, restaurants and wholesale food distributorships, garment manufacturing, juke boxes and vending machines, nightclubs, trade associations, trucking, and waste disposal. Profits from these endeavors are then mixed with those from illicit activities to form the sums necessary for the final stage of infiltration--big business. Some affected areas that Salerno listed are banking, construction, credit card companies, entertainment, hotels and motels, insurance, mortgages, real estate, labor and financial securities.

Three stages of corruption parallel the progression of organized crime into big business. At the first stage, organized criminals corrupt the criminal justice system. At stage two, the operation of legitimate businesses, the corruption occurs among "licensing agency officials and others employed in supervisory or regulatory agencies." Finally, at the third stage, organized criminals work directly with the highest political officials in the nation, as other leaders in big business have also been doing for decades. Salerno claimed this last step was neither an "over dramatization" nor a "ridiculous conclusion."

The progression of organized crime that Salerno identified is clearly historical. However, an important question must be asked: What definition of organized crime can be used to evaluate Salerno's classic pattern? If organized crime were a singular entity, then this would be the dramatic heart of its history. However, if organized crime is less structured and hierarchical than many suggest, then the pattern or some variant of it would be repeated from one generation of criminals to the next. Consider, for example, La Cosa Nosra, which many believe is a commission of the leaders of twenty-four rather strictly organized Italian-American gangs across the United States. La Cosa Nostra should have reached a commanding position in U.S. life, according to Salerno's theory. What if La Cosa Nostra was more fiction than fact, however, a compound of political and policing necessity given shape and form by academics working with little reliable data? Would a looser structure in the social world of organized crime invalidate the classic pattern? Before these questions can be answered, a discussion of La Cosa Nostra is necessary.

The Question of La Cosa Nostra

Belief in La Cosa Nostra as a nationwide crime syndicate has varied since the early 1960s, when the term first surfaced in the testimony of informant Joe Valachi. This key perception derived from the Senate's Special Committee to Investigate Organized Crime in Interstate Commerce, commonly called the Kefauver Committee after its chairman, Senator Estes Kefauver of Tennessee. The committee's major mark came in the spring of 1951, when it moved to New York for a hearing on the alleged real bosses of organized crime. The New York hearings covered many facets of organized crime, including bookmaking, drug racketeering, political connections, and waterfront crime. The major focus, however, was on the members and structure of a supposedly giant crime syndicate primarily directed by Frank Costello, Joe Adonis, and Meyer Lansky. To penetrate this syndicate the committee utilized the testimony of two primary witnesses, Costello and William O'Dwyer, who had recently retired as mayor of New York. In its report the committee condemned O'Dwyer:

Neither he nor his appointees took any effective action against the top echelons of the gambling, narcotics, waterfront, murder, or bookmaking rackets. In fact, his actions impeded promising investigations of such rackets. His defense of public officials who were derelict in their duties, and his actions in investigations of corruption, and his failure to follow up concrete evidence of organized crime, . . . have contributed to the growth of organized crime, racketeering, and gangsterism in New York City.[37]

In the halcyon days after World War II, when the United States stood supreme, its major antagonist became the enemy within--the ubiquitous Communist subversive, to which the Kefauver Committee added another type of traitor, the organized criminal. The Kefauver Committee changed the basic view of organized crime, designating organized criminals and criminal syndicates as Organized Crime--the Big Conspiracy. The great fear of subversion that enveloped so many areas of U.S. life in the post-war years worked its influence on crime as well. The big conspiracy was characterized by its national scope and alien origin. The usually submerged issue of ethnicity was brought back into political and criminological discourse. As I have said elsewhere, "the lineal descendant of the Kefauver Committee's conclusions is La Cosa Nostra."[38]

Reuter and Rubinstein noted that the Kefauver conclusions were solidified in a series of Senate hearings over the course of a decade. Then in 1967, President Lyndon Johnson established the Commission on Law Enforcement and the Administration of Justice, which "Provided the most influential endorsement of the Kefauver conclusions."[39] Reuter and Rubinstein provided an important insider's view of this commission's work. Organized crime was not one of the commission's original topics but was included "after the FBI argued that organized crime represented a threat to national security."[40] A so-called task force consisting of only one staff member and a budget of $30,000 was hastily set up. Several academic consultants were brought on board, and they prepared five papers dealing with different aspects of organized crime. Four of the papers were published, and, as Reuter and Rubinstein have remarked, in view of their subsequent significance, it is vital to grasp the published papers' limitations.

For the purpose of establishing the history and sociology of La Cosa Nostra, the paper by Donald Cressey was the most important. Cressey affirmed that "'families' of criminals of Italian and Sicilian descent either operate or control the operation of most of the illicit businesses--including gambling, usury, and the wholesaling of narcotics--in large American cities, and that these 'families' are linked together in a nation-wide cartel and confederation."[41] Though Cressey placed the academic imprimatur on La Cosa Nostra, Reuter and Rubinstein questioned his evidence: "Nowhere did he describe the nature of the data on which this conclusion was based or his access to it."[42] They claimed that Cressey did have some data but that it was impossible to evaluate. Cressey did admit to a lack of detailed information about La Cosa Nostra's code of conduct. Reuter and Rubinstein suggested that he "substituted intuition for argument, claiming that the similarity of structure of organized crime in America and the Italian-Sicilian Mafia enabled him to infer the code of the former from what was known of the code of the latter."[43] However, his knowledge of the latter was deficient. Nonetheless, the belief in La Cosa Nostra, which took a deserved drubbing during the 1970s as revisionist sociologists and criminologists looked at the work sponsored by President Johnson's commission never quite died. It was kept alive by hosts of popular writers, film makers, and the odd sociologist.

The situation now, however, is quite different. Over the course of the past several years, the revisionists of the 1970s have been attacked for doubting the existence of La Cosa Nostra. The oft-discredited testimony of Joe Valachi in 1963, especially his supposed insider pronouncements on mob history, has been resurrected and retroactively confirmed by federal wiretaps placed in mobsters' hangouts, offices, cars, and homes, during the 1980s. More importantly, a series of extraordinary prosecutions of organized criminals has taken place that seem to prove La Cosa Nostra's existence and power. John C. Keeney, the acting assistant attorney general summed up the Justice Department's stunning victories while testifying before the Senate in 1988: "The mob leadership in our major cities has been crippled. Boston, Buffalo, Chicago, Kansas City, Cleveland, Los Angeles, New Orleans, New York, Philadelphia--all have seen La Cosa Nostra . . . bosses, underbosses and capos convicted, sentenced to long prison terms and stripped of their assets."[44] David C. Williams, director of the Justice Department's Office of Special Investigations, added to Keeney's comments, claiming that "between 1983 and 1986, over 2,500 LCN members and associates were indicted, and sixteen mob bosses convicted."[45] It seems clear to many that Salerno's classic pattern reflects La Cosa Nostra's history except for, of course, LCN's recent fall under sustained federal attack.

Beyond the guilt or innocence of important mobsters in particular cases, what precisely has been established by federal prosecutors? Have they uncovered the big conspiracy of Kefauver days, and have they traced a verifiable history of La Cosa Nostra? They certainly have observed big conspiracies and plenty of interaction among primarily Italian-American criminal syndicates and many associates. For believers in La Cosa Nostra, few issues are more difficult than finding a slot in which to put non-Italian-American criminals who work with the LCN. The phrase used most often is "non-member associate," which thereby allows for the preservation of LCN's organizational integrity. It is, however, difficult to get a precise fix on what differentiates "non-member associates" from members. That issue aside, the last step in verifying La Cosa Nostra's existence has not been adequately managed by the theory's supporters. The history of La Cosa Nostra as recently presented before congressional panels and by President Ronald Reagan's Commission on Organized Crime suffers from elementary errors probably more egregious than those committed by Cressey.

At the same 1988 Senate hearing at which Keeney and Williams testified, a "Chronological History of La Cosa Nostra in the United States" was offered by the Justice Department's Organized Crime Intelligence and Analysis Unit. The history began with the 1890 murder of David Hennessey, who was superintendent of police in New Orleans. This murder and related ones in New Orleans "created perhaps the first significant public awareness of the La Cosa Nostra."[46] This statement, however, is an example of "prolepsis which describes an event as happening before it could have done so."[47] It cannot be true that the Hennessey murder made anyone aware of La Cosa Nostra because the term was not invented and certainly not popularized until seventy-three years later. The Organized Crime Intelligence and Analysis Unit was confused. This is particularly apparent when the same event--the Hennessey murder--was said to have introduced the term Mafia into American society. One cannot argue that the Mafia and La Cosa Nostra are synonymous unless both designations already exist.

The Organized Crime Intelligence and Analysis Unit also had another date for the formation of La Cosa Nostra. LCN's influence emerged during Prohibition (thirty years after the Hennessey murder), "which enabled the small, but powerful LCN to capitalize upon its international contracts, its reputation for ruthlessness, and--above all--its rigidly disciplined structure of cooperating gangs to establish the position of unrivaled eminence it holds in the American underworld today" (my emphasis).[48] To prove this, the report rattled off murder after murder, beginning with the killing of Big Jim Colosimo in May 1920 and ending with the April 1931 shooting of Giuseppe Masseria, "boss of all bosses." This decade of reported mayhem, however, contradicts the idea that La Cosa Nostra was by 1920 composed of rigidly disciplined cooperating gangs. Gangster killings indicate a history of underworld violence, nothing else. Additionally, no evidence showed that the compact early LCN had any international contacts, another important part of its alleged development.

In sum, the history of La Cosa Nostra is virtually unknown and its sociology barely understood. The recent and often remarkable law enforcement triumphs over organized criminals from powerful criminal syndicates should not be held as proof of the big conspiracy. Salerno's classic pattern is not the history of La Cosa Nostra, but rather a history of what some criminals have accomplished, what others will accomplish, and most importantly, what is attainable for organized criminals within the political economy of the United States.

Organized Crime and Capitalism

Some time ago I argued that real progress could be made in understanding the history of organized crime by concentrating on urban underworlds. In these areas the business of crime is planned, contacts are made, some crimes are carried out, the fruits of crime are often enjoyed, and the methodologies for the integration of organized criminals into civil society are established.[49] Recognizing the existence of such underworlds was only a first step, however. Like all other quasi-institutions, urban underworlds changed in response to outside pressures, such as population growth, ever more rapid urbanization, and industrialization. These quantitative and qualitative changes in urban structures and economies accounted for different patterns of organized crime in the nineteenth and twentieth centuries. Modern capitalism created lucrative new enterprises for criminals. Economist and historian David Landes captured the essential changes.

> Mass production and urbanization stimulated, indeed required, wider facilities for distribution, a larger credit structure, an expansion of the educational system, the assumption of new functions by government. At the same time, the increase in the standard of living due to higher productivity created new wants and made possible new satisfactions, which led to a spectacular flowering of those businesses that cater to human pleasure and leisure: entertainment, travel, hotels, restaurants, and so on.[50]

Urban organized criminals who were specialists in vice, violence, and corruption penetrated segments of licit pleasure businesses while also controlling illicit ones. The pleasurable commodities and leisure businesses are heavily regulated by the state. This control, however, creates a climate for criminal conspiracies that thrives on the systematic avoidance of regulation. In fact, the variety of criminal conspiracies in the economic sector devoted to pleasure and leisure enterprises (i.e., narcotics syndicates, bootleg syndicates, linen and good suppliers to hotels and restaurants who monopolize through violence, sports entrepreneurs connected to gambling syndicates with interests in prostitution and pornography, and vending machine operators that terrorize their way into choice locations) represents one of the most significant arenas for organized criminal expansion within the past two centuries.

Organized crime also reflects the structure and tension in civil society, the opportunities for profit and power, and the contradictions in political economy. And if, as Immanuel Wallerstein suggested, the "mark of the modern world is the imagination of its profiteers and the counter-assertiveness of the oppressed," then organized criminals must play a powerful role within that drama.[51] The criminal conspiracies highlighted above clearly reflect the imagination of profiteers and function within the place modern capitalism and the bourgeois state have set aside for the sellers of illicit goods and services. Insofar as they operate as labor disciplinarians in the interests of owners and managers, organized criminals thwart to some degree the "counter-assertiveness of the oppressed." Nevertheless, contemporary organized crime is a method of integrating segments of the urban poor into the political economy of capitalism. Naturally, the modes of integration differ according to the size and ethnicity of the urban poor, the structure of law enforcement, the power of trade unions, and the economies of particular cities.

Since the Gilded Age (1890s), organized crime in the United States moved into tertiary industries and the control of significant unions and has infiltrated the other aspects of modern capitalism mentioned by Professor Landes. Organized criminal syndicates are deeply enmeshed in both distribution facilities and credit structures. In addition, organized criminals who for decades have worked closely with political officials have overwhelmed the government's new functions, particularly those associated with the regulation of the construction industry and the protection of the environment.[52]

A few brief illustrations taken from Project Alpha, a government sting operation run by the New Jersey State Police in the late 1970s, demonstrates this political corruption. The government bugged the offices of a phony trucking company, Alamo Transportation. Alamo was run by Patrick Kelly, now in the Witness Protection Program, who decided to manage this sting rather than face prosecution on several serious charges, and by an undercover state police detective.

Kelly recorded daily summaries of organized criminals' meetings and activities. In the second week of February 1977, for example, racketeers discussed a waterfront deal put together by mobster Russ Bufalino that utilized Alamo to channel money for "payoffs to the officials in the Port of Camden," and "the Mayor of Camden."[53] Four days later, a corrupt public official told Kelly that he had a connection in Baltimore through U.S. Senator Harrison Williams for construction performance bonds "where the bond agent will push bonds through and take a point to a point and a half under the table."[54] In the following weeks, Kelly reported that racketeer Tino Fiumara had an appointment with the "head of the Housing Commission Tuesday night along with one of the councilmen. This is in reference to the housing project we're involved in with Tino on Walnut Street."[55] On 19 April, Kelly and a corrupt attorney met with the "head of the [state office of the] EPA concerning" a landfill. This was followed by a meeting on the same matter with the head of New Jersey's Public Utility Commission.[56] In the middle of March, a deal with Conrail officials was discussed that called for a mob takeover of a Conrail landfill in the Bronx and another in Newark, New Jersey.[57] A couple of days later, Fiumara's contact with "the head of urban renewal in Newark" was reviewed. Subsequently, a Conrail official came to the Alamo office to tell Kelly and others how funds for a "gubernatorial campaign" were being diverted into other projects.[58] These are but a few of the many examples of the collusion between some of the public officials whose duties include the regulation of waste disposal and construction and organized criminals.

About the Documents

A word of caution: This documentary study of organized crime's penetration and control of several areas of U.S. industrial society is composed of reports by state and federal investigative bodies and court documents, particularly civil and criminal indictments that are related to the Mafia and La Cosa Nostra. The documents represent organized crime as synonymous with the LCN, a view I have taken some time to critique. Nonetheless, the important issue is not whether the Mafia in particular controls an industry such as waste disposal but that organized crime does. That investigators have found Italian-American organized criminals as major decisionmakers in national trade unions and their "non-member associates" as controllers of the dispersal of millions of dollars from union pension funds is of incalculable importance in understanding the failures to regulate and police by major American institutions such as the Department of Labor and the Environmental Protection Agency as well as the power of organized crime. The point is not ethnicity, but criminality. In using the quite remarkable cache of material produced by the government on organized crime, readers will need to be able to separate the significant from the sensational, the probable from the problematic.

The readings are divided into three sections, although there is some overlap among the documents selected. I have chosen these particular documents for several reasons. First, I include material from each of the past three decades in order to firmly establish what is available about organized crime for contemporary social historians, historically minded sociologists and criminologists, and, of course, students in these disciplines.

Second, one of the important themes of the documents is the capture and control of particular trade unions by organized crime and the invaluable financial leverage this brings. Therefore, there is much material about "union," or "industrial," racketeering, especially concerning Teamster-organized crime connections and mobster control of union pension and welfare funds. Concerning the latter, it is apparent that major organized crime figures have had the ability to appropriate these funds as though they were acting as private banks. The control of vast repositories of cash has been a primary avenue of organized crime advancement and expansion, whether in the form of huge real estate investments or the virtual takeover of banks and savings and loan institutions. Many bankers, for example, have been so eager to secure large pension and welfare deposits that they have knowingly joined with racketeers in various bank-financed illicit activities. In some cases, gangsters who have delivered large union funds for deposit have been rewarded with important positions on banks' loan committees.

Third, the presentation of these documents enables us to follow governmental response to organized crime over the past three decades. Some of the early documents demonstrate that the best that honest lawmakers could really hope for was publicity about some quite flagrante criminality, prosecution of some of the malefactors, and some incremental tinkering with the rules and regulations governing the affected parts of the economy. Hence, the documents in the first two sections are examples of the government's lack of effectiveness in the face of concerted organized criminality. The documents in the final section, however, reflect potential fundamental changes in governmental tolerance and procedure toward organized crime.

Before presenting a more detailed description of the material, I should point out that much of it centers on New York. New York has had much organized crime activity, its professional criminals have had a national impact by restlessly engaging in working illicit activities across the country, and its investigators and prosecutors have worked on more important cases than others anywhere else in the nation. In fact, one could reasonably argue that the New York State Organized Crime Task Force and the Southern District (Manhattan) Federal Strike Force have been at the forefront of introducing innovations to combat organized crime. What might appear at first glance as eastern ethnocentrism is not the case--the New York focus neither distorts nor invalidates the general purposes of the study.

The first section of readings contains two reports generated in the 1960s that dealt with the process of organized crime's move into already extant legitimate businesses. Chapter 1 contains a 1965 New York State Commission of Investigation report that painstakingly revealed loansharking as a criminal method of taking over a wide range of businesses, including restaurants and brokerage firms. Additionally, the commission pointed out the woeful inadequacy of legislation in providing sanctions against loansharks. The next chapter is a report released in the spring of 1967 by the Senate Permanent Subcommittee on Investigations. Over time, this subcommittee has done more to oppose organized crime than any comparable federal legislative body. In this instance, it concentrated on a particular New York-based racketeer and several of his associates, showing how they developed and used their influence, under the guise of labor consultants, to subvert labor-management disputes in order to enrich themselves. The subcommittee also revealed how union benefit programs were undermined by these same racketeers and their partners.

Part 2 contains five chapters, one of which is composed of more than one document. The chapters are arranged to reflect a broad range of affected industries and workers. For instance, Chapter 4 deals with organized crime's depredation of New York's clothing industry. It is a compilation of investigations centered on the general exploitation of immigrant labor in garment manufacturing, which ties into organized crime's domination of the whole industry.

The next two chapters focus on commercial transportation. Chapter 5 examines the movement of air freight through New York's Kennedy Airport in the mid-1960s in a report compiled by the New York State Commission of Investigation. In line with the classic pattern of criminal domination, legitimate businesses were taken over, trade unions captured and used to serve racketeers' purposes, and mobster-owned companies gained preferential treatment. Organized crime had almost total control of air freight through Kennedy Airport and their illicit profits raised consumer prices--the all-to-familiar taxing power of organized crime. The increased costs that provide organized criminals their cut are ultimately passed on to consumers. The document in Chapter 6 recounts a long federal investigation into waterfront corruption from Miami to New York during the 1970s and early 1980s. It describes how sophisticated organized crime syndicates were able to expand their illicit interests from New York to other parts of the country.

Chapter 7 concentrates on an industry--waste disposal--that until fairly recently was considered neither very significant nor a part of organized crime's domain. The document is a report by the New York State Assembly Committee on Environmental Conservation that details criminal syndicates at work in the region's garbage industry. Although not reported in this chapter, it should be noted that the move of waste racketeers in the New York metropolitan area into southern and midwestern states has become more apparent. Indiana, for instance, has been running public service television ads depicting eastern garbage racketeers invading small towns in the Hoosier state.

The last chapter in Part 2 is a short but critical statement by a repentant conspirator about insurance corruption, showing how organized crime's control of the Hotel Employees and Restaurant Employees International Union and the International Brotherhood of Teamsters, allowed it to manage the exceptionally lucrative union insurance industry. Through the use of nominees, front men, and associates a multitude of schemes were carried out.

The final part presents two documents that represent the beginning of the government's most interesting counterattack against organized crime's grip on the U.S. economy. Once again, the Senate's Permanent Subcommittee on Investigations came to the force. Chapter 9 presents the subcommittee's scathing report of government laxity in tolerating organized crime's domination of the International Brotherhood of Teamsters. The Department of Labor's peculiar behavior in supposedly policing the Teamsters and the Central States Pension Fund during the 1970s was placed under the subcommittee's microscope. The final report, printed in 1981, shows precisely how racketeers turned the nation's largest trade union into a private treasury, in apparent full view of the Department of Labor.

In addition, the subcommittee's investigation may have had an important impact on the internal structure of the Department of Labor even before the 1981 report came out. While the subcommittee was conducting its preliminary investigation, the Labor Department formed a new Office of Investigations and instructed some of its other offices to work hand-in-glove with the Department of Justice's Organized Crime Strike Forces.[59]

The document in Chapter 10 continues to examine the government's counterattack upon organized crime's control of the Teamsters. Using innovative legal arguments derived from the civil remedies provisions of the Racketeer Influenced and Corrupt Organizations Statute, the government asked the judiciary to remove the Teamster's corrupt leadership and place the union under a court-appointed trustee. A case against the infamous New Jersey Teamster Local 560, in which Judge Harold A. Ackerman appointed a union overseer, was cited as a precedent.[60]

Notes

1. In addition, something must be said about a common perception found in a segment of the social science community that data taken from government sources are not very useful. For instance, it is often argued that "the files of government law enforcement agencies were never intended as research sources; they are police intelligence files focusing on the types of information necessary to seek indictments and hopefully obtain convictions of individual criminals." And given this orientation such data "tell little about how crime activities organize themselves and nothing of the relationship between organized crime and other sectors of American society." Robert J. Kelly, "Criminal Underworld: Looking Down on Society," in Kelly, ed., Organized Crime: A Global Perspective (Totowa, NJ: Rowman & Littlefield, 1986), 11.

This argument is somewhat taxing to follow because there are so many different types of government documents germane to the issue: court records of various kinds, including trial transcripts, indictments, sentencing memoranda, exhibits and affidavits; police intelligence files; and hearings and reports by investigative groups at the local, state, and federal levels. But even taking the most problematic example--police intelligence files--they are simply not limited in the fashions described above. What I believe to be their usual construction reveals this: name; aliases; nativity; residence; physical description; social security number; telephone number; crime family; former residences; banking, marital status; family history; legitimate business or corporation associates; criminal record; military record; education; hangouts; tax information; and surveillance reports. There is obviously important information on ethnicity, residential mobility, the organization of criminal activities, and most especially the relationship between organized crime and other sectors of U.S. society. All this is or should be grist for the mills of social historians, urban economists, sociologists, anthropologists, and criminologists.

Another consideration, rarely spoken but obviously important, is not whether police intelligence files have the right sort of information, but that it is objectionable to use such information in any case. After all, the police themselves are known to be often venal and corrupt. But this has little bearing upon the majority of intelligence files dealing with organized crime, which are built from mostly verifiable sources, layer upon layer over time. Police intelligence files are far more accurate than many corporate annual reports, which are habitually utilized by social scientists for analytical purposes.

2. Robert Lacey, Ford: The Men and the Machine (Boston: Little, Brown, 1986), 367.

3. Ibid.

4. Ibid., 368.

5. This point also seems to cause an inordinate amount of academic squabbling, particularly concerning the availability of information. Kelly raises it, noting that "data concerning [organized crime's] infiltration into legitimate businesses are often closely guarded by law enforcement groups," (p. 11). It is impossible to deny this claim of guardianship, but it is of only marginal consequence. There have been literally thousands of exceptions. For decades law enforcement groups have gone to great lengths to provide detailed material on organized crime's "infiltration into legitimate businesses."

6. Alan A. Block and William J. Chambliss, Organizing Crime (New York: Elsevier, 1981), 14-15.

7. Ibid., 16.

8. U.S. Senate, Committee on Government Operations, Permanent Subcommittee on Investigations, Hearings: Organized Crime and Illicit Traffic in Narcotics, Part 2 (Washington, DC: Government Printing Office, 1963), 621-622.

9. Waterfront Commission of New York Harbor, "Statement of William P. Sirignano, Executive Director and General Counsel in Support of the Following Bills: Senate Nos. 705, 706, 708," 26 June 1969, 1.

22

10. Ibid., 3.

11. Ibid., 5.

12. Ibid., 9.

13. New York State Senate Select Committee on Crime, Papers: Digest of Testimony of Congressman Steiger, 4 March 1970.

14. New York State Senate Select Committee on Crime, Papers: Nevada Attorney General Lee Johnson, "Report, Sportservice Corporation," n.d., 2.

15. Ibid., 3.

16. New York City, Department of Investigation, "Katz Brothers and the Harlem Check Cashing Corp.: Supplemental Report," 20 December 1944, 1.

17. Ibid., 7.

18. U.S. Drug Enforcement Administration, "Report of Investigation," File No. XFR2-78-4117, File Title PIANCONE, Michael, et al. 1 October 1978.

19. Ibid., 4.

20. U.S. Court of Appeals for the Sixth Circuit, "United States of America v. James A. Russo; Vincent Meli; Roby G. Smith," 20 May 1983; and David J. McKeon, Attorney in Charge, Detroit Strike Force, to Strike Force Chiefs, Field Offices, Strike Force 18, "MEMORANDUM: United States v. Russo, Meli and Smith," 25 May 1983.

21. Peter Reuter and Jonathan Rubinstein, "The Structure and Operation of Illegal Numbers, Bookmaking, and Loansharking in Metropolitan New York: Draft Report" n.d., Chapter 4, 3.

22. Ibid., 3.

23. Ibid., 7.

24. Peter Reuter, Disorganized Crime: The Economics of the Visible Hand (Cambridge, MA: MIT Press, 1983), 42.

25. United States District Court, Southern District of New York, United States of America -v- Vincent Joseph Rotondo, a/k/a "Jimmy," Michael J. Franzese, Benedetto Aloi, a/k/a "Benny," Antonio Peter Napoli, a/k/a "Anthony," a/k/a "Tony Nap," Carlo Enrico Vaccaressa, a/k/a "Carlos," Leonard Carl Di Maria, a/k/a "Lenny," Francesco Di Stefano, a/k/a "Frankie the Hat," Jesse David Hyman, a/k/a "Doc," Melvin Cooper, Joseph M. Biasucci, Chaim Gerlitz, Oscar Louis Albenga, a/k/a "Al," Alan Albenga,

Stanley Gramovot, Anthony Charles Capo, Jr., and Joseph Nicholas Lipari, Defendants, INDICTMENT 84 crim 479.

26. U.S. District Court, Southern District of New York, USA v. Jesse David Human, a/k/a "Doc," Melvin Cooper, et al., Sentencing Memorandum s 84 Cr. 479 (LBS), filed 16 October 1985, 18.

27. Ibid.

28. Ibid., 14.

29. Ibid.

30. Ibid., 12.

31. Ibid., "Government Opening," 5.

32. Ibid., 7.

33. The following material comes from Alan A. Block and Frank R. Scarpitti, Poisoning for Profit: The Mafia and Toxic Waste Disposal in America (New York: William Morrow, 1985), 228-236.

34. Elizabeth, New Jersey, Police Department, "Sensitive Report, Informant Interview--Murder of Gabe San Felice," (1978), 7.

35. Ibid., 8.

36. My copy of Salerno's paper, "The Classic Pattern of Organized Crime," was in the New York State Senate Select Committee on Crime Papers.

37. U.S. Senate, Special Committee to Investigate Organized Crime in Interstate Commerce, The Kefauver Committee Report on Organized Crime (New York, 1951), 125.

38. Alan A. Block, East Side--West Side: Organizing Crime in New York, 1930-1950 (New Brunswick, NJ: Transaction Press, 1983), 123.

39. Reuter and Rubinstein, 8.

40. Ibid., 9.

41. Ibid., 10.

42. Ibid.

43. Ibid.

44. U.S. Senate, Committee on Governmental Affairs, Permanent Subcommittee on Investigations (PSI), Hearings: Organized Crime: 25 Years After Valachi (Washington, DC: Government Printing Office, 1988), 452d.

45. Ibid., 500.

46. U.S. Department of Justice, Criminal Investigative Division, Organized Crime Section, Organized Crime Intelligence and Analysis Unit, "Chronological History of La Cosa Nostra in the United States, January 1920--August 1987" (October 1987), included in ibid., 294. Although the history supposedly begins in 1920, the text starts with the Hennessey murder in 1890.

47. David Hackett Fischer, Historians' Fallacies: Toward a Logic of Historical Thought (New York: Harper & Row, 1970), 43. Fischer's work was aimed at professional historians who committed logical and other philosophical errors time and again. It seemed that no historian, however prominent, escaped Fischer's attention. Of course, historians are not the only ones to either write or invoke history to explain current phenomena, nor are they the only ones who must be called on to account for mistakes.

48. U.S. Senate, PSI, 296.

49. These ideas were first presented in my paper titled "Some Thoughts on the State of Comparative Research in the Study of Organized Crime" presented at the 1977 annual meeting of the Society for the Study of Social Problems. The paper was later incorporated into Block and Chambliss, Chapter 6.

50. David Landes, The Unbound Prometheus: Technological Change and Industrial Development in Western Europe from 1750 to the Present (Cambridge: Cambridge University Press, 1969), 9.

51. Immanuel Wallerstein, The Modern World-System: Capitalist Agriculture and the Origins of the European World-Economy in the Sixteenth Century (New York: Academic Press, 1977), 357.

52. On these topics see New York State Task Force, Corruption and Racketeering in the New York City Construction Industry: An Interim Report (Ithaca, NY: ILR Press, 1988); Andrew Szasz, "Corporations, organized Crime, and the Disposal of Hazardous Waste: An Examination of the Making of a Criminogenic Regulatory Structure," Criminology, Vol. 24, February 1986; and U.S. Senate, PSI, Profile of Organized Crime: Mid-Atlantic Region (Washington, DC: Government Printing Office, 1983), 230-252, 402-468.

53. New Jersey State Police, Project Alpha Transcript--K-0004.

54. Ibid., K-0007.

55. Ibid., K-0061.

56. Ibid., K-0068.

57. Ibid., K-0032.

58. Ibid., K-0033, K-0035.

59. U.S. Department of Labor, Office of Inspector General, "Employee Orientation and Reference Book," n.d.

60. Local 560, run by notorious organized crime figures, was seized by the government in the first ever application of the civil RICO (Racketeer Influenced and Corrupt Organizations Act) remedy for this purpose. Judge Ackerman removed the gangsters as officers and members of the Executive Board and appointed Joel R. Jacobson as the trustee to administer the union. Unfortunately, Ackerman and Jacobson disagreed about the procedures for freeing the union from organized crime's control. After overseeing extensive and fundamental changes in the structure and personnel of 560, Jacobson was nonetheless removed from the trusteeship. Jacobson concluded that Judge Ackerman, who appointed in Jacobson's place Edwin Stier, the former director of the New Jersey Division of Criminal Justice, "did not want a trade unionist to continue as trustee: he wanted a cop." Joel R. Jacobson, "'Guilty Until Proven Innocent': How the Teamsters' Trusteeship Turned Sour," New Jersey Reporter, Vol. 17, March 1988, 19.

PART ONE

The Process

2

An Investigation
of the Loan-Shark Racket

A Report by the New York State Commission of Investigation, 1965.

Introduction

Problems arising from money lending have vexed mankind from its earliest history. However, loan-sharking, the charging of unconscionably high and onerous rates of interest in loans of money, as an organized criminal enterprise, is a fairly recent development. The loan-shark racket as we know it today was developed by the same lawless elements that turned the streets of American cities to battlegrounds during Prohibition.

There was a time when a "respectable" racketeer looked down his nose at the usurious money lender. He was regarded with the same contempt accorded to the common procurer.   The czars of the underworld and their highly organized minions were then engaged in other pursuits--protection rackets during the earlier part of the century, and bootlegging, after the passage of the Volstead Act. It was not until the repeal of the Prohibition Laws that the organized crime syndicates, with tremendous capital at their disposal, started looking around for new enterprises. Expansion of gambling, vice and the traffic in narcotics took up the slack caused by repeal. This produced new and greater profits. The underworld sought a racket to put this money to work and in a way that would produce "legitimate" revenue. They found it in loan-sharking.

By the end of the Thirties, crime syndicates were fully engaged in usurious money lending operatios. This venture soon proved its tremendous potential for making money. Racket controlled money lending operations were not affected by governmental regulations of legitimate lenders nor was organized criminal loan-sharking ever encumbered by considerations of proper banking practices, procedures and ethics. Competition for business, in the normally accepted sense, was never a factor. In the years that followed, the racket flourished.

The Commission's investigation and hearing, conducted in 1964, revealed that loan-sharking, today, has become a major and most lucrative operation of the criminal underworld. Moreover, loan-sharking is a principal avenue by which crime syndicates have invaded legitimate businesses. These businesses, when taken over by the loan-sharks, are used to further other criminal enterprises. With this growth of power, the loan-shark has become a serious threat to our economy and a menace to society.

Clearly then, the importance of this investigation and report is not only to alert the public to the ever-growing danger of loan-sharking, but to help bring it within effective control of the law.

A. The Investigation

As part of its continuing program dealing with organized crime, the Commission had gathered substantial information regarding the activities of crime syndicate members in the money lending business. In the fall of 1963, the Commission, deeply concerned about the situation, authorized a full investigation into all aspects of the loan-shark racket.

Investigative leads were developed and witnesses who could provide direct evidence about the racket were located and questioned. Businesssmen, laborers, doctors, lawyers, manufacturers, restaurant owners, real estate men, artists, bankers, liquor dealers, "finders," night club entrepreneurs, bakers and housewives--this is merely a sampling of those questioned at length, to determine the scope of loan-sharking.

But before testimony was secured, the ever-present obstacle of fear had to be surmounted--fear engendered by loan-shark tactics in collecting loans. Uppermost in the minds of so many witnesses was their personal safety and the well-being of their wives and children. Questions were often answered by such counter-queries as: "My son walks to school every day. Who's going to watch him?"; "My wife has already been hospitalized for a nervous breakdown over this. What will happen next?" Questions such as these were not lightly treated, and it was necessary to establish a relationship of trust and mutual confidence between the Commission and the witness before the truth could be recorded.

In some instances the Commission was able to obtain valuable testimony on a confidential basis from individuals who had been on the "inside" of the racket. Significant assistance was also provided by brother law enforcement agencies.

B. The Public Hearing

The six day public hearing, climaxing the investigation, was held in the Commission's Hearing Room at its office in New York City, on December 1, 2, 3, 7, 9 and 10, 1964.

The report which follows will detail the evidence presented at the public hearing. For completeness, additional material from the investigation and private hearings is included.

At their request, and for obvious reasons, the identities of several witnesses who testified publicly were not divulged. In this report, these and other witnesses afforded anonymity will be given a simple alphabetical designation, according to the order in which they appear in the report.

The commission's statement upon the commencement of this public hearing, in pertinent part, outlined the scope and purpose of the hearing:

> Law enforcement officials have long recognized that one of the principal and most lucrative operations of the criminal underworld is the loan-shark racket. Together with gambling operations, labor racketeering and trafficking in narcotics, loan-sharking, in its various aspects, has engaged in the major efforts of law enforcement in the battle against organized crime. Yet comparatively little is known by the general public about loan-sharking. Most disturbing is the fact that enforcement efforts in this area have been handicapped seriously by weak and confusing anti-usury laws--laws under which the most nefarious and vicious practices are often legal.
>
> Today, this Commission commences a public hearing which will expose this racket, and the problems in dealing effectively with it, to public scrutiny.

Underworld Operation of the Loan-Shark Racket

In the months of investigation that preceded the public hearing, it became clear to the Commission that the usurious money lending business had become a major enterprise, and a principal source of revenue of the crime syndicates. Loan-sharking, once considered of small consequence, was recognized by underworld leaders as having a number of highly attractive features.

A. *Crime Syndicates in the Money Lending Business*

The usurious money lending business was particularly adaptable to successful operation through existing underworld organizational structures. With potential for great profits, it presented an open avenue to the world of legitimate business and the means of returning racket revenues to usable legitimate capital. The absence of effective usury laws in New York State served to make these prospects all the more inviting.

These conclusions by the commission were unanimously confirmed by a number of law enforcement officials who testified at the public hearings.

The Hoodlum Hierarchy. Organization of the loan-shark racket as a syndicate venture is composed generally of three principal echelons. On the first or top level is the underworld boss. He is the original source of money and the person to whom all others owe their absolute allegiance. Assistant District Attorney Frank Rogers of New York County, in testifying about the hoodlum hierarchy of loan-sharking, stated that the bosses distribute unlimited amounts of money; "millions of dollars" are entrusted to chief lieutenants and under-bosses who comprise the second echelon. The amount of money these men receive from the top is determined by their stature, past performances and volume capabilities. This second echelon pays one percent vigorish weekly for its money.* There is absolute responsibility for the use of this money on all levels. This includes the distribution of funds to borrowers and the profitable return of capital and interest to each source. Each man is an independent contractor and knows that there are no excuses for failure to perform his part of the "contract."

The chief subordinates act as middlemen and loan monies to a third echelon comprised of the hoodlums who deal with borrowers--the ultimate victims of this underworld financial empire. Rates charged to the third level generally are from one and one-half percent to two and one-half percent weekly. The third level loan-shark lends money to the borrower at rates of interest usually not less than five percent per week.

Distribution does not always follow the general pattern as outlined. In fact, there are several loan-sharks who, law enforcement officials agree, are chief lieutenants in the second echelon and who handle their own distribution. These are among the major loan-sharks in New York City who can loan a million dollars at a time to a borrower.

One such transaction was described at the hearing. In this instance, the borrower needed one million dollars to finance a construction project. In his conference with the loan-shark, a chief lieutenant of a syndicate and one of the most prominent loan-sharks in New York City, the borrower talked about credentials and collateral. The loan-shark clearly acquainted him with the facts of such a loan:

> And the loan-shark quite frankly stated to him that he doesn't need any credentials, number one. The man who had sent the borrower, the prospective borrower into him, he was enough, his word that you, meaning the prospective borrower are okay, is enough for me.
>
> And the borrower also didn't require any collateral. The borrower couldn't understand this too well. He was simply told in no uncertain terms that 'Your body is your collateral.'
>
> The borrower then understood the type of loan that he was getting.

---

*Vigorish is the underworld term for interest and other penalties or charges imposed on a usurious loan.

The testimony adduced at the public hearing showed that one hundred twenty-one of the high echelon members of the five recognized criminal syndicates operating in greater New York were engaged in loan-sharking.*

It appears that either membership in or affiliation with one of the syndicates is necessary in order to move money into the usurious money lending business. The "Newsboy" Moriarity case illustrates this fact. Moriarity, a professional gambler who operated a number or policy racket in Jersey City, was characterized as an "overlook." This term is applied to a criminal who operated on a scale larger than generally recognized and who escaped being absorbed by the syndicates. Consequently, ". . . he couldn't move his money to hide it from the government and the tax people. He couldn't put it in banks and he couldn't move this money out without the assistance of the mob. Therefore, he had to hide it." He did just that. In July, 1962, approximately 2.5 million dollars in cash were found crammed in a Jersey City garage and generally acknowledged to be the proceeds of Moriarity's illicit business.

There are also instances of top loan-sharks who are not recognized syndicate members. However, they cannot operate unless they have a direct connection with the syndicate. This usually comes in the form of a syndicate "partner" who supplies "prestige and brawn."

Syndicate Discipline--"The Sit-Down." One significant aspect of underworld control of the loan-shark racket is the desire to operate in a discreet and cautious manner. Syndicate money lenders have generally recognized the need for good "public relations" which will allow them to function with a minimum of police attention and public clamor. Rather than solve internal disputes by gang warfare or to resort unnecessarily to violence, the syndicates now tend to arbitrate differences by a more "civilized" technique known as the "sit-down." The full power of the underworld's absolute authority, iron discipline and enforcement machinery is behind such arbitration.

When disputes arise in connection with any aspect of the underworld lending business, the opposing parties will arrange for a "sit-down" with a mediator. There the matter will be peaceably settled as quickly as possible rather than engaging in "open shooting wars which bring the hue and cry of the public and prosecutors on top of them. . . ." A high ranking member of the underworld presides over every "sit-down" and his decision is final.

The "sit-down" is also used to adjudicate a claim against a borrower whose interest and penalty assessments have increased his indebtedness to a point where it is no longer collectible. In such cases, an amount will be decided upon in full

---

*These syndicates are identified by the names of their alleged leaders as follows: Vito Genovese, Carlo Gambino, Joe Colombo, successor to Joseph Profaci, Thomas Luchese, Joe Bonanno.

settlement of the obligation.* This type of "kangaroo court," never requires a loan-shark to accept a sum less than the original loan. Invariably the arbitrated figure is three or four times that amount.

Connection with Other Rackets. The close connection between loan-sharking on the one hand, and bookmaking and narcotics distribution on the other, was also revealed at the hearing. The bookmaker who sustained high losses as a result of the unforeseen shut-out of the Yankees in the 1963 World Series, for example, obtained re-financing through the loan-shark. The narcotics importer who needs instant credit to meet an exceptionally large drug shipment also goes to the syndicate usurer. In another situation, the New York City Police Department arrested a narcotics "pusher" and found records on his person indicating that he was "not only pushing those doses of junk, but also shylocking them (the addicts) when they were unable to make their payments (for drugs).

Instances were found in which a racket union in the construction field actually used loan-sharking as a concession at construction sites. These concessions were sold or granted to others and operated by criminal underlings as a continuing source of revenue.

The Profit Incentive. Of all the factors that led to popularity of loan-sharking as a principal crime syndicate activity, its fantastic profit was undoubtedly the most compelling. Just how much profit was illustrated at the public hearing by Sergeant of Detectives Ralph Salerno of the Criminal Intelligence Bureau of the New York City Police Department:

> MR. SALERNO: A big racket boss could have a Christmas party in his home, to which he invites ten trusted lieutenants. He doesn't have to write their names down. He knows their names. They are friends of his. They can come to his home.
>
> MR. VERGARI: They are part of the underworld, and in the underworld parlance, they belong to him.
>
> MR. SALERNO: Yes. He can take one million dollars, which is not an inconceivable amount in cash, and distribute that one hundred thousand dollars per man to these ten men. All he has to tell them is, I want one percent per week. I don't care what you get for it. But I want one percent per week.
>
> He does not have to record their names. He doesn't have to record the amount. These are easy enough to remember. And if you stop and think, that 365 days later, at the next year's Christmas party, the only problem this gang

---

*Fixing a final figure by arbitration or a "sit-down" is known in the loan-shark racket as "stopping the clock," connoting the cessation of the accumulation of weekly vigorish and penalties. This only happens when the borrower has convinced the loan-shark that he cannot continue paying weekly vigorish. The loan-shark will stop the weekly accumulation of interest and penalties and settle upon a lump sum payment at a specific time.

leader has is where is he going to find five more men to hand out half a million dollars that he earned in the last year on the same terms.

MR. VERGARI: In other words, he is making ten thousand dollars a week on his million dollars. Is that right?

MR. SALERNO: Yes. $520,000 a year.

Carrying this illustration out along the succeeding echelons of the racket, a matter of simple mathematics, further underscores this great profit making potential. The third echelon lender charges, on the average, five percent weekly vigorish. Therefore, a million dollar "investment" at this level can produce as much as $50,000 a week or $2,600,000 a year. Of this amount, $15,000 to $25,000 a week, or up to $1.3 million a year in vigorish alone, is returned to underworld superiors.

Deputy Inspector Arthur C. Grubert, Commanding Officer of the Criminal Intelligence Bureau of the New York City Police Department testified that "there is far less risk with every bit as much profit coming from the loan-shark racket as there is in the gambling operations." The expense involved in maintaining a lucrative loan-shark business is relatively less. Unlike the gambler, a loan-shark does not need a network of controllers, runners and bankers without which the successful policy operator could not operate. The bookmaker requires an office or a wire room and must be generally available at a fixed location with well paid sheet writers and the like on the payroll. Loan-sharks can get along without experience or specialized training, which are absolute necessities for professional gamblers.

Loan-sharking also has become a convenient vehicle for turning so-called "black money" into "white money," or legitimate funds. Major racketeers have great fortunes available to them, the proceeds of their illicit trade in narcotics and gambling. These underworld leaders have found that by loaning money out to their chief lieutenants, for further distribution in loan-sharking, they can gain control of many legitimate businesses. A business take over gives the hoodlum not only a corporate cover, but a new source of money--this time, legitimate.

Loansharks have constantly used corporate borrowers as a cover, or concealing device for themselves and other hoodlums. Typical was the instance in which a loan-shark took his weekly vigorish payments in the form of a salary check from an automobile dealer to whom he had loaned money. The gangster appeared on the corporate books as an outside salesman. He never sold a car. When questioned, he was able to claim legitimate employment, at least insofar as a weekly paycheck would indicate.

Opportunity to realize unusual profit in loan-sharking was also disclosed in the case of an heir to a large sum of money in trust, who attempted to sell his inheritance rights for a loan-shark loan, at one-third the actual value of the trust fund. The Commission also received testimony of an attempt by "the mob" to take over a bank which had as its objective the use of the bank as a cover for usurious money lending operations.

There was testimony at the hearing of yet another and little recognized advantage accruing to the criminal through loan-sharking. Money-lending has prestige value which feeds the gangster's ego and makes him a success in the eyes of his fellow criminals. The hoodlum enjoys the feeling that comes with making a loan to a member of the legitimate business or professional community. Not only has the loan-shark made a profit on his transaction, but there is "an additional profit in the sense of loyalty from this man (the borrower) to a racketeer (the lender). The unique position of the loan-shark in the underworld was summarized:

> It is a demonstration of power. You have something which, I think, is unique in criminal fields in loan-sharking.
> They have raised the status of loan-sharking to a height and to a degree in their own criminal circles that I have never seen duplicated anywhere.
> It seems to be an unwritten law that even if you are a criminal even if you are a top guy, you always pay the shylock.*
> The Gallo gang, for example . . . . I know that this very same group which challenged the criminal empire, still very diligently paid the shylocks. Certainly not out of a sense of fear, but this is the status that it has achieved in their circles. You borrow money, you pay it back. They weren't afraid of the shylock. But they didn't know when they might need him again. So they very diligently paid the shylock.

Ineffective Laws--An Invitation to Crime. Startling as it may seem, the Commission found, and all official witnesses agreed, that the absence of effective usury laws in this state was a significant factor in the underworld's move into loan-sharking. The criminal usurer can, and generally does, operate within the law. A reliable informant advised that "every hood in the world knows you can charge any amount of 'vig' you want on $800 or up." This is indeed the case.** This situation was pointed up by the testimony of Assistant District Attorney Rogers who testified that prosecutions for "pure loan-sharking" are rare. Police and prosecutors must look for other criminal violations in

---

*The term "shylock" or its derivations "shy" and "shell" are generally used in the underworld to refer to anyone in the money lending business. As will be noted several witnesses used the expression "shylock" when referring to loan-sharks in their testimony.

**See pp. 80-84 [of original document] for a discussion of the shortcomings in New York State statutes concerning usury which permit loan-sharks to operate within the law.

seeking to combat the loan-shark, including extortion, assault and other crimes of violence. However, as noted, arbitration through the "sit-down" was designed to avoid such problems. Overt and actionable violence is rarely necessary. The loan-shark's reputation alone, is generally enough to instill fear.

Loan-Sharking--How Big? The scope of the underworld's financial empire is described in this testimony of Assistant District Attorney Rogers at the public hearing:

> COMMISSIONER LANE: Mr. Rogers, can you give us an estimate in dollars and cents of this loan-sharking operation in the United States? I know that it is an estimate. Could you give us one for the United States?
>
> THE WITNESS: It is very hard to say, Commissioner Lane. I can give you an idea from one particular loan shark that I was very familiar with. Perhaps you could get it from this.
>
> From reliable information we know that in approximately 1959 and in 1960, there was made available by the leader to his chief subordinates approximately a half a million dollars, $500,000. Again, from reliable information, from the best accounting we could obtain of this, we now believe that that $500,000 has been pyramided to seven and a half million dollars.
>
> COMMISSIONER SARACHAN: Seven and a half million dollars?
>
> THE WITNESS: That this man now is worth seven and a half million dollars.
>
> COMMISSIONER LANE: One person in New York County?
>
> THE WITNESS: Yes.
>
> COMMISSIONER LANE: It is reasonable to expect, there is roughly five hundred million to one billion dollars.
>
> THE WITNESS: That would be very easy, sir. Here in New York City, in New York County, there is [sic] at least ten men who are comparable to him. A loan shark that we know of lent a million dollars in the morning and a million dollars in the afternoon.
>
> COMMISSIONER LANE: So it would sound as if it were in the billion dollar class, if you take the entire United States.
>
> THE WITNESS: Yes, very easily.

B. *Jiggs and Ruby*

At a private hearing before the Commission, a well-informed and reliable witness, who will be called A, was asked: "Who is the biggest loan shark in the City of New York?" His answer was quick--"Jiggs Forlano. I would call him the biggest in the five boroughs. The biggest. And Ruby Stein is his partner." He was referring to Nicholas "Jiggs" Forlano and Charles "Ruby" Stein. "Jiggs and Ruby" may sound like characters in a comic strip, but they hold key positions in the intricate network of criminal usury operations in the New York area.

Nicholas Forlano is 48 years old and lives modestly in a semi-detached house in Long Island City, Queens. Few people know him by any other name than "Jiggs," and this alias is duly noted on the record of his criminal past. His record dates back to 1930. In 1935 he was sentenced to the Northeastern Federal Penitentiary after having been found guilty of trafficking in narcotics. He was also convicted on bookmaking and policy charges in 1943. Forlano and Stein were part of a gathering of notorious underworld figures picked up at a raid in January 1961 at a White Turkey Restaurant in Manhattan. Among others arrested in that raid and charged with consorting with known criminals were Carmine "Snake" Persico, Philip Gambino and Albert Gallo, brother of Joseph "Crazy Joe" Gallo.

Charles Stein has been connected with loan sharking and bookmaking for many years. Known as "Ruby" and "Charles Rice," he has a criminal record dating back to the 1940s, when he was arrested twice for bookmaking. In 1954 he was sent to the United States Penitentiary in Atlanta on a tax evasion charge. Stein gives a Jackson Heights address, but maintains a plush Park Avenue apartment.

A was asked to explain the way in which Forlano and Stein operate, particularly with regard to the sources of their capital. He outlined the chain of command in what he chose to call the "Mafia." Heading the syndicate, he explained, are the bosses, whose power is complete and absolute. The position of Forlano and Stein is such that they deal directly with the bosses.

The rackets are the life blood of the syndicates. It is generally known that bookmaking, narcotics, policy--all generate fantastic profits. As A put it, ". . . the boss must push it out to make profit with it, so that eventually this money can turn from no good money to good money." "Now, how do they do that?" **Mr. A** answered his own question. "They go ahead and they give this kind of money to people like Jiggs Forlano."

Forlano, in A's terms, is a wholesaler of money, a "shylock's shylock." With the syndicate boss as his direct source of capital, he borrows vast sums at the rate of one percent weekly. A testified that Forlano loans out this money to other loan-sharks and "bookmakers, policy operators or businessmen with the type of operation he feels he could step into." Forlano's vigorish rate to the lower echelon loan-shark is from one and one-half to two and one-half percent a week.

Forlano originally came out of the Brooklyn syndicate headed by the late Joseph Profaci. However, his sources of capital are not confined to his old syndicate. His reputation for moving money quickly and efficiently at great profit is generally known to underworld bosses. As a result, his capital sources have no bounds. Any syndicate chieftain will entrust Forlano with unlimited funds, confident that a return on his investment will be assured. Because of his reputation and contacts, Forlano is the decision maker in his partnership with

Stein. "Ruby" Stein is the mathematician of the business.* He is also used as the contact man who actually handles the money. A has witnessed Stein handing packages of money to borrowers.

Bar and restaurant owners are favorite clients of Forlano because as part of the loan transaction they are required to permit him to set up shop on the premises. Invariably he acquires "a piece" of the business. Word goes out to the select clientele regarding the various locations where business is being conducted. According to A, Monday was the busy day in Forlano's operation. People who wanted money were told to come in on Monday, and vigorish was regularly due on the same day. "Everybody pays Monday," explained A, "Monday always comes."

The site for transacting business has varied from a large cafeteria in midtown to a quiet, elegant East Side steak house. Operations were not limited to Manhattan. Forlano and Stein, for a time, were doing a thriving business right on Queens Boulevard, just a stone's throw from the Criminal Courts Building in Kew Gardens.

In addition to money, the successful loan-shark at any level requires an "enforcer." Some usurers, such as Forlano, are feared in their own right because of their reputation. Forlano is not known "to do his own dirty work." He is too big and above that, A explained. At one time, Forlano, to collect debts, used the services of the infamous Gallo gang of Brooklyn, on a contract basis.

Both Stein and Forlano were subpoenaed for the public hearing. They appeared but invoked their privilege against self-incrimination.

The Forlano-Stein business combination has reaped a vast harvest of ill-gotten gains. The magnitude of the profits to be made in loan-sharking at this level is indicated in A's considered estimate of the volume of this business. He stated that Forlano and Stein have had as much as $5,000,000 "on the sheet" at one time. And at an average of two percent a week return, these money wholesalers make for themselves and their underworld bosses at least $100,000 weekly.

C. First National Service and Discount Corporation--
A Typical Underworld Loan-Shark Operation

An individual approaching the doors of the First National Service and Discount Corporation** would never guess the real nature of its business.

---

*Stein is reputed to be a mathematical wizard capable of swift and accurate computation of complicated problems. This talent is particularly valuable in the bookmaking business in which he and Forlano are also engaged.

**Hereafter referred to as First National.

Tucked away in a Fifth Avenue office building, First National's title was a euphemism at best. The "service" it dispensed was intimidation and fear. Its "discounts" were limited to loans which called for the payment of five percent weekly vigorish as long as the loan was outstanding.

First National was a loan-shark operation and its principal operating force was Julio Gazia, alias Julie Peters. The names Gazia and Peters were used interchangeably by many witnesses and the Commission found that he was equally well-known by either name. In the text of this report, he will be referred to as Gazia; in the quoted excerpts from private and public hearing testimony, his name appears as both Gazia and Peters.

The operation of First National and its hoodlum masters and employees will serve to illustrate almost every sinister aspect of underworld loan-shark operations.

"I am a Shylock--A Five Percenter." The history of First National and details of its operation were provided by a witness, who will be referred to as **B.** An attorney, **B** was retained by Gazia around 1955 to represent him in a bankruptcy matter in Buffalo, New York. Gazia was referred to **B** by another attorney with whom **B** was associated at the time.

In time, the professional relationship between **B** and his client grew more friendly and personal. On one of their frequent flights together between Buffalo and New York City, Gazia spoke rather freely to **B** about the true nature of his business. **B** testified:

BY MR. COMETA:

Q. It was at this time that Peters informed you as to the true nature of his profession, is that correct?
A. Yes.
Q. Did he characterize his profession in his own words?
A. Yes, he said 'I am a shylock.'
Q. As simple as that?
A. A five percenter, he called himself.
Q. A five percenter?
A. Yes.

Gazia went on to explain the various aspects of his business. **B**, interested and, of course, knowing that Gazia's claim against the bankrupt debtor was $80,000, asked about the source of his capital:

Q. Did you ask Mr. Peters where he got the $80,000 to loan this man?

---

*This witness testified at the Commission's public hearing as John Doe.

A. Yes. He told me that he had been shylocking all the time, or lending money at five percent, and then he told me that there were fantastic amounts of money that could be earned at this rate of interest, and that he had a clientele that couldn't be beat, going into doctors, stockbrokers, the highest people that you want to meet. They were paying him five percent on tremendous sums of money and there couldn't be a nicer existence to live on that kind of income.

Q. Is that five percent a week . . .?

A. That is five percent a week.

B was to become a close business associate of Gazia's and an active participant in his money lending business.

The Corporate Cover. Some time later, Gazia and B established the First National Service and Discount Corporation. Records filed with the office of the New York County Clerk indicate that First National was incorporated on April 12, 1960 and that its certificate was filed on May 4, 1960.

Soon after its incorporation, First National started business in a suite of rooms at 475 Fifth Avenue, New York City. Customers were no problem--in the country's largest city there is an abundance of those to whom the traditional channels of credit are closed. First National proceeded to loan money, at first only to corporate borrowers. B testified:

Q. The corporation proceeded to loan money?

A. Yes.

Q. To individual borrowers?

A. No, it lent money to corporate borrowers and later it went into individual cases.

* * * *

Q. Was there any particular reason for this?

A. Because there is no usury statute with respect to corporations.

Gazia's Underworld Sources. While a substantial clientele of borrowers was acquired readily, the sources of First National's capital were unorthodox, to say the least. B, who was active in the management and affairs of the corporation explained:

Q. When this corporation . . . was established, did Peters actually bring into it a certain amount of capital?

A. Not as capital. As loans he did, yes.

* * * *

There was never any capital in the company.

Q. He, Peters, was borrowing from other sources?

A. Yes.

Q. And in turn he would loan out the money that he borrowed from other sources?

A. Yes.

Q. What were the sources that he borrowed from?

A. The sources were Ruby Stein and Thomas Eboli.*

Q. Is Mr. Eboli also known as 'Tommy Ryan?'

A. Yes, he is.

Q. In addition to these two people, were there others also involved--Mike Genovese and Joe Ross?

A. Yes, Mike Genovese*** gave his money and Joe Ross gave his money on isolated occasions.

Q. What is Joe Ross' real name?

A. Joseph De Nigris.****

The monies which were thus loaned Gazia, were in effect the investment made by these underworld figures in First National.

Money wasn't always on hand to cover all borrowers' needs. In the event that Gazia needed additional financing to make a particularly large loan, he would borrow accordingly from Ruby Stein, Tommy Eboli and others. These individuals charged Gazia a rate of interest of one and one-half percent to two percent a week. This proved to be an ideal way to make money, especially since Gazia risked no capital of his own. He succeeded in making an average profit of three percent a week on this money.

It was hardly expected that the testimony of First National's principals would present a complete picture of the manner in which it was doing business. Accordingly, pursuant to service of a subpoena, a number of corporate ledgers and other records such as checks, statements and assorted index cards were produced for examination by the Commission staff.

---

*Eboli, who is alternately known as Tommy Ryan, Tommy Rye and Tommy De Rosa, lives comfortably in Englewood Cliffs, New Jersey. Together with Gerardo Catena, also a New Jersey resident, Eboli acted as an underboss in the Vito Genovese syndicate. It is generally believed that in the absence of Vito Genovese, Eboli is acting chief of the Genovese criminal empire.

***Relatively little is known about Michael Genovese, brother of Vito Genovese. He is referred to, in inner criminal circles, as the "wise man." When questioned at both private (June 8, 1964) and public (December 1, 1964) hearings, Genovese invoked his constitutional privilege against self incrimination in answer to all questions.

****De Nigris, alias "Joe Ross," is known as a reliable old "soldier" in the Vito Genovese syndicate and a close aide of "Tommy Ryan" Eboli. His criminal record, dating back to 1914, includes convictions for larceny, burglary, forgery and counterfeiting.

The records clearly indicated the relationship of Genovese, Eboli and Stein to Gazia and First National. Although these individuals loaned sums of money to the corporation from which they reaped the rich return of two percent per week, they were, in fact, capital investors in a loan-shark venture. Because of the constant flow of this money in and out of the corporate treasury, by way of loans and repayments, **B** found it difficult to testify with regard to the indebtedness of First National to any of these men at one particular time. Typical weekly debit entries relating to "Tommy Ryan" Eboli, carried on the books as "TR" and to Stein, referred to as "R.S.," were discussed with **B**:

Q. By the 'books,' you are referring to the blank indexed ledgers which you also submitted to the Commission . . .?

A. Yes. If you will look at the card of June 19th you will find it is written in ink up to a certain point, and every one of the payments in ink were payments that were received by check and entered by me. You will find payments in pencil and they were the cash payments that were turned over to Julie (Gazia). And he would supply that to me. In the same week you will find another payment to Tommy Ryan of $300 and you will find a Ruby Stein, 'R.S.,' $300 both of them.

Q. On the calculation of two percent of the outstanding indebtedness per week, how much money would have been outstanding with regard to Tommy Ryan at that time, based upon that $300 vig payment?

A. Around $15,000.

Q. And the same would be true with regard to Ruby Stein, is that correct?

A. Yes.

Q. Based upon that computation, which you just made, could you give us any indication of how much money was outstanding on a monthly or weekly basis from these two payments? Was that the usual amount? I am talking now about borrowings from either Tommy Ryan or Ruby Stein.

A. No, there was nothing unusual about it. The money would be taken as it was needed for a specific loan. There was nothing that was ever carried as just carrying of a loan as such.

Gazia and his investors met at a variety of Greenwich Village restaurants. **B**, present on many of these occasions, "heard them discussing money and payments of money that were due between them." On other occasions, Eboli was seen in the offices of First National. **B** testified that on one occasion he saw Eboli hand Gazia a substantial sum of money. Gazia explained to **B** that the business needed capital for a particular loan and that Eboli brought the money for that purpose.

The Delinquent Loan-Shark. Gazia's relations with his financial bosses were not always smooth and untroubled. Gazia was, of course, bound by stern racket discipline which, on transactions between Eboli and Gazia, required prompt and full payment of vigorish--in this case two percent weekly. **B** had numerous conversations with Gazia about his weekly obligations and actually observed Gazia making payments of money to Eboli.

Like many other borrowers with "vig" obligations, Gazia himself fell behind in his payments to the underworld leaders. Eboli, in keeping with the code, was not one to let arrears pile up. According to **B**, he applied immediate and constant pressure on Gazia for payment.

Gazia was a heavy gambler and loser--a fact which was largely the reason for his periodic failure to pay weekly vigorish to his racket sources on time. It was as a result of Gazia's gambling losses that **B** met the notorious "Jiggs" Forlano. The witness found Forlano going through Gazia's desk at First National. **B** was not sure who the stranger was at the time and ordered him to leave, but not without asking the purpose of the search. Forlano told him that Gazia owed Ruby Stein some money and that he was sent to get it.

When Gazia returned to the office, **B** asked for an explanation and at that time was told who "Jiggs" was. Gazia confessed that he was heavily indebted to Stein as a result of a baseball gambling system which Gazia had devised and which was supposed to be foolproof. Gazia apparently picked the wrong teams and ended up a big loser, owing Stein between $125,000 and $150,000. When Gazia realized that Stein was pressing for the money, "he beat it for one or two days, and then went running to Mike (Genovese) for protection." Later, a compromise was arranged under the auspices of Michael Genovese.

Uncle "Mike" Genovese. The name "Genovese" is woven throughout the fabric of First National's story. Julio Gazia is related by marriage to Vito and Mike Genovese. The corporate books clearly indicated that "M.G.," code for Mike Genovese, invested money in First National and profited handsomely on his investment.

Further evidence of Gazia's connection with and subservience to the crime syndicate headed by Vito Genovese was obtained during the investigation. Michael's brother, Vito, was arrested by the federal government on a narcotics charge, tried, convicted and sentenced to serve a fifteen year term at Atlanta Penitentiary in April 1959. The cost of Vito's defense was substantial--a great deal of money was spent on legal fees. At one point during the lengthy litigation, Michael Genovese discussed this matter with the principals of First National. The corporation, as a syndicate enterprise, was assessed $5,000 as a contribution to the defense fund.

A Cadillac--Gratis! Mike Genovese, who referred to First National as "our business," received other dividends for his investment in the company. It was agreed at the inception of the corporation that he was to be a one-third partner in the business although he received no share of corporate profits as such. However, one of the rewards for his financing the company was a new Cadillac convertible purchased ostensibly for the corporation and used solely by him. **B** testified that First National purchased the car for Genovese and paid for garage and maintenance costs with corporate funds. Shortly after its purchase, at Mike's direction, the car was sold. B was instructed to transfer title to the automobile. He did so and testified that thereafter, he saw neither the car nor the proceeds of the sale.

The Borrowers. What of the unfortunates who were desperate enough to borrow money from the Gazia operation? The case of an independent photographer who found himself caught in the loan-shark's iron grip serves to illustrate the high-interest payment exacted from borrowers. Some time ago, the photographer, who shall be called C, met Gazia and borrowed $200 from him.

C had no collateral of any kind and was unable to secure a loan from any reputable financial institution. C was asked about the terms of the loan:

BY MR. COMETA:
Q. What did you agree to pay him?
A. He wanted me to pay him an interest of ten dollars a week.
Q. Did you understand that this ten dollars a week would have any effect on the two hundred dollars you owed him?
A. None whatever.
Q. None whatever?
A. That's right.
Q. So that, in fact, you were obligated to pay ten dollars ad infinitum?
A. As long as I keep the $200.

* * *

Q. Did you, in fact, thereupon, begin to pay him weekly ten dollars?
A. I did.

C found it impossible to keep current with his "vig" payments. Upon default, he immediately heard from Gazia, who threatened him with bodily harm if he didn't pay what Gazia said he still owed him. The witness testified that his weekly $10 payments for a period of over two years totaled between $1,000 and $1,500. None of this was applied to payment of the principal amount. C admitted that he was fearful "most constantly" and that he was "always aware that something could happen to me."

The Easily Accessible Loan-Shark. One might well wonder how a borrower like C finds a loan-shark. Criminal usurers do not advertise nor are they listed in any business directories. Their seeming ubiquity and ready accessibility to borrowers is attributable chiefly to one other cog in the underworld money lending apparatus--the "steerer." This individual, normally not a syndicate member or employee, refers borrowers to the money lender. According to law enforcement officials and other reliable sources the number of steerers who stand ready to recommend a loan-shark is legion. These are found in the vast army of doormen, elevator operators, bartenders, hat check girls, cab drivers, cigar stand operators and others who have daily contact with many people.* Such people usually earn a small fee for their service.

The case of an East Side restaurant owner, D, is in point. D, after years of working in the restaurant field in a number of capacities, finally accumulated enough money to become sole owner of a fine French restaurant. His business was successful by most standards, but in making the jumps from employee to partner to sole owner, D became financially overextended. Not being able to obtain a loan at his bank, he found a "temporary solution" which he has long since regretted. When examined at a private hearing, he readily admitted borrowing money from First National. D dealt with Gazia, who loaned him $5,000 for which he agreed to pay $250 a week vigorish as long as he held the money. However, to repay the loan in full, he was obligated to pay back to Gazia the sum of $6,000 regardless of the amount of vigorish previously paid.

It is interesting to note the route which D traveled to get to the loan-shark. He testified that he had become friendly with a doorman at an expensive East Side night club. At one point, D confided to the doorman that he was in need of quick cash. The doorman referred him to a cab driver, who, in turn, recommended First National.

Borrowers Live in Fear. Typical of all loan-sharks, Gazia was able to instill great fear in the minds of his borrowers. These individuals lived in dread that defaults in payment of vigorish would bring abuse and violence down upon them.

The criminal in the money lending business doesn't ask for collateral, but he is a secured creditor in the most dramatic sense of the term. The health of the borrower is his security, and upon every default, no matter how short in time, the possibility of bodily harm is brought home to him. D, the restaurant owner, testified regarding his fears:

Q. Are you fearful of these individuals, as far as what might happen to you if you did not pay them?
A. Not to myself . . .

* * *

. . . but suppose they try to harm my children or my wife or my business.

* * *

. . . I am fearful of the whole bunch of them, not just one shylock.

---

*In certain instances a "steerer" may be held liable as a guarantor on the loan. This usually occurs when the "steerer," as a friend or business associate of the borrower, urges the granting of the loan and an understanding, express or implied is reached, that he will make good on the loan in the event of a default.

Another borrower, E, went to First National for a small loan. His fortunes became progressively worse and he found himself falling behind in his payments. Gazia began a blitz campaign of telephone calls to E and his wife. Mrs. E testified that Gazia cursed her and generally subjected her to abuse and humiliating and filthy language. She once found an obscene note in her mailbox. An asthmatic, Mrs. E found all of this so sickening, she was stricken by a serious attack and was hospitalized for two weeks. Believing that Gazia was "crazy enough to do anything" Mrs. E lived in dread that "my son would be in any way subject to harm or my husband or myself."

The Gazia operation employed two hoodlums as its collectors, Anthony Scala and Anthony "Junior" De Franco. De Franco has two convictions for violation of Section 1751 of the Penal Law, which deals with the possession and use of narcotic drugs. His partner, Scala, likes to be called "the leg breaker."

The Business Takeover. The loan-shark is very anxious to accommodate the impecunious business corporation. There are several reasons for this, one of them being that if he and his henchmen can actually gain control of a company in legitimate business, they obtain important benefits beyond financial gain. The underworld is constantly looking for "cover," that is, a front which will serve to mask criminal activity. Known criminals are most anxious to appear as employees on the payroll of any going enterprise so that they may show some legal source of income. When the loan-sharks take over a business, the gates are opened and hoodlums become non-working "salaried employees."

Money, however, is the prime consideration. When a corporate executive approaches the loan-shark, the company itself will be subjected to a thorough scrutiny, for today's usurer is a sophisticated man, and if he cannot size up the possibilities of a business, someone who can is just a phone call away. If the business is beyond recall, it will be run into the ground at a profit to the loan-shark. This method of corporate rape, known as the "bankruptcy caper" will be discussed in a subsequent section. If the business can make money, the loan-shark will see to it that he receives his weekly vigorish from the executive borrower and also a sizeable share of the proceeds of the business itself.

F was a fairly successful business man in the optical field before he met Gazia. In need of quick cash for corporate development, he was referred to First National by a New Jersey businessman.

First National agreed to loan $22,000 to F for which he was obligated to pay vigorish at a five percent weekly rate. Usually a loan-shark is not primarily interested in repayment of the principal. He is content with indefinite weekly vigorish payments. This was undoubtedly true in F's case. No matter how many times he paid his $1100 weekly "vig," he still owed the entire principal of $22,000. When asked how he came to agree to such an exhorbitant rate, F simply replied ". . . I needed the money."

Three weeks later, **F** borrowed an additional $6500 without reducing the principal of the first loan. Now he found himself burdened by a $1425 weekly vigorish payment. In a short time, his fortunes hit rock bottom and he found himself running from friend to friend in an effort to borrow money to meet the loan-shark's demands.

Gazia's patience ran short when **F**'s resources completely disappeared. The men at the top were also becoming concerned about their investment return and efforts were initiated to salvage what they could. To plot their future course, Gazia met with Eboli and one Don Ferraro* at a Greenwich Village restaurant. Witness **A** was also in attendance and testified about the details of the "sit-down." At this meeting, which **A** referred to as a "kangaroo court," the future of **F**'s corporation was decided.

Ferraro was assigned to operate the corporation's plant in West Virginia and **F** was required to relinquish virtually all control over the fortunes of his company to him. In fact, he did not even have the authority to co-sign checks under the Ferraro regime. Eboli, as top man at the "sit-down" decreed that **F** was to be held to complete repayment according to their terms. The entire principal and as much interest as could be squeezed out of **F** and his company was to be recovered.

Numerous other meetings were held concerning the fate of the company. Notorious underworld figures such as Santos Trafficante were present. Some of these meetings took place in Miami, and at least one was held at the Englewood Country Club, Englewood, New Jersey, one of Eboli's frequent haunts. Another participant in this series of meetings was Louis P. Coticchia,*** better known as "Lou Brady," who was presented to **F** as the "cure-all" who might possibly effect the merger of **F**'s company with another enterprise.

Not too many months elapsed before the inevitable bankruptcy came. The company was completely drained and liquidated under the auspices of the loan-shark and his underworld cronies. **F** had not only paid back $25,000 in interest but lost his business as well.

---

*Dominick Ferraro has an extensive criminal record. He was convicted for armed robbery in New Jersey early in his career and in 1936 was convicted on a felonious violation of the U.S. Postal Laws, in that he operated a fake lottery known as the Montreal Post Graduate Hospital Fund Sweepstake.

***Coticchia's criminal record includes convictions for the crimes of receiving stolen goods and assault with intent to commit rape. His criminal record reflects entries from such varied cities as Hot Springs (Arkansas), Los Angeles, Miami, Baltimore and Dallas.

Gazia's Testimony. Gazia did not testify at the public hearing. Subpoenaed to appear on December 1, 1964, he entered Columbus Hospital for minor surgery three days before the hearing commenced. However, he appeared at four private hearings conducted in the earlier stages of the usury investigation. The fourth of these private sessions was on the occasion of his release from Civil Prison, where he had been remanded for his contumacious refusal to answer certain questions put to him by the Commission.

During each of his four private hearings, Gazia frequently indulged in emotional outbursts and was, for the most part, beyond the control of his attorney. Rambling incoherently, it was nearly impossible to obtain a direct answer to most of the questions asked of him. He denied that he was ever a principal of First National, that he made decisions as to the operation of the company, that he borrowed from Thomas Eboli, Ruby Stein, Michael Genovese, or others for the lending business. He did state that he worked as an investigator for the company.

The Profit Picture. First National's books and records were the subject of an extensive analysis. An accountant on the Commission's staff testified at the public hearing regarding his detailed examination of approximately six thousand entries, covering a two year period. Ninety-four borrowers transacted 410 separate loans for a volume of $400,000 in business during a twenty-five month period. The accountant's analysis further indicated a profit to First National on this business of about $150,000.

He was questioned about the very high profit margin of this operation. Using a ledger page from the corporate books as an example, he explained one instance of First National's extraordinary money-making techniques. In that case, a borrower received a loan of $2,500 for which he agreed to pay weekly interest of $125. He managed to pay the interest at first, but thereafter could not pay for several weeks. At a time when he had already repaid $2,375 in interest, the borrower made a $3,000 payment toward principal--a total payment, at that point, to First National of $5,375 in principal and interest. However, as a result of his failure to make all weekly interest payments on time, he was penalized to such an extent that his ledger sheet indicated a balance due of $1,750. If the unhappy borrower paid this last amount in one lump sum, he would end up by paying the loan-shark $7,125 on an original indebtedness of $2,500--all in a period of less than one year!

Under corporate cover, well-financed by the upper echelon of the underworld, and being able to operate within the law, the Gazia venture prospered for several years. Using fear as a method of enforcement, large profits were made at the expense of human suffering and abasement. Evidence adduced at the Commission's public hearing put a powerful spotlight on the actions of Gazia and his ilk. First National Service and Discount Corporation has ceased to operate.

D. Syndicate Discipline and Control of Loan-Shark Operations

Direct ties with organized crime syndicates are clearly manifested in loan-shark businesses as conducted by Julio Gazia and the First National Service and Discount Corporation. The disclosure of Gazia's sources of capital and underworld superiors and his established allegiance to the Vito Genovese group definitely place him in the high echelons of syndicate money lending operations.

The investigation revealed that the strong arm of the crime syndicates reached out to control, influence and discipline smaller and more obscure loan-sharks, operating in the seeming backwaters of the usurious money lending business.

1. The Case of the Timid Bookie. Witness G was a neighborhood bookie in Yonkers, New York. For many years he operated out of a small smoke shop front, taking bets on horses. Information about G came to the Commission's attention during its investigation of gambling and law enforcement in Westchester County. Bookie G was noted for being a very careful, if not timid, operator. In sixteen years of bookmaking at one location, he was never arrested. He handled his own bets with known bettors, made minimal and discreet use of the telephone, avoided lay-off complications and paid all his obligations promptly. G had substantial "cash on hand" from the proceeds of his bookmaking business. In about September, 1961, he decided to put some of it to work. Through an intermediary, he gave $8,000 in cash to one Thomas Manzo as an investment "to make money with it." Manzo was a loan-shark.

The Local Loan-Shark. If one needed a case in point that loan-sharks thrive at every level of our economic, business and social life, Thomas Manzo would serve admirably. He resides in a small private home in a moderate income residential area of Yonkers. His "cover," while not nearly as imposing as a fancy corporate name on a Fifth Avenue office door, was no less effective. Manzo was on the payroll of the Department of Sanitation of the City of Yonkers, with duties as an emergency repair man, on call between the hours of twelve midnight and eight o'clock in the morning. This, of course, left ample time for his money lending activities.

Information available to the Commission indicates that Manzo operated as a loan-shark in the Yonkers area. A borrower from Manzo testified that in 1962 he borrowed $1,000 from him at five percent a week interest. This witness, an admitted and inveterate horse player, was referred to the loan-shark by his bookmaker. Up to the time of the hearing in December, 1964, the witness had been paying $50 a week vigorish, more or less regularly. He was not able to fix the total amount of vigorish that was paid over the more than two year period. However, he still owed the principal amount of $1,000.

Unlikely as it may seem, G's venture with Manzo was to create a conflict that was marked by shootings and threats and only settled finally through the imposition of syndicate discipline by a top underworld figure. The rather bizarre chain of events which ultimately led to an underworld "sit-down" was sketched by testimony obtained from **G** himself and from reliable information obtained through underworld sources. **G**, obviously frightened, was an extremely reluctant and evasive witness. Despite being granted immunity, he at first refused to testify. Contempt proceedings were brought and an order for his commitment to jail had to be obtained before he would give any testimony.

The Dispute. Bookie **G** had turned over his $8,000 to Manzo without receipt or other evidence of the transaction. He denied that any specific agreement had been entered into respecting return on his investment. Nevertheless, every week between September 30, 1961 and February 10, 1962, he received regular payments which totaled about $2,000, indicating weekly vigorish to him of about 1.5 percent. After February 10, 1962, payments stopped abruptly. **G** stated that he waited until April, 1963 before he contacted Manzo directly in an effort to get his money. Never one to ignore "heat" **G** had closed shop during the Commission's gambling investigation in Westchester which was accompanied by county-wide raids in March, 1962. "Things were bad" according to **G** and his need for cash forced him to seek the repayment directly from Manzo. He was turned down.

Shortly thereafter **G** was put in contact with an individual named James De Masi, alias "Jimmy Dimps." "Dimps," previously convicted of larceny, gambling and assault charges, is a known hoodlum in Westchester County and a strong-arm man and enforcer for New Rochelle loan-shark and racketeer Joseph Calandruccio.*

---

*Calandruccio, known also as "Joe Cal" and "Joe the Baker," came under investigation as part of the loan-shark inquiry. His criminal record includes convictions for felonious assault and gambling. He is an associate of members of the Vito Genovese syndicate. A number of borrowers from Calandruccio were identified and questioned. No other group in the entire investigation were so patently in terror of speaking. In a few instances where witnesses admitted borrowing money from "Cal" they insisted that they had paid no vigorish and that the loans were given as personal favors. One borrower, severely beaten by "Dimps" and Bruno Capio, another strong arm employee of Calandruccio, would not identify them as his assailants. He explained "All I know is I found a note under my door. It said 'keep your mouth shut if you know what's good for you.'" Another borrower, urged to testify truthfully, replied "I'd rather go to jail for perjury. At least in jail I would be alive." Calandrucio fled to California a short time before the public hearing. Information was received by the Commission that he was directed to leave the jurisdiction by his underworld superiors. The exceptionally brazen and vicious manner in which he conducted

(continued...)

At a meeting in a New Rochelle diner, "Dimps" agreed to try to collect the money. Such "contracts" generally call for the payment of a substantial fee to the collector. However, G denied such an arrangement:

Q. Isn't it a fact, Mr. G, that you knew that this Jimmy Dimps was a strong arm man and a hoodlum from the New Rochelle area?
A. No, I never heard of him. I didn't know any such thing.
Q. You still haven't answered the Commission, what was Mr. Dimps going to do to collect the money that you couldn't do yourself?
A. I don't know what he was going to do.

Whether G knew or not, "Dimps" obviously started action. Shortly after the meeting, Manzo's wife received a phone call late at night from an individual who, using filthy and abusive language, demanded that Manzo pay G the money due him. Manzo returned the compliment with a phone call to G's wife. G, frightened, sent $100 and a message to "Dimps" to "stop whatever he is doing," but G had started a chain of events which he was powerless to stop. Within a short time, a shotgun blast was fired into the rear of his car which was parked in the driveway of his home. G continued:

Q. Mr. (G), did you get a telephone call immediately after the shotgun blast in the back of your car?
A. Yes. They said the next time it would be me.

"Dimps" had not ceased in his efforts to collect.
Some days later, G met Manzo, who was brief and to the point--"you better get this guy off my back. I work for Frank Sacco." The connection to Manzo's lending operations with the higher echelons of the underworld were revealed for the first time to G. Sacco was a notorious hoodlum, convict and loan-shark with a reputation for viciousness surpassed by none.*
Frightened, G arranged through friends to meet with Sacco himself. The cutting of the electric power line leading into his home, which occurred about

---

*(...continued)
his activities had made him "too hot" and the subject of concentrated attention by law enforcement authorities.

*An associate of top members of the Vito Genovese syndicate, Sacco's criminal record includes convictions for felonious assault, forgery and interstate shipment of stolen securities and other property. He is presently serving a five year term in federal prison on convictions for interstate shipment of stolen property and bankruptcy frauds. Other loan-shark activities of Sacco are discussed at pages 38 to 41 and 43 to 45, ifra.

this time, added to his acute feeling of urgency. In a meeting at an automobile dealer's office in Yonkers, G asked Sacco for help. Sacco told G that Manzo owed him $12,000 and "when I collect mine, I will see what I can do for you." Reliable information received by the Commission corroborates the facts indicated by the statements of Sacco and Manzo to G concerning their relationship. Sacco was Manso's underworld superior and a source of funds for his lending operation.

Sacco, of course, had no interest in helping G to collect his money. However, with a hood's instinct for sensing weakness and a ready mark, he set up G for a shakedown. Another mobster was flushed out of the woodwork for this job--James Palmisano, alias "Jimmy Vee."*

G was called to a second meeting, this time with both Sacco and Palmisano, who took over. He told the bookie that for $1,500 he would "settle" the loan for $4,000. G agreed to this extraordinary proposition. "I got panicky," he explained. At this point, G's prime interest was the safety of his hide; the money became secondary.

The $4,000 settlement proved to be a note in that amount, payable two years from date, and executed by Manzo. The note was signed "Thomas Manzo, Pres." yet contained nothing to indicate that it was in any way a corporate obligation. G recognized it for what it was--a worthless scrap of paper.

BY MR. VERGARI:

Q. Are you telling us Mr. (G), that you agreed to give $1,500 in good hard cash for this note payable two years later?
A. Right.
Q. And this was to satisfy your entire claim with respect to the eight thousand dollars?
A. Right.
Q. And you agreed to that?
A. Yes.

* * *

Q. So far as you are concerned, what is this note worth to you?
A. What this thing is worth to me, nothing.

THE CHAIRMAN (Commissioner Grumet): Did you pay him fifteen hundred dollars for that note, for that?
THE WITNESS: Yes.

---

*Palmisano was convicted of grand larceny, growing out of assault and robbery charges and of O.P.A. violations. He, like Sacco, is a known associate of the Vito Genovese syndicate.

THE CHAIRMAN: On top of the eight thousand dollars?
THE WITNESS: Yes sir.

G had indeed panicked. The manner in which he paid the $1,500 "fee" further evidenced his fear. He was instructed to go that evening with $1,500 in cash in an envelope, to the lounge of the Town House Motel in Yonkers. There, he was to leave the envelope under a table at which Sacco would be seated. Following his instructions, G appeared with the cash at the appointed place and time and found Sacco seated at a table with one Anthony Plata.* He sat down briefly, dropped the envelope under the table and left without a word.

G fully realized that he was playing in a league that was far over his own timid head. Howver, the game was not over for him. There were innings to be played.

G did receive something more for his money at the meeting in the auto agency. Palmisano gave him a telephone number in Florida to call "in case there was trouble." The trouble came.

Apparently the word had gone out in the underworld that this bookie, with ready cash, was a push-over for a shakedown. Some time after dropping the $1,500 cash "fee" at Sacco's feet, G was called from his home to a meeting on a Yonkers street corner. Two men, described by G as rough looking characters, attempted another shake-down, offered to protect G and to help him with his problems for a fee of $15,000.

The now distraught G called Palmisano in Florida who instructed him "to see a fellow by the name of "Joe The Wop**" on Mulberry Street and have him call me."

G visited Gennaro at a coffee shop at 121 Mulberry Street, in New York City, and as instructed, asked him to call Palmisano in Florida. Gennaro placed the call and later told G that "everything would be all right."

In spite of G's request that he cease and desist, James "Dimps" De Masi continued his efforts to collect from Manzo. Information indicates that "Dimps" and his bosses, "Joe Cal" did not wish to give up their valuable "contract" to collect the $8,000 from Manzo. G testified:

---

*Plata, known as "Tony Plate" has been identified as a member of the crime syndicate headed by Carlo Gambino. Plate, known as an enforcer, has been convicted of assault and armed robbery.

**Joseph Gennaro, with aliases "Joe the Wop" and "Pete Russo" is known for long and unsavory criminal associations. He is a suspected loan-shark and is reported to have taken over Carmine Lombardozzi's activities during the latter's incarceration. Lombardozzi is a leader in the Carlo Gambino syndicate.

Q. After the meeting with Gennaro, what happened to you?
A. What happened to me?
Q. I am talking about specifically on November 3, 1963.
A. My house got shot up.
Q. Tell us what happened.
A. I was sleeping and the dog got shot at.
Q. Somebody fired shots through your front door?
A. Yes.

According to a reliable informant, this shooting brought an end to syndicate patience with the entire affair. G's venture into the world of loan-sharking had to be brought to a final conclusion. A "sit-down" was called at a restaurant in the lower East Side of New York City. The presiding officer was drawn from the top ranks of the underworld, Thomas Greco, alias "Tommy Palmer." Palmer, identified as a group leader in the Vito Genovese syndicate, called for the attendance of Sacco, Plate, Manzo, "Dimps" De Masi, representing Calandruccio, and G. The decision was predictable and perhaps, by underworld standards, appropriate. "Dimps" was to cease all efforts to collect on behalf of G. Sacco, Plate and Manzo were to leave G alone. For his part, G was told that he must abandon any claim to his $8,000 investment. The $1,500 paid by G to Sacco and Plate was to be marked off as a fee for their services in arranging the temporary settlement. And perhaps as a final lesson, G was required to pay $1,000 to Palmer in appreciation for his achieving the final settlement.

Nothing has happened since 1963 to indicate that this "injunction" handed down by Palmer has been violated in the slightest respect.

2. *A Matter of Priorities.* The disciplined and peaceful settlement of racket disputes growing out of opposing loan-shark claims was reflected in another case which involved extreme provocation--a brawl and shooting fracas. In conflict were two loan-sharks, Frank Sacco and John Massiello. Each had made separate loans to a restaurant owner referred to as H* and each claimed prior right of payment.

In 1957, Witness H, with a parcel of real estate worth $13,000 and personal and family cash resources of an equivalent amount, built a modern restaurant and banquet facility in Yonkers, New York. An additional $60,500 was raised by first and second mortgages on the property placed with legitimate lending sources.

---

*References to H's dealings with loan-sharks will be principally to private hearings and statements given to investigators in private interviews. At the public hearing H became highly emotional and sought to deny the accuracy or truth of much relevant testimony given by him in private.

The initial capitalization proved to be insufficient and in the latter part of 1957, H borrowed an additional $10,000 from one Maitland Brenhouse. H did not seem to be sure of the rate of interest on this loan, which was secured by an additional mortgage on the property. However, he did admit paying $125 a week on the loan with only "very little" applied to principal.

H opened the restaurant in May, 1958 and business was good. Nevertheless, his debt load was so great that he had difficulty in meeting his obligations. Defaults in payment led to threats of foreclosure and general harassment from creditors. One of the creditors was Brenhouse, who told H "Don't worry about your money, when you get on your feet, you will pay me." Brenhouse, a loan-shark himself, was obviously not acting out of kindness. Unpaid interest and penalties were added to the mortgage and compounded so that within a year, the principal amount owing had increased from $10,00 to $25,000.

In September, 1959, Brenhouse advised H that he had to assign the mortgage to Frank Sacco, with whom he was associated in a money lending firm known as Yonkers Factors, with offices at 900 Nepperhan Avenue, Yonkers, New York.* Another principal in that firm was one Simon Geller. Sacco, with strong syndicate connections, was the undisputed boss of that lending operation, which included at least two other firms known as Valbretto Factors and H M R Realty, located at the same address. H testified that he knew of Sacco's reputation and voiced strong objections to the assignment of the mortgage to him. Brenhouse told H that he had no choice in the matter. Sacco was "calling the tune." Call the tune he did, with H paying the piper most dearly. Within three days of the assignment, the loan being in default, Sacco demanded full payment and threatened H with foreclosure. Unable to make any payment, H accepted an alternative offer by Sacco. He signed notes for a further increase in the principal amount of the loan to $29,000. By March, 1960, the principal amount was raised to $35,000 through further imposition of interest and penalties. This was done in spite of the fact that H received no additional capital over the original $10,000 and had paid some $18,000 in vigorish during the period. This unconscionable treatment of a borrower is typical of loan-shark transactions.

However, of major interest in this particular matter was the conflict which developed between Sacco and John Massiello. It was in testifying on this part of his experience that H became highly emotional and agitated. Some time in

---

*Maitland Brenhouse, who had been involved in the money lending business with Sacco for many years, was found dead of a gunshot wound in the head at his home at Hastings, New York, on April 5, 1962. The matter is carried as an open homicide investigation by Westchester County authorities.

the early part of 1960, H borrowed $2,000 from Massiello. He would not discuss the interest rate on this loan, insisting "Massiello did not shylock me."

On the evening of June 1, 1960, Massiello and his henchmen held a large dinner party at H's restaurant. At about ten that night, Sacco came into the bar and asked H for a vigorish payment. Not having the cash, H went to the dining room and asked Massiello for part payment on the dinner party bill. Massiello asked why and H explained his problem with Sacco. H was instructed to tell Sacco that Massiello wanted to see him in the dining room. Sacco accepted the invitation and a brief but heated argument ensued between the loan-sharks. Priority of their respective claims was the bone of contention. Sacco was apparently annoyed that part of the cost of the party was to be applied to the Massiello loan, money that he might otherwise have collected himself. The argument was taken to the street. Massiello and several henchmen walked out with Sacco. When they returned a few minutes later, Sacco appeared to have taken a rather severe beating. In a rage, Sacco went to H's office and used the phone. H testified that Sacco called his associate, Simon Geller, and overheard him order Geller, to "bring over my piece." Extracts from a statement by H to a Commission agent follow:

> Shortly thereafter, Sy Geller appeared at the restaurant and handed Sacco an automatic pistol. Sacco and Geller, followed by H, went into the back room where Massiello and several of his men were sitting. Sacco threatened Massiello with the gun. At one point, he had the gun buried in Massiello's stomach but it failed to fire when he pulled the trigger. Sacco then levered a fresh round into the chamber but must have had his finger on the trigger when he worked the slide. During the ensuing brawl, a wild shot was fired which struck a radiator and ricocheted into the hand of one of the group.

Cooler heads apparently prevailed. Although the police were called, no complaints were made or charges placed. The shooting was reported as an accidental discharge of a weapon by Geller who was licensed to carry a gun. All agreed that any criminal prosecution growing out of the melee could imperil the restaurant license, as well as present personal difficulties for those involved.

Such an incident, a near murder, might well have started a shooting war. Quite the opposite occurred. Apparently syndicate discipline and influence once more asserted itself and underworld policy for peaceful settlement or disputes prevailed. Within a few days, Massiello's claim was merged with the total debt to Sacco, who was charged with collecting on the entire account and paying Massiello his proportionate share. Some time later, the two loan-sharks who had once nearly killed each other showed up together dunning H for payment. At this point H had been removed from his restaurant business and was operating a bar and grill owned by him at another location. During that visit, the loan-sharks demanded that H sell this business in order to pay their claim.

H refused. Three days later a shotgun was fired through the window of these premises. This shooting occurred ten minutes to two o'clock in the morning, when H, alone in the premises, was preparing to close.

A postscript should be added. H was finally forced into bankruptcy. He lost the restaurant and the bar and grill and all other assets.

E. *Borrowers Coerced into Criminal Acts*

> To enforce a debt, they will go very far--I have known them to go as far as hanging a man out of a window by his feet, fifteen stories--he got the money up in one hour--after you are frightened, you will come up with it--the only time a man gets killed is when he has defied their law completely--when he has it and just doesn't want to pay it--then it pays to make an example of him.

This sworn testimony was given by an individual who had been inside the underworld as a friend, confidant and some-time employee of well known racket figures. That it was stated in a calm, matter-of-fact way, made it no less frightening. Investigation clearly indciated that "to enforce a debt" they will, indeed, "go very far." One extent to which they do go has most tragic consequences on the lives of borrowers. Through intimidation and harsh, unyielding pressure, borrowers are virtually forced to commit criminal acts to provide money to meet vigorish payments. Ever ingenious, loan-sharks devise criminal ventures that fit the borrower's particular situation and capabilities.

Sergeant of Detectives Salerno of the Criminal Investigation Bureau, New York City Police Department, testified of a hair-dresser who operated a beauty salon in a fashionable area of New York City. His clients included wealthy women who possessed jewelry of great value, a fact which did not escape the loan-shark. When it became apparent that the hairdresser could not meet his substantial vigorish payments, he was pressed into service as a "fingerman" for a burglary ring.

The hairdresser was able to identify those clients who owned gems, to ascertain their value and to obtain addresses and apartment numbers. Casual conversation during a coifing session would elicit information such as a husband's working hours, the maid's day off and other facts vital to the planning of a burglary. After each successful jewel theft, the hairdresser's share of the proceeds of the crime were given to the loan-shark as a vigorish payment.

Another case which also demonstrated loan-shark ingenuity involved a prominent sports announcer. This individual had become so hopelessly in debt to several racket lenders that a "sit-down" had to be held. The indebtedness was consolidated and two of the loan-sharks were entrusted with devising a means of collection. A crooked dice game was set up. The broadcaster, with numerous friends and contacts among affluent and "sporting" people, was required to act as a "steerer" for the game. A percentage of the proceeds of this "razzle-dazzle" was applied to satisfy his indebtedness. Investigation by the Commission disclosed similar instances.

   1. A Trucker Forced to Ship and Store Stolen Property. Witness J* is the Secretary and Vice-President of a small trucking and warehouse corporation in the Bronx, New York. This corporation is family owned and J and an elder brother operate the business. Serious illness in the family adversely affected management efficiency. This problem, together with high medical costs, had completely drained cash resources. The usual sad pattern of events developed. Credit with legitimate lending sources was exhausted.

   In 1957, the firm started borrowing from loan-shark Frank Sacco. Over a period of four years, through 1961, the firm borrowed a total of $40,000, paying and receiving loans averaging about $10,000 a year. These loans were ostensibly obtained from other Sacco "cover" firms, Hub Factors and Certified Discount Corporation. Most transactions were negotiated with Simon Geller and J's direct dealings with Sacco during the early years of their relationship were limited. J claimed that she did not at first fully realize who and what Sacco was. This may have very well been so, but she eventually learned.

   On Election Day 1961, J's brother was arrested on a charge of receiving stolen property. New York City Police found a truck, belonging to J's firm and parked in J's garage, loaded with stolen transistor radios. J and her brother, who had handled the shipment, claimed innocence of any knowledge of the nature of the truck's cargo, although the brother eventually entered a plea of guilty to the charge. They would not implicate Sacco or his men and as late as the hearings in 1964, both continued to insist that Sacco had nothing to do with the stolen property. Information from reliable sources indicates that quite the opposite was true. Principals of the J firm were coerced into transporting and storing the stolen property out of fear of Sacco.

   This fear and their reluctance to testify against Sacco is readily understood in light of an incident which occurred in about April, 1962. J saw Sacco's picture in a newspaper and read that he was questioned and being held on bail as a material witness in the Maitland Brenhouse homicide investigation. She told Sacco that she wanted to discontinue their lender-borrower relationship and asked that he stop visiting the office. An argument ensued, in which Sacco claimed that the J firm owed him substantially more than J's books then indicated. J testified:

> Q. Did he claim in this argument that you owed him a much greater amount
>   than you, in fact, believed you did, or knew you did?
> A. He did claim I owed him much greater than I knew that I did.

---

*The letter J is not being used in this report as a witness designation. "J" testified as Jane Doe at the public hearing.

Q. Did you express to him rather clearly that you had no--
A. I not only expressed it to him, but I showed him in black and white.
Q. You expressed it to him much clearer, that you wouldn't pay this great amount that he claimed you owed him?
A. Yes.
Q. Did you have any heated exchange about that?
A. No. I was the one who was heated at all times in this particular discussion.
Q. All right. But you were firm about that?
A. Yes, sir.
Q. You weren't going to accede to this demand on his part?
A. Definitely not. That's right.

A short time later, Sacco sent an emissary demanding immediate payment of vigorish. Still angry, J refused to pay and ordered the collector out. Her testimony continued:

Q. What happened?
A. That evening I received a telephone call, stating that--just stating that--I believe--to the effect that I should see my car outside, and whatever happened to that was going to happen to me next. And it just so happens that I didn't own a car then, but a car that I had previously owned I had given to my brother-in-law. My brother's car was directly outside of my house. I looked outside and there was nothing wrong with the car. So I laughed the whole thing off. However, the following morning, my brother-in-law, who then was the owner of a car that I originally owned, came into my home, and, of course, told me that the car, supposedly mine, was bombed.
THE CHAIRMAN: Was what?
THE WITNESS: Bombed.
COMMISSIONER LANE: Blown up?
THE WITNESS: Well, the windows were shattered and the seats were shattered, et cetera.
Q. Were you able to recognize the voice of the person who called you and told you, in effect, see what happened to your car, the next time it will be you?
A. Yes. The voice that I recognized was Frank Sacco.

J paid off the debt to Sacco in full.

Loan-Sharks in the Securities Business

Ever since the underworld realized that loan-sharking was a safe and highly lucrative enterprise, it has devised increasingly sophisticated ways of using loan-sharking to invade the business world. The loan-shark may no longer be stereotyped as an unshaven thug standing on a corner dispensing money by the traditional "six for five" formula.

In the development of our free enterprise system, we have become a nation of stockholders. Millions of Americans own countless shares of stock in business corporations. The "board" rooms of brokerage houses across the country daily are filled with anxious customers who watch carefully the progress or decline of their favorite securities. Our expanding economy has brought on a corresponding expansion of the securities business, especially in the organization of many new over-the-counter firms.* Occasionally, some of these brokerage houses are undercapitalized and find it difficult to meet the strictly enforced monetary ratio requirements of the federal government. Enter the loan-shark.

The Commission's investigation revealed several instances where loan-sharks were able to gain control of the operations of brokerage houses through usurious loans. Stockbrokers who became deeply indebted to the underworld money lenders were forced into high pressure schemes involving the sale of thousands of shares of worthless stock resulting in great losses to the investing public. . . .

The recent public hearings of the State Commision of Investigation disclosed, for the first time, that the organized criminal underworld, its agents and other unscrupulous operators are conducting a vast and highly lucrative usurious money lending business in this State. This element charges unconscionable rates of interest of 260% per year and in some cases 2000% per year, and enforces its obligations by fear, threats and violence.

Loan-sharking has become a major source of revenue for the underworld and a principal avenue by which crime syndicates have invaded legitimate businesses, including, in some instances, manufacturing and merchandising firms, brokerage houses, restaurants and night clubs. These businesses, when taken over by loan-sharks, are used to further other criminal enterprises.

Most shocking was the revelation that this racket has grown to tremendous proportions, producing millions in revenue, in large measure because of the serious vacuum which exists in the usury laws of this State.

---

*The term, over-the-counter, is generally used to designate a brokerage firm which specializes in unlisted issues, that is, the stock of companies not appearing on the boards of the New York, American or other major stock exchanges.

Traditional organized crime operations such as narcotics, gambling and prostitution carry, in varying degree, substantial risks of prosecution and severe penalty. No comparable handicap exists for the loan-shark. He is, in a sense, invited into the money lending business by the lack of strong criminal laws against unconscionable usury.

The criminal loan-shark can, and generally does, conduct his business wholly within the law, operating under high-sounding business names, with offices and other trappings of legitimacy. The criminal usurer is fully cognizant of the laws' shortcomings and sets his business policies accordingly. An underworld "insider" and others have testified that the loan-shark knows that no criminal penalty attaches to loans made to corporations regardless of how onerous and unconscionable a rate of interest is imposed. He is also aware that this same absence of criminal penalty prevails in loans to individuals in excess of $800.

From the law enforcement standpoint, it is clear that existing statutes do not provide adequate weapons for attacking the problem. Laws against extortion and coercion are of only limited value, since the loan-shark rarely needs to resort to overt and actionable intimidation. His own reputation is usually enough to instill fear. Furthermore, when such acts become necessary, they are usually carried out by strong-arm underlings.

To seek out and prosecute usury as such, law enforcement authorities have available only two usury laws which carry penal sanctions. One is Section 357 of the Banking Law, the other, present Section 2400 of the Penal Law.

Section 357 is part of Article 9 of the Banking Law, which regulates the small loan business. Section 357 penalizes as a misdemeanor, loans of $800 or less bearing more than the authorized rate of interest, made to individuals by unlicensed lenders. This section is of some use only against the distinctly small-time "six for five" type of street corner loan-shark. It is less than adequate for that breed because its violation constitutes only a misdemeanor. Moreover, it provides no remedy at all against the higher echelon, underworld connected loan-shark whose activities constitute this major law enforcement problem and the principal threat to the safety and economic well-being of the community.

The other present law, Section 2400 of the Penal Law, penalizes usury as a misdemeanor only when tools, implements of trade or household goods are taken as security. This section is limited and its prohibitions in no way reflect any present day loan-shark activity. Loan-sharks do not find it necessary to trouble themselves with collateral of this nature.

Full consideration of the facts about modern loan-shark operations makes clear the urgent necessity to strike boldly at the heart of the probelm--to legislate where the law is silent. The existing vacuum in law, in which the criminal loan-shark has operated with impunity, must be filled by meaningful and effective legislation.

3

Labor Racketeering Activities of Jack McCarthy and National Consultants Associated, Ltd.

Report of the Committee on Government Operations, United States Senate, Made by Its Permanent Subcommitee on Investigations Together with Individual Views, April 24, 1967.

The Senate Permanent Subcommittee on Investigations received a considerable number of complaints during the years 1965-66 relating to the role of labor relations consultants in the important field of collective bargaining between management and labor. Certain of these disquieting reports centered upon the highly questionable activities of a labor consultant named Jack McCarthy, whose business is located in the metropolitan area of New York.

It was alleged that he and his associates represented employers in collective bargaining with labor unions which McCarthy reportedly dominated and controlled. Information received by the subcommittee also indicated that conflict of interest situations existed which emanated from dubious financial transactions between labor consultant McCarthy and certain union officials. It was alleged that McCarthy and the officials acted in collusion on labor matters. Other improprieties and abuses were reported which involved purported misuse of welfare funds for highly questionable dental, optical, and medical benefits.

Under the authority granted by the Senate,* the Permanent Subcommittee on Investigations conducted a preliminary inquiry to determine whether the

---

*Sec. 2, S. Res. 183 89th Cong. 2d sess., authorizing and directing the Committee on Government Operations and the Permanent Subcommittee on Investigations to conduct "an investigation and study of the extent to which criminal or other improper practices or activities are, or have been, engaged in the field of labor-management relations or in groups or organizations of employees or employers, to the detriment of interests of the public, employers, or employees, and to determine whether any changes are required in the laws of the United States to protect such interests against the occurrence of such practices and activities."

allegations were substantiated by facts, and whether existing laws were adequate to correct the reported improprieties and to prevent their recurrence. The subcommittee's interest was particularly directed toward those sections of the Labor-Management Reporting and Disclosure Act of 1959 which deal with the activities of "middlemen" or labor consultants in labor-management relations.

As a result of information developed during the preliminary inquiry, the subcommittee held public hearings on September 27-28 and October 4, 1966. Twenty-four witnesses were examined under oath, and additional evidence was received in the form of exhibits and sworn affidavits.

Dual Role of McCarthy as Union Official and Labor Consultant

The date of Jack McCarthy's introduction into the labor movement is not known. In 1950 he was associated with Local 1430 of the International Brotherhood of Electrical Workers (IBEW), located at 165 West 46th Street, New York City. McCarthy was business manager of this local for a number of years until he resigned on July 19, 1962.

McCarthy also was an organizer for Local 225 of the International Jewelry Workers Union (IJWU) as early as 1957. This union also was located at 165 West 46th Street. Daniel Kapilow, a close associate of Jack McCarthy for a number of years, was president of local 225 during the period 1957 to 1960 and has been vice president from 1962 to the present. Kapilow also was associated with Jack McCarthy in Local 1430, IBEW. Kapilow has been a business agent in this local from 1960 to the present.

In November of 1954, McCarthy and Kapilow became business partners in the Linsan Trading Co., located at 113 West 42d Street, New York City. This partnership, which is still in operation, lends money to businesses which deal in window cleaning and maintenance of commercial offices. The company receives chattel mortgages on the service contracts as collateral for its loans.

The subcommittee did not determine when McCarthy first entered into his dual role of union official and labor consultant. In August of 1961, McCarthy, while still a union official, was shown to be associated with Westminster Associates, Ltd., a labor consulting firm with offices at 509 Fifth Avenue, New York City. Westminster Associates, Ltd., was incorporated in the State of New York on July 26, 1960.

In July of 1961, McCarthy became associated with another labor consulting firm called National Consultants Associated, Ltd. (NCA). This firm was incorporated in the State of New York on July 6, 1961, with Louis Basis as president, Jack McCarthy as secretary-treasurer, and J. Kenneth O'Connor as director. All three of these individuals were connected with Westminster

Associates, Ltd. Both consulting firms shared the same address, 509 Fifth Avenue, New York City.

McCarthy faced certain legal problems in being a labor consultant and at the same time occupying a position in labor unions. The Taft-Hartley law prohibits the receipt by a union official of moneys from an employer with whom he negotiates a union contract. McCarthy was precluded, as an officer in National Consultants Associated, Ltd., from receiving money from employers who dealt with Local 1430, IBEW, and Local 225, IJWU, unions with which he was associated. Testimony showed that this legal impediment was circumvented by causing the payments from the employers to be made directly to Louis Basis, at 509 Fifth Avenue, New York City, and located at the same address. Evidence to illustrate this maneuver was presented to the subcommittee involving negotiations with the Klavier Corp., formerly Capehart Corp., in Richmond Hills, N.Y. This company had collective bargaining agreements with Local 1430, IBEW, and Local 225, IJWU. Examination of the company's records showed that all payments were made directly to Louis Basis. At that time, McCarthy not only controlled the two unions, but his associate in NCA, Louis Basis, had represented the employer, Capehart Corp, since 1958, in labor matters involving the two local unions. During this period McCarthy himself owned stock in the Capehart Corp. He purchased 500 shares of common stock on September 12, 1958. On January 19, 1961, he sold his stock in the company.

The conflicting positions of McCarthy, as a union official affiliated with Local 225, IJWU, and as a labor consultant at the same time, occurred in 1961. This situation involved House Beautiful, a curtain manufacturer located at 605 Fifth Avenue, New York City. The owner of House Beautiful was Harry Schechter. The firm's employees were nonunion when Schechter obtained control in the middle of 1961. Schechter had approximately 150 employees, both skilled and unskilled. Approximately 20 of the unskilled employees signed up to join Local 225, IJWU. On Friday, August 11, 1961, according to testimony before the subcommittee, 20 of the employees who had signed up with the union walked off the job. Picketing began on Monday, August 14, 1961. On Tuesday, August 15, the second day of picketing, one of Schechter's employees contacted Jack McCarthy. Shortly thereafter McCarthy appeared and identified himself. He gave Mr. Schechter his card, representing himself as a member of Westminster Associates, Ltd. McCarthy stated that he could help settle the strike. Schechter asked what charge he would ask for his services. According to Mr. Schechter, McCarthy replied that "he has charged for his services up to $25,000." Schechter told McCarthy he was not interested.

Later on the same day, a union official of local 225 met with Schechter and told him that the union had a majority of the employees of House Beautiful signed up and demanded that Schechter sit down with the union and sign a contract. At that point, Daniel Kapilow, an associate of Jack McCarthy in the union, signed a contract on behalf of the union.

The financial records of National Consultants Associated, Ltd., disclose a link between that company and Westminster Associates, Ltd. Books of the latter show that the following sums of money were received by National Consultants Associated, Ltd., from the Westminster firm during the years indicated:

1961	$ 9,025
1962	13,366
1963	5,225
1964	$ 1,513
TOTAL	$29,129

Although the books of Westminster Associates, Ltd., do not reflect any direct payments to Jack McCarthy for services rendered, the records show that both Louis Basis and McCarthy shared equally in the moneys funneled into National Consultants Associated, Ltd., from Westminster Associates, Ltd.

Financial Success of National Consultants Associated, Ltd.

National Consultants Associated, Ltd., which was controlled by McCarthy and Louis Basis, was a relatively prosperous business from its formation. During its first year of operation, July 1, 1961, to June 30, 1962, NCA had an income of $97,633. An analysis of this figure disclosed that McCarthy and Basis took from this corporation, for their own benefit, approximately 92 percent of the total income during this period. Each man received $25,200 in salary, and additionally they received the following amounts, as indicated:

Reimbursed expenses	$ 9,053.81
Pension fund	27,089.82
Travel and entertainment	$ 2,274.01

During its first year of operation NCA spent only $243.32 for office expenses, $53.61 for organizational expenses, and $60 for telephone services. NCA was then and is today a one-room office operation with no office staff.

McCarthy's Control of Certain Local Unions Dealing with NCA

Jack McCarthy's financial success as a labor relations consultant depended upon his giving satisfactory service to the employers who retained him. As a labor official, McCarthy had gained wide experience and contacts in negotiating union contracts with employers. In its study of his activities, the subcommittee sought to determine how McCarthy could guarantee satisfactory service to employers. One answer which was indicated was that he controlled the unions with which he dealt as an agent for employers.

Such control could lead to the arrangement of "sweetheart" contracts for the employers. The subcommittee heard testimony that a contract of this type was arranged involving Local 1430, IBEW, after McCarthy resigned his position in that union. McCarthy was retained by the employer as a labor consultant to deal with his former union associates. Equally enlightening testimony was received about previous events which occurred while McCarthy, as a union official, supposedly was making efforts to organize the company's employees. The employer involved was Jay Wells, president of Wells Television, Inc. He testified that during 1961 and 1962 he purchased a total of $1,000 worth of advertising in a publication called the National Labor Record. Wells thought that the publication was affiliated or connected with Local 1430, IBEW. Testimony established that the periodical had in fact been exposed and repudiated publicly as early as 1955, by George Meany, president of the AFL-CIO, because it had no legitimate connection with organized labor.

Testimony was received that the National Labor Record was owned, prior to 1955, by McCarthy's brother-in-law, Joseph Costa. It was then sold to David Kohler, a nephew of Daniel Kapilow, McCarthy's business associate.

The chairman elicited the following explanation from Mr. Wells as to why he purchased advertising space in the National Labor Record:

Mr. Wells: These folks had been after us for a half dozen or 10 years, and we had not unionized. It was our feeling that if we bought these ads, just the couple that we bought didn't amount to much, that it would place us on a basis where they would not keep chasing after us.

The Chairman: In other words, you would get rid of them for a whole if you bought some ads?

Mr. Wells: If you want to use those words.

The admission by Mr. Wells that this was in fact a purchase of "labor peace" was made in answer to a question by Senator Ribicoff:

Senator Ribicoff: So basically you were trying to purchase quiet not in the hospital corridors but quiet from being organized by the McCarthy union?

Mr. Wells: I think that is a proper way to put it.

McCarthy resigned from Local 1430, IBEW, in July of 1962. The last ad placed in the National Labor Record by the employer was on November 30, 1961. McCarthy was retained as a labor consultant by Wells Television, Inc., around February of 1963. Prior to McCarthy's retention as a labor consultant by this firm, William Maude, union official of Local 1430, IBEW, attempted to organize the Wells Television employees. Approximately 9 months after McCarthy was retained as a labor consultant, the employer signed a collective bargaining agreement with Local 1430, IBEW. Mr. Wells admitted that McCarthy suggested that he sign up with the union.

Harry Scher, manager of the engineering division of Wells Television, Inc., who appeared as a witness with Mr. Wells, testified that employees of the company did not wish to join a labor union because they would receive no benefits from unionization. Their existing wage scale exceeded that which the union requested from the employer. The employer arranged to pay the initiation fees for the employees who joined the union by giving them a raise in salary. According to Mr. Scher, the arrangements for the unionization of the employees had been handled by Mr. Wells; Mr. Scher said that he, in fact, was not aware that McCarthy was on the payroll as a labor consultant to advise about labor matters.

The subcommittee tried to gauge properly McCarthy's influence and control over certain local unions by means of a detailed analysis showing the various clients of National Consultants Associated, Ltd., and those local unions with which their employees were affiliated. It was found that National Consultants Associated, Ltd., had 122 clients from 1961 through the time of the hearings, and that 43 percent of the business was linked with seven local unions, which were identified as follows:

Local 1430, International Brotherhood of Electrical Workers, 165 West 46th Street, New York City.

Local 225, International Jewelry Workers Union, 165 West 46th Street, New York City.

Local 1922, International Brotherhood of Electrical Workers, 59 Urban Avenue, Westbury, NY.

Local 2066, International Brotherhood of Electrical Workers, 790 Broad Street, Newark, NJ.

Local 3108, Carpenters Union, 2607 Nostrand Avenue, Brooklyn, NY.

Local 436, International Union of Electricians, 164-09 North Boulevard, Flushing, NY.

Local 1233, International Brotherhood of Electrical Workers, business manager, June 1962 to August 1964.

McCarthy's business partner, Daniel Kapilow, was a key union official in four of the seven unions listed above. Kapilow held the following positions with these unions:

Local 225, International Jewelry Workers Union, president, 1957-60; vice president, 1962 to present.

Local 1922, International Brotherhood of Electrical Workers, business manager, 1959 to present.

Local 1430, International Brotherhood of Electrical Workers, business agent, 1960 to present.

Local 1233, International Brotherhood of Electrical Workers, business manager, June 1962 to August 1964.

Significantly, 31 of the 122 clients of NCA had collective bargaining agreements with Local 1922, IBEW, the union in which Daniel Kapilow was business manager from 1959 to the time of the hearings. The result was that McCarthy negotiated union contracts for management, through NCA, with his business partner, Daniel Kapilow, who was a top union official in local 1922.

The testimony of Stanley Greene explained how this collusive arrangement between McCarthy and Kapilow operated. Greene indicated how they used National Consultants Associated Ltd., as a vehicle to negotiate a "sweetheart" contract. Greene testified that he was president, in 1961, of Estey Electronics, a firm located in the New York area, when Local 1922, IBEW, attempted to unionize certain of Green's employees. When he learned that a number of his employees wanted to join a union, Greene, accompanied by his attorney, met with Frank Mancuso, a business representative of Local 1922, IBEW. During these preliminary negotiations, Mancuso, representing the union, made unrealistic demands which Greene felt he could not accept. Approximately one week after this first discussion, Mancuso arranged another meeting, which Mr. Greene attended without his attorney. During this meeting Mancuso made it clear that a mutually satisfactory contract could be worked out. At this point Mancuso stated that he would like Greene to meet with another person.

Mancuso departed, soon returning with Daniel Kapilow, Mancuso's superior in the union. Kapilow suggested that Mancuso leave, and Kapilow and Greene were alone to discuss the union contract. Kapilow indicated that he could arrange a contract which would be satisfactory to Greene, but that the difference between the union's original demand and the agreement which could be worked out amounted to a considerable sum of money over a period of a year. Because the company would save money under the proposed contract, it was suggested that it would be logical for Greene to make some form of payment for this service. According to Greene's testimony, Kapilow suggested a cash payment of $2,000 as a consideration for the acceptance of Kapilow's proposal. Greene testified that he objected to making this payment in cash and suggested that the payment could be made if an invoice were sent to him. Kapilow mentioned that it could be arranged to make the payment through a labor consulting firm.

Senator Muskie questioned Mr. Greene about the payment:

> Senator Muskie: Did you consider such a payment for such services a proper one at the time?
>
> Mr. Greene: Not proper, as such, no, but I must say, Senator, that in operating a company with manufacturing facilities and transportation requirements, that from time to time we have been put in a position where we have had to make certain payments in order to expedite our own operations, and I consider this as another type of expenditure in that category.
>
> Senator Muskie: How do you describe such an expenditure? How do you describe such a payment?
>
> Mr. Greene: I don't understand the question, How do I describe it?
>
> Senator Muskie: You used the expression that this was another one of those payments you have to make. What kind of payments? How do you categorize it? How do you describe it?
>
> Mr. Greene: It is an expeditious payment to accomplish a smooth operation within a corporation.
>
> Senator Muskie: Did you think of it as in the nature of a bribe, for example?
>
> Mr. Greene: Unfortunately, I realized it was, and that it was improper, and yet in order to have peace in my operation and not curtail our flow of shipments, I felt that the amount of money was worth making if I could at least put it through our normal bookkeeping.
>
> Senator Muskie: Did you consider it an illegal payment?
>
> Mr. Greene: It would be; yes. I realized it would be.

Approximately 1 week after Greene met with Kapilow--the meeting at which the $2,000 was mentioned--Kapilow again communicated with Greene, suggesting that he meet with Louis Basis, McCarthy's associate in NCA. Kapilow advised Greene that Basis would be in touch with him within a few days.

Subsequently, a meeting was held between Basis, accompanied by Frank Mancuso, and Greene and his attorney, at which the final points in the contract were worked out. Greene testified that approximately 1 year later he received an invoice for $2,000, which he did not pay because he did not think it was from Louis Basis. To his best recollection, it was from National Consultants Associated, Ltd. Mr. Greene did not then connect Louis Basis with that labor consulting firm. The invoice was set aside and never paid.

Mr. Greene testified that he had subsequent conversations with Daniel Kapilow, at which time Mr. Kapilow told him not to pay the bill for $2,000.

According to Greene's testimony, Daniel Kapilow was aware that Greene had appeared upon request at the district attorney's office in New York County. Shortly after Greene's appearance at that office, Kapilow advised him not to pay the invoice for $2,000. Greene further testified that about April of 1963 Kapilow again communicated with him and advised Greene to state that the invoice from NCA for $2,000 was intended to apply to future services in connection with Greene's California plant. It was Greene's view that Basis wanted to represent Greene's plant on the west coast.

Approaches utilized by Kapilow to bring his union into contact with McCarthy's labor consulting firm, NCA, were not always so subtle as that shown in the testimony of Stanley Greene. When Kapilow thought it appropriate, he openly recommended to the employer that NCA be retained by the employer to handle labor matters. The subcommittee heard testimony relating to this practice from Milton Paulenoff, president of Macrose Distributors, Inc., located in New Hyde Park, N.Y. According to Mr. Paulenoff, Daniel Kapilow of Local 1922 of the IBEW recommended that Louis Basis of NCA be retained to handle labor matters. Within one week after this recommendation, Paulenoff hired Basis. NCA was still retained, at the time of the hearings, by the employer at $100 a month. Mr. Paulenoff admitted in his testimony that it was not until after he hired Louis Basis that a collective bargaining agreement was negotiated with Local 1922 of the IBEW through Mr. Kapilow.

Additional testimony was introduced into the record concerning Kapilow's recommendation of Louis Basis to an employer. Marvin Schwartz, secretary of the Amplex Corp, located in Carla Place, Long Island, N.Y., stated in a sworn affidavit that in 1958 Daniel Kapilow represented Local 1922 of the IBEW during contract negotiations with the company. In 1961, Kapilow recommended to Mr. Schwartz that he hire Louis Basis. Shortly thereafter, Schwartz stated, he did retain Basis to handle labor matters.

Jack McCarthy's relatives also played important roles in several of the seven local unions that McCarthy dominated and controlled. Joseph Costa, a brother-in-law of Jack McCarthy, was an official in four of the seven unions as indicated below:

Local 225, International Jewelry Workers Union, secretary-treasury, 1959-60; president, 1960 to present.

Local 2066, International Brotherhood of Electrical Workers, recording secretary 1960, 1961, and 1962.

Local 1430, International Brotherhood of Electrical Workers, office manager, 1959 to present.

Local 3108, Carpenters Union, recording secretary, 1960, 1961, 1962, and 1963.

The testimony showed that union official Joseph Costa was active not only as a union officer, but assisted his brother-in-law, Jack McCarthy, in matters relating to the management side of labor relations.

During an investigation by the New York City Police Department into the activities of Jack McCarthy in January of 1964, it was established that NCA had no office staff. The correspondence of NCA and Westminister Associates, Ltd., contained the initials "jc" in the lower left hand corner. It was believed that this typing was done by Joseph Costa. On January 10, 1964, detectives of the New York City Police Department went to the office of Local 225, IJWU, in New York City, in order to determine whether the correspondence of NCA was in fact typed on typewriters located in the office of Local 225 of the IJWU and Local 1430 of the IBEW. Laboratory tests showed that the correspondence was typed on machines in the union office. Joseph Costa was the principal officer in both these unions during this period.

Evidence disclosed that Joseph Costa was not performing these services for NCA without compensation. His receipt of money from NCA was indicated by the testimony of Assistant Counsel LaVern J. Duffy of the subcommittee's staff:

Mr. Duffy: Union official Joseph Costa received money from NCA. In examining the financial records of NCA, we found a number of checks from NCA made payable to cash and endorsed by Joseph Costa. These checks are dated from November 10, 1961, to September 7, 1962. I would like to place in the record at this time a number of checks from NCA endorsed by Costa indicating he received cash from NCA.

The Chairman: He was a union official at the time he was receiving this money?

Mr. Duffy: He was a union official, Mr. Chairman.

Another McCarthy brother-in-law, Richard Costa, was an official in five of the seven McCarthy-dominated unions. His affiliations are listed below:

Local 225, International Jewelry Workers Union, recording secretary, 1959-64.

Local 1922, International Brotherhood of Electrical Workers, business representative, May-December 1960; November 1961-November 1962.

Local 2066, International Brotherhood of Electrical Workers, vice president, 1960-61; treasurer, 1962.

Local 3108, Carpenters Union, conductor, 1960, 1961, 1962, and 1963.

Local 436, International Union of Electricians, vice president, 1962; president, 1963 and 1964 (December).

Richard Costa's involvement with NCA through Local 436 of the IUE was of interest to the subcommittee. The history of local 436 illustrated how McCarthy, through NCA, managed to obtain control of a local union from the time its charter was issued. After National Consultants Associated was instrumental in the chartering of this local union, Richard Costa turned up immediately as the union's vice president. Thereupon, a contract was negotiated with the union through NCA.

The testimony established that Rotating Components, Inc., of Flushing, N.Y., had retained J. Kenneth O'Connor as attorney in 1959. O'Connor had previously been affiliated with Westminister Associates, Ltd., and has been a director of National Consultants Associated, Ltd., since it was incorporated in July of 1961.

Local 463, IUE, attempted to organize Rotating Components, Inc., in 1959. After a lengthy and costly strike, the employer refused to deal further with local 463. Finally a 3-year union contract was signed on December 24, 1959, with district 4 of the IUE. In April of 1962, O'Connor recommended to the employer that National Consultants Associated, Ltd., be retained, including the services of McCarthy. On April 17, 1962, NCA started receiving $500 per month from Rotating Components, Inc. When O'Connor recommended NCA to the employer, in April of 1962, he was aware that the employer's contract with district 4 of the IUE was to expire in 1962.

After the charter was issued in July of 1962, O'Connor prepared a letter dated July 12, 1962, which was signed by James H. Mills, secretary and treasurer of Rotating Components, Inc., advising the firm's employees not to vote for local 463 in an impending NLRB election. The newly chartered local 436 thereupon won the election. Richard Costa, McCarthy's brother-in-law, was then vice president of the local, and became its president in January of 1963.

Richard Costa's versatility as a union official was illustrated by the testimony of Richard Lee Cash, president of Ranken Trimming Co. in New York City. According to Mr. Cash, in 1958 and 1959 he was shopping around for a local union which could give him a favorable union contract for his newly acquired company. After Local 225, IJWU, was selected, Richard Costa was placed on the payroll by the company purposely to organize its employees from within.

Mr. Cash admitted this in reply to a question by Chief Counsel Donald F. O'Donnell:

> Mr. O'Donnell: But the primary reason, actually, he was put on the payroll of the company was in order to organize the employees to join 225 because you were concerned with district 65 coming in and organizing, and probably putting you out of business. You wanted a more favorable contract that 225 could give you; is that it?
> Mr. Cash: Yes.

In 1960, Mr. Cash acquired another small nonunion company. Local 225, IJWU, was again selected by the employer to represent the employees. In this instance, Mr. Cash went directly to Daniel Kapilow of Local 225, IJWU, to sign a collective bargaining agreement.

Mr. Cash testified to the discussion between him and Kapilow in the following colloquy:

> Mr. O'Donnell: Did you go out to Kapilow's residence?
> Mr. Cash. Yes sir.
> Mr. O'Donnell: That was with your family in a car. You left the family and you went in to talk to him; is that correct?
> Mr. Cash: That is correct; right.
> Mr. O'Donnell: After you had talked to him about negotiating with the company, what did he say to you relative to his financial remuneration in union activities and so forth?
> Mr. Cash: He mentioned something to me to the effect that he found it slightly difficult to live on his salary, and suggested that I might give him $1,000. I said at that time, "I don't exactly carry $1,000 with me." When I got back in the car, I started to think and I thought, "I wonder if he wanted to borrow the money or what"?
> But it was never mentioned again. He never said anything to me and I never said anything to him and it was never discussed again until recently when I spoke to you about it.

Jack McCarthy's techniques for control and domination of certain unions were not limited to using his relatives and associates in high union positions. One device he utilized was lending money to union officials with whom he dealt in collective bargaining. He also arranged for certain union officials to receive substantial profits through usurious loans set up by McCarthy and Kapilow. These activities of McCarthy had the effect of destroying the proper "arm's length" relationship that must be maintained between labor and management during collective bargaining.

An understanding of the usurious loans which were arranged by McCarthy for certain of his union friends requires background material about the company that received the loans. On October 20, 1960, Joseph Hirsch, a friend of McCarthy's, arranged to buy the Lock Haven Electrical Equipment Corp. in Lock Haven, PA. The down payment for the purchase of the company was $100,000. Daniel Kapilow advanced $45,000. Testimony disclosed that Alan Segal provided the remainder of the down payment, $55,000. The company's name was later changed to General Armature & Manufacturing Co.

Alan Segal has an extensive background of hoodlum connections and of involvement in loan shark operations. Charges upon which Segal has been arrested include grand larceny, interstate transportation of stolen property, bail jumping, and violations of the business law of the State of New York. During 1962, Segal was heavily indebted to shylocks.

In June of 1963, the Chicago Police Department informed the New York City Police Department that Ernest Rocco Infelice, a well-known hoodlum from Chicago, and other racketeers, were then in New York City to take over the Living Room nightclub because of debts owed them by Alan Segal, whose brother owned the club. Information received from a confidential source at that time, according to testimony, disclosed that Alan Segal had put up a block of stock of the General Armature & Manufacturing Co. as collateral when he was unable to pay his debts to loan sharks. An examination of certain records of General Armature disclosed that the interest charged by and paid to Alan Segal for his $55,000 investment in the company amounted to $20,500. This was a return of more than 37 percent on the principal for the 3 months the loan was in existence. There were significant developments after the usurious loan was made by Segal to Joseph Hirsch, enabling Hirsch to gain control of the General Armature Co. After the initial down payment was made, the balance due on the purchase price of the corporation was $405,000. Hirsch then incorporated a new company called General Armature & Manufacturing Co., Lock Haven, PA. The name of the old Lock Haven Electrical Equipment Corp. also was changed to General Armature & Manufacturing Co.

The General Armature companies were then merged and the firm name was retained. Hirsch was president of the company. The $405,000 still due on the purchase price was obtained through Talcott Corp., a financial and factoring organization in New York, after the assets of the new General Armature Co. were pledged as collateral. When Hirsch incorporated the new General Armature Co., prior to the merger, 5,000 shares of stock were issued at $1 par value per share, a total of $5,000. Hirsch gave the company a note for $5,000 and the 5,000 shares were listed in the name of Joseph Hirsch. Jack McCarthy and Daniel Kapilow were listed as beneficial owners of 550 shares each.

Hirsch, McCarthy, and Kapilow were in control of the company after Kapilow and Segal financed the $100,000 down payment which made the purchase possible. When control was complete, the corporate assets were depleted through usurious loans by McCarthy's union friends. These loans were arranged by Hirsch and McCarthy, as indicated by a letter from McCarthy to Hirsch dated May 8, 1962. This letter is quoted in full:

May 8, 1962

Mr. Joseph Hirsch
General Armature Manufacturing Co.
Lock Haven, PA

Dear Joe: Pursuant to our telephone conversation, please find enclosed several checks which represent loans to your company for a 60-day period at 10 percent interest.

These checks are as follows:

Mrs. Dorothy Husted	$ 5,000
Frank Mancuso	5,000
Mike Manley	12,000
National Consultants Associated, "voluntary fund"	27,500
TOTAL	50,000

When you are next in New York we can get together and make up the proper notes to cover these loans made by the above persons.

With best wishes, I am,
Sincerely yours,
Jack McCarthy

Dorothy Husted is international representative of the IBEW for New York, New Jersey, Delaware, and Pennsylvania. Her work involves service to the various IBEW locals with which McCarthy negotiates collective bargaining agreements through National Consultants Associated, Ltd., on behalf of employers. Frank Mancuso is an official in a number of the IBEW locals that negotiate with McCarthy's consulting firm.

The letter quoted above indicates that McCarthy arranged for the loans on behalf of certain union officials. The 60-day loans were all renewed for an additional 60-day period at 10 percent. Prior to the renewals, General Armature paid Dorothy Husted $500 by check for the interest on her $5,000 loan, for 2 months, at 10 percent. Mancuso received a similar check. In the latter part of 1962, the Maremont Corp., Chicago, IL, purchased the General Armature & Manufacturing Co., and assumed its outstanding obligations. On December 10, 1962, Dorothy Husted was paid, through the Maremont Corp., $5,583.33 in full payment of her notes to the General Armature Co. On the same date Frank Mancuso was paid a similar amount, in full payment of his note.

In summary, Dorothy Husted and Frank Mancuso each loaned $5,000 for about 7 months, and each received $1,083.33 in interest, or 21.7 percent.

In an affidavit submitted to the subcommittee, Dorothy Husted admitted that Jack McCarthy approached her to make the loan to General Armature Co.

Mrs. Husted acknowledged that, as an international representative of the IBEW, she handled organizational campaigns, contract negotiations, grievances, arbitration sessions, and shop and committee meetings in connection with all four of the IBEW local unions which were under the control of Jack McCarthy.

Frank Mancuso admitted in an affidavit filed with the subcommittee that Daniel Kapilow first mentioned the General Armature loan to him. Kapilow then put Mancuso in touch with McCarthy, who convinced Mancuso that it was a good investment.

Daniel Kapilow was instrumental in fostering the labor career of Frank Mancuso. Mancuso's affidavit stated that he was active in all seven local unions that are dominated and controlled by McCarthy. Kapilow helped Mancuso to organize Local 2066 IBEW. Kapilow also assisted Mancuso in his affiliation with Local 3108, Carpenters Union, and brought Mancuso into Local 1233, IBEW.

Jack McCarthy and Daniel Kapilow also made use of their partnership, Linsan Trading Co., to make loans to union officials who negotiated union contracts through National Consultants Associated, Ltd. One of these union officials, Andy Bellamare, received a $3,000 loan from the Linsan Trading Co. Bellamare was an officer of Local 225, IJWU, and of Local 2066, IBEW, which were two of the seven local unions under McCarthy's control.

The subcommittee sought to obtain the records of the Linsan Trading Co. from McCarthy and Kapilow in order to determine what other loans had been made to McCarthy's union friends. McCarthy and Kapilow refused, under subpoena, to make these records available to the subcommittee for review. When they appeared before the subcommittee, both men invoked their constitutional privilege under the fifth amendment to decline to answer any questions relating to Linsan Trading Co. on the grounds that truthful answers might tend to incriminate them.

Purity Maintenance Co.,Inc., and Preferred Building Maintenance Co., Inc.

The Purity Maintenance Co. was incorporated in the State of New York on February 5, 1959, and Preferred Building Maintenance Co., Inc., was incorporated on May 21, 1959. Both firms are located at 261 Berry Hills Road, Syosset, Long Island, N.Y. They supply certain services to employers, including cleaning and waxing of floors. Joseph Maake, another brother-in-law of Jack McCarthy, was an equal partner in these two companies with Fred Ferrara, alias Fred Gladstone, who is president of Local 11 of the Hotel & Restaurant Workers Union in New York. Ferrara sold his interest in the companies in March of 1965. Testimony disclosed that certain of McCarthy's union friends, including his business associate, Daniel Kapilow, had recommended the cleaning and waxing firms to employers with whom they negotiated union contracts.

An affidavit submitted to the subcommittee from Marvin Schwartz of the Amplex Corp., Carle Place, Long Island, N.Y., states that Amplex had a collective bargaining agreement with Local 1922, IBEW. Daniel Kapilow signed the agreement for the union. Kapilow not only recommended McCarthy's labor consulting firm to Amplex, but also recommended the Purity Maintenance Co., Inc., for cleaning and waxing operations. Both NCA and Purity Maintenance Co., Inc., were retained by the employer.

Robert Ross, president of the Ace Spray Finishing Co., Bronx, N.Y., stated in an affidavit filed with the subcommittee that he had a union agreement with Local 225, IJWU. In 1961, Daniel Kapilow recommended to Mr. Ross that his company retain the Purity Maintenance Co., Inc., and shortly thereafter the Purity company was retained by the employer.

The sponsorship of these cleaning firms by McCarthy's union friends was a contributory factor in the income of Fred Ferrara, who received a total of $36,606 from the two firms during the period 1960 to 1965. Joseph Maake, who kept the records of the companies and ran their daily operations, refused to answer any questions, invoking the fifth amendment, about Ferrara's role as a partner in the operations of Purity Maintenance Co., Inc., and Preferred Building Maintenance Co., Inc. A possible motive for placing Ferrara on the payroll of these two companies was indicated in the following exchange between Senator Jackson and witness Maake:

> Senator Jackson: Was this method the one utilized by Mr. Jack McCarthy to pay off Fred Ferrara as president of Local No. 11 for favorable treatment during the contract negotiations with employers that hired McCarthy as labor consultant?
> Mr. Maake: I refuse to answer that question on the ground that it may tend to incriminate me.

The basis for Senator Jackson's question is found in earlier testimony of Jerome Brody, former president of Restaurant Associates in New York. In 1961 McCarthy had been retained by Mr. Brody for $7,800 annually, as a consultant. This was done upon Ferrara's recommendation. Ferrara was president of Local 11 of the Hotel and Restaurant Workers Union and had, during this period, negotiated a union agreement with Restaurant Associates. McCarthy received a total of $15,600 from Restaurant Associates until his services were terminated in early 1963, following various unfavorable press accounts of McCarthy's union activities in the New York area.

Fred Ferrara sold out his interest in Purity Maintenance Co., Inc., and Preferred Building Maintenance Co., Inc., on March 25, 1965. Mrs. Florence Richter, McCarthy's mother, purchased Ferrara's interest in the two companies and placed the stock in the name of McCarthy's wife, Dorothy, to be retained for the benefit of McCarthy's seven children.

The subcommittee, seeking to determine Ferrara's involvement with McCarthy, subpoenaed Ferrara to appear as a witness at its public hearings, which began on September 27, 1966. An affidavit, dated September 26, 1966, was filed with the subcommittee by Ferrara's doctor, which stated, in effect, that Mr. Ferrara had been admitted to St. Claire's Hospital in New York on September 25, 1966, and was unable to appear as a witness before the subcommittee.

Windfall Profits--59 Urban Realty Corp.

In late 1958 and early 1959, Jack McCarthy and Daniel Kapilow were trustees of the Tri-Union Welfare Fund, which operated on behalf of members of Locals 1430, 2066, and 1922, IBEW. They arranged a "windfall" profit for Mrs. Florence Richter, McCarthy's mother, in a transaction which was an obvious breach of their fiduciary responsibilities as trustees of the fund.

McCarthy resigned as a trustee of the welfare fund shortly after this transaction was arranged, but he retained his union office as business manager of Local 1430, IBEW. Daniel Kapilow presently is administrator and trustee of the Tri-Union Welfare Fund.

In late 1958, Kapilow arranged to move the union offices of Local 1922, IBEW, of which he was business manager, to a new location on Long Island, N.Y. Through Kapilow's arrangements, a private residence, located at 59 Urban Avenue in Westbury, N.Y., was selected to house both local 1922 and the Tri-Union Welfare Fund. On December 12, 1958, the 59 Urban Realty Corp. was incorporated. On January 6, 1959, the residence was sold to the 59 Urban Realty Corp. The president of this corporation was Florence Richter, also known as Florence McCarthy. On January 16, 1959, the 59 Urban Realty Corp. obtained a mortgage for $15,000 from the Long Island National BAnk of Hicksville, Long Island. On January 16, 1959, Florence Richter made a down payment of $5,500, which with the $15,000 mortgage, equaled the total purchase price of $20,500. On March 13, 1959, the house and property were transferred from the 59 Urban Realty Corp. to Florence Richter. On July 13,

1959, the 59 Urban Realty Corp. was dissolved. However, prior to the dissolution, on March 2, 1959, the 59 Urban Realty Company was set up to do business and to collect rents for Florence Richter.

On February 1, 1959, two 10-year leases on this property were entered into. Both leases were to run through January 31, 1969. One lease binds the Tri-Union Welfare Fund to pay rent of $1,800 per year for the first 5 years and $2,100 per year for the second 5 years. The other lease, for local 1922, IBEW, binds the local to pay $3,000 per year for the first 5 years and $4,200 per year for the second 5 years. At the end of 10 years, on January 31, 1969, about $45,780 in profits will have been realized either by McCarthy's mother, who is the ostensible owner, or by McCarthy himself.

Testimony established that if the union and the welfare fund had purchased the house initially instead of leasing it, there would have been significant savings. Both organizations had adequate funds to purchase the house. At the end of the 10-year period, these organizations will have paid $58,500 in rent, whereas the initial price of the property was $20,500 and required a down payment of only $5,500. With the exception of about $720 a year in real estate taxes, all other expenses are being borne by the union, according to the leases. Based upon Mrs. McCarthy's cash investment of $5,500, she will have received 832-percent income return over her investment for the 10-year period, or an average of 83.2 percent annually.

An examination of Jack McCarthy's bank accounts disclosed that he siphoned moneys from the rents collected through this arrangement. As early as July 7, 1960, a withdrawal by bank check for $3,000 was made payable to Florence Richter--Florence McCarthy, and endorsed by Jack McCarthy. McCarthy deposited the check in his account in the Chase Manhattan Bank.

Misuse of Union Welfare Funds

Loans from Tri-Union Welfare Fund to Linsan Trading Co.

As indicated on page 3 of this report [in original], the Linsan Trading Co., located at 113 West 42d Street, New York City, was a business partnership of Jack McCarthy and Daniel Kapilow which was registered in the State of New York in November of 1954. The firm, which is still in operation, lends money to window cleaning and office maintenance businesses and receives chattel mortgages on their service contracts as collateral for the loans. In 1959, the New York Insurance Department audited the Tri-Union Welfare Fund which provides welfare benefits for members of three local unions of the International Brotherhood of Electrical Workers, Locals 1430, 1922, and 2066. Daniel Kapilow is presently administrator of the welfare fund. The records of the fund indicate that the trustees had loaned $21,600 to the Linsan Trading Co. between the years 1954 and 1957. McCarthy and Kapilow were both trustees of the fund during this period. The loans finally were repaid in 1959.

Amalgamated Dental Plan

Shortly after Jack McCarthy resigned from Local 1430 of the IBEW in July of 1962, he arranged, with the aid of certain union officers and other individuals in the New York area, for the establishment of the Amalgamated Dental Plan (ADP) which, according to testimony, resulted in the unconscionable waste of approximately $200,000 in union welfare funds over a 2-year period.

The funds dissipated in this scheme belonged to the Tri-Union Welfare Fund, administered by Daniel Kapilow, McCarthy's business associate, and to the Industrial Welfare Fund, administered by McCarthy's brother-in-law, Joseph Costa. Jack McCarthy was paid $20,800 from the plan for bringing these unions into the plan. In addition to paying McCarthy, the plan also employed five bookmakers or known gamblers.

The details relating to the Amalgamated Dental Plan were supplied to the subcommittee by James J. Higgins, supervising insurance examiner for the New York State Insurance Department. He testified that pursuant to New York insurance law, regular statutory examinations were made during 1963 and 1964 into the affairs of a number of welfare funds, including ADP, whose president was Sam Kushner. Dr. Jerold Goldin was secretary-treasurer. Approximately $200,000 was expended from the welfare funds during the period September 1, 1962, to August 31, 1964, as indicated by the schedule below for a dental program which provided minimal benefits to the members. The ADP was discontinued in 1964. . . .

The plan did not offer direct dental care and was not licensed to practice dentistry in any form. It was paid approximately $200,000 merely for furnishing a list of dentists who were willing to accept specified fees for enumerated services. In other words, the welfare funds were expended for a referral service. Dental X-ray examinations and cleaning were supposedly available from the participating dentists at "no charge." However, in its circulars to the prospective panel of dentists, the ADP stated:

> Past performance records indicate that very few of these prospective patients will avail themselves of this free service without arranging for full dental care.

None of the money funneled into the dental plan from the welfare funds was paid to the participating dentists for the free services. In all cases, the cost of dental care was paid directly by the patient to the dentist. No machinery was established to determine whether the applicants were, in fact, eligible, whether the fee schedules were actually adhered to, or how the plan was working out.

Apparently neither the participating dentists nor the welfare funds involved kept any records of the operation. The officers of the Amalgamated Dental Plan flatly refused to make any records available to the New York State Insurance Department. Furthermore, the trustees who paid welfare funds into the dental plan failed to arrange for access to the plan's records after a formal request was made by the New York State Insurance Department examiner. By direct communication with a majority of the dentists who comprised the panel, the examiners obtained the following information.

1. Actual utilization by the members appeared to be so negligible as to be virtually nonexistent.
2. No records whatever were submitted by the dentists to the ADP or to the participating welfare plans.
3. The dentists were unaware that large sums of money were being paid by the welfare funds to the ADP for referral service.
4. The dentists joined the plan chiefly in response to the circular letter from the ADP.

Accountants of the subcommittee's staff made an examination of the financial records of the Amalgamated Dental Plan, finding that Jack McCarthy had received from the ADP a total of $20,800 for the period of October 1962 to August 1964. It was also determined that the five bookmakers or professional gamblers who were placed on the payroll during the period September 1962 to June 1963 had received a total of $16,800.

Cyril T. Jordan, a detective with the New York Police Department, supplied the subcommittee with significant information concerning the five "bookies."

The criminal record of one of the bookies, Arthur Sonnenschein, showed 19 arrests and three convictions, primarily for bookmaking. Sonnenschein was an associate of John "Sonny" Franzese, a known racketeer in the New York area, and of "Black Sam" Nastasa, who works for John Franzese. Sonnenschein also was an associate of known gamblers Marty Hirsch and Philip Shobert. Detective Jordan testified that Sonnenschein's poor reputation should have been known to the individuals who placed him on the payroll of the ADP.

Following is a summary of information about the other bookies who were placed on the payroll of ADP:

John Iovieno, also known as John Marino, listed in the New York Police Department known gamblers file--32 arrests and 15 convictions.

Morris Lipsky, listed in the New York Police Department known gamblers file--Six arrests and three convictions.

Philip Biscoglio, listed in the New York Police Department known gamblers file--Nine arrests and seven convictions. Biscoglio died in 1963.

Jacob Lipsky, listed in the New York Police Department known gamblers file--Five arrests and three convictions. Lipsky died in 1966.

Sam Kushner, president of the Amalgamated Dental Plan, and Dr. Jerold Goldin, secretary-treasurer of the plan, were subpoenaed by the subcommittee. They refused to answer all questions, invoking their constitutional privilege under the fifth amendment. Kushner and Goldin refused to furnish any information about McCarthy's role in the formation of the ADP and about what influences, if any, were used to recruit the various welfare funds that joined the dental plan.

Kushner and Goldin also refused to answer whether they had kicked back to union officials any of the money paid into the plan. They both declined to tell the subcommittee why they placed the five bookies on the payroll and whether the bookies shared the money they received with officials of the plan. Two of the bookies, John Iovieno and Morris Lipsky, were also called to testify concerning the dental plan, but they refused to answer any questions, invoking the fifth amendment on the grounds that a truthful answer might tend to incriminate them. Jack McCarthy, in his appearance before the subcommittee, also refused to answer any questions and invoked the fifth amendment.

Optical Benefits

The New York State Insurance Department also investigated the optical benefits supposedly provided to participants and beneficiaries of the Industrial and Tri-Union Welfare Fund and the Welfare Trust Fund of Local 11 of the Hotel & Restaurant Workers Union. A total of $313,500 was expended from these three funds for optical benefits during the years 1959-66. . . .

The findings of the New York State Insurance Department concerning the optical benefits furnished participants and beneficiaries of the funds were similar to those reported for the Amalgamated Dental Plan.

The three funds had written contracts for optical benefits with Dr. Morris Zucker, located at 134 West 34th Street, New York City. The trustees of the fund had arbitrarily awarded the original contract without cross-studies, comparisons with other plans, or requests for bids from competing optical plans. Increased charges to the funds were arbitrarily granted subsequently without supporting data to justify the need for them. The trustees failed to be guided by utilization control data which was available.

Dr. Zucker originally flatly refused to allow the examiners of the New York State Insurance Department to have access to his files. The trustees who paid Dr. Zucker failed to arrange access to Dr. Zucker's records. Findings of gross overcharges were verified in August of 1966 when the New York State Insurance Department succeeded in gaining access to Dr. Zucker's case records. Analysis of the actual records showed that for the years 1962-65, the funds had paid Dr. Zucker at the following average prices per pair of single-vision glasses:

Tri-Union Welfare Fund	$46.32
Industrial Welfare Fund	43.81
Local 11 Welfare Trust Fund	46.21

The New York State Insurance Department made an analysis of 55 reports that had been made for other optical plans in the New York area, and determined that the average price per pair of single vision glasses within the 55 plans was $6.19. The New York State Insurance Department thereupon made formal charges of fund depletion against the trustees of the funds in the following amounts:

Tri-Union Welfare Fund	$ 50,171
Industrial Welfare Fund	19,301
Local 11 Welfare Trust Fund	156,364
TOTAL	$226,036

In September of 1966, certain trustees of the Local 11 Welfare Trust Fund, the Tri-Union Welfare Fund, and the Industrial Welfare Fund, representing both union and management, were cited by the New York State Insurance Department to show cause why they should not be removed as trustees and/or why they should not be charged with depletion of fund assets. The union trustees cited were Daniel Kapilow, Joseph Costa, James Duffy, and Andy Bellamare.

Dr. Zucker's contract with Local 11 Welfare Trust Fund has been terminated. Dr. Zucker's current optical contracts with Industrial Welfare Fund and the Tri-Union Welfare Fund are presently on a fee-for-service basis.

The subcommittee also received in the testimony of James J. Higgins, insurance examiner of the New York State Insurance Department, a full account of the department's report and findings relating to the expenditure of welfare funds for medical benefits in the three union trust funds.

Medical Benefits

Dr. Irving Epstein, of 36 West 34th Street, New York City, contracted to provide certain medical benefits for the participants and beneficiaries of the Industrial and Tri-Union Welfare Funds and the Welfare Trust Fund of Local 11. The three funds expended $451,150 for medical benefits. . . .

The New York State Insurance Department found the same pattern prevailing for medical benefits as was found for the optical and dental plans of the funds.

The original contract was awarded without cost studies, comparisons, or requests for competitive bids. Subsequent renewals were unsupported by studies of past usage or analyses of the cost of the services. The trustees neither kept records of utilization nor requested access to Dr. Epstein's utilization records. Dr. Epstein said he was willing to make his records available to the New York State Insurance Department examiners upon receipt of a written authorization from the trustees, who failed to arrange for such authorization.

On July 21, 1966, the New York State Insurance Department served a subpoena on Dr. Epstein. He appeared before the appropriate authorities on August 10, 1966, but refused to answer any pertinent questions. On August 17, 1966, in response to another subpoena, he testified at length, but still refused to divulge utilization information on the ground that he would be disclosing confidential communications between doctor and patient. The record of testimony and supporting documents of the New York State Insurance Department were forwarded to the attorney general of New York on August 26, 1966. On September 7, 1966, an order was returned requiring Dr. Epstein to show cause why he should not be compelled to answer the questions put to him pursuant to the subpoena.

The Industrial Welfare Fund, on April 1, 1966, entered into a new arrangement with Dr. Epstein on a fee-for-service basis. The Tri-Union Welfare Fund advised the New York State Insurance Department on September 16, 1966, that henceforth its arrangement with Dr. Epstein would also be on a fee-for-service basis. Local 11 Welfare Trust Fund, by contract dated April 1, 1966, increased its annual payment to Dr. Epstein from $40,000 to $55,000.

Finances of Jack McCarthy

The subcommittee's staff made a thorough check of the finances of Jack McCarthy. This effort was hampered throughout its course because McCarthy refused to make his financial records available for review.

Preliminary inquiry showed that McCarthy had used devious methods to cover up his finances. For example, he deposited checks in commercial checking accounts, then withdrew cash and deposited it in various savings accounts. He also made deposits of checks and cash in savings banks, which were subsequently withdrawn either in cash or bank checks.

Despite the lack of cooperation from McCarthy, the subcommittee's staff uncovered 10 different bank accounts in Jack McCarthy's name. A schedule was made of the deposits of seven of these accounts. Three of the bank accounts were not tallied because the amounts involved were relatively small. The schedule of the bank deposits is printed below:

Jack McCarthy and Dorothy McCarthy, Etc.

Schedule of bank deposits compared with income per tax returns (exclusive of interest earned on bank accounts)

Banks	1959	1960	1961	1962
1. East River Savings Bank (Jack McCarthy)	$ 4,035.02	$ 4,544.12	$ 9,840.00	$ 0
2. Union Dime Savings (Jack and Dorothy McCarthy)	18,311.05	7,000.00	0	$ 11,697.00
3. The Seaman's Bank for Savings (Jack and Dorothy McCarthy)	71,247.29	0	0	19,800.00
4. Meadow-Brook National Savings (Dorothy McCarthy and T.F. Children)	1,539.86	842.68	5,622.00	1,845.00
5. Federation Bank & Trust Co. (Jack McCarthy)	5,837.25	13,450.46	277,338.58	12,305.86
6. New York Bank for Savings (Jack McCarthy)	0	0	5,622.00	10,172.00
7. Franklin National Bank-Savings (Dorothy McCarthy)	0	0	630.00	1,238.50
Total deposits	100,970.47	25,837.26	299,103.64	66,058.36
Income, per IRS tax returns:				
Salary, Local 1430, IBEW	9,360.00	9,360.00	9,360.00	5,580.00
Salary, Preferred Book Co.	2,080.00	1,920.00	3,500.00	3,600.00
Salary, Bookmobile Co.	950.00	2,400.00	0	0
Salary, National Consultants Associated	0	0	7,800.00	33,000.00
Linsan Trading Co.	1,807.40	1,978.43	3,167.36	1,196.10
Commissions	4,500.00	9,800.00	4,500.00	2,700.00
Excess reimbursements for expenses	1,588.00	1,588.00	1,588.00	0
Interest earned on loans	0	0	3,190.00	2,338.69
Capital gains	9,220.19	0	4,785.71	5,913.48
Total income, per tax returns	29,505.23	27,046.43	37,801.07	34,328.27
Deposits to be accounted for	71,505.23	(1,209.17)	261,212.57	11,730.00
Total of deposits in excess of reported income (1959-62 inclusive) (may be accounted for in whole or part as loans or exchanges)				343,198.73

As indicated by the schedule above, during the year 1959, Jack McCarthy deposited in excess of $100,000, but his reported income for tax purposes was only $29,505.23. Deposits which were not accounted for during this year were in excess of $71,000.

Jack McCarthy's union salary during the years 1959, 1960, and 1961 was $9,360 annually. The figure dropped to $5,580 in 1962, when McCarthy resigned his union position in July.

In 1961, McCarthy's bank deposits skyrocketed to approximately $300,000, while his declared income on his tax returns was only $37,891.07. In summary, there were $343,198.73 in bank deposits in excess of the amount of income reported on tax returns filed by McCarthy for the years 1959 through 1962 inclusive.

Analysis of McCarthy's finances in 1961 disclosed that he made large withdrawals from certain bank accounts and loaned this money to Martin Rarback, a secretary-treasurer of district 9 of the Painters Union in New York.* Payments also were made by McCarthy to Frank Grattano, formerly an official of the same union. These loans totaled $188,300 and were made by McCarthy to Rarback and Grattano during the years 1960 and 1961. Rarback received $123,800 and Grattano received $6,450. Included in the overall $188,300 figure was a $30,000 check from the Linsan Trading Co.

On May 15, 1961, McCarthy received a check for $96,350 from Martin Rarback in partial payment of this large loan.

Maurice A. Eichenholtz, subcommittee staff accountant, was asked whether the $96,350 paid to Jack McCarthy as partial repayment of the Rarback loan could be considered as a reduction of the $343,198.73 in known bank deposits of Jack McCarthy which were in excess of his declared income. Mr. Eichenholtz testified that the staff was unable to determine the sources from which McCarthy obtained the $94,000 to lend to Rarback. (The $96,350 total included $94,000 plus 5 percent interest for 6 months or $2,350, making a total of $96,350.) However, even if the total of known bank deposits were reduced by $96,350, there still remained a balance of $246,848.73 above declared income to be accounted for by Jack McCarthy. . . .

McCarthy refused to answer any questions, including all which related to his finances, on the grounds that the answers might tend to incriminate him.

---

*On October 18, 1966, Martin Rarback was indicted by District Attorney Hogan's office in New York on charges of conspiracy with other persons to obtain unlawfully all maintenance painting contracts of the New York City Housing Authority, and on charges of bribery in connection with that conspiracy. He is presently awaiting trial.

Specifically, he refused to explain how he was able to accumulate large sums of money, particularly during the periods 1959, 1960, and 1961, while still a union official who received a salary of less than $10,000 annually. During this period he managed to withdraw from a number of bank accounts a total of $188,300 to make loans to various individuals.*

---

*Jack McCarthy and Louis Basis, partners in National Consultants Associated, Ltd., were indicted by a Federal grand jury in the Southern District of New York on March 29, 1967, on 38 counts of conspiracy to violate Section 302 of the Taft-Hartley Act, and for violation of the Labor-Management Reporting and Disclosure Act. U.S. Attorney Robert Morgenthau announced that the indictments were related to activities of the two men which were disclosed during hearings of the Senate Permanent Subcommittee on Investigations, which took place approximately 6 months earlier. The indictments are concerned with the activities of McCarthy and Basis relating to Local 1430 of the International Brotherhood of Electrical Workers. Mr. Morgenthau also said that the indictment charging violation of the Labor-Management Reporting and Disclosure Act was the first such indictment to be brought under the appropriate section of the Act.

PART TWO

Industries Under Siege

4

The Return of the Sweatshop

Part II of an investigation by State Senator Franz S. Leichter 29th S.D., Manhattan; Glenn F. von Nostitz, Legislative Counsel; and Maria J. Gonzalez, Special Assistant, February 26, 1981.

A report by my office released in late 1979 revealed the existence of several thousand garment factory sweatshops throughout New York City. That report chastised the New York City Buildings Department, the Fire Department, and Federal agencies for not enforcing safety and wage laws in these dangerous establishments.

Continuing investigation by my office of sweatshops has now reached these additional startling conclusions:

-Organized crime families are apparently substantially in control of the sweatshop industry. Through use of their dominated garment trucking companies, they finance new shops, arrange for work for these shops, and transport the finished garments from the shops to midtown warehouses. Through inflated rates and other means, these trucking concerns rake in enormous profits. My conservative estimate of the "take" from trucking overcharges in Chinatown, alone, exceeds $9 million a year. This siphons off money that could pay higher wages to garment workers, most of whom earn no more than $15 for an eight-hour day.

-Major Seventh Avenue (SA) garment manufacturers are equally responsible for conditions in the sweatshops. My staff has identified numerous major SA manufacturers having their work done in Manhattan sweatshops, and the International Ladies Garment Workers Union estimates that about half the sportswear made in the City is now produced in sweatshops. Yet while inflation has been escalating shop operating costs, prices SA manufacturers pay for sweatshop work has declined considerably over the past few years, forcing shop owners to cut back even more on safety and wages.

-Retailers claim to have no knowledge of where garments sold in their outlets are made. However, some of the labels seen by my staff being manufactured in Manhattan sweatshops can be found (and have been seen) on the racks at major midtown department stores . . . .

-The government on all levels--Federal, State and City--remains indifferent and callous to the plight of workers in sweatshops. Laws that are on the books are not enforced, new legislation is ignored, and enforcement action against sweatshop exploiters is nil.

-I am urging a legislative and enforcement action campaign to end the sweatshop scandal in New York by:

1. Asking the Federal Organized Crime Strike Force to look into the organized crime control and operation of the sweatshop industry.
2. Strict enforcement of wage, child labor and safety laws by the Federal Occupational Safety and Health Administration (OSHA), the Federal Employment Standard Division of the United States Labor Department, the New York State Attorney General's Office and the New York City Fire Department and Buildings Department.
3. A special investigation by the New York State Department of Taxation and Finance into the failure to pay taxes and maintain employee records by garment shop operators and trucking companies serving these shops. . . .

Sweatshops: A Growth Industry

Both the ILGWU and the United States Labor Department estimate that just ten years ago there were fewer than 200 garment factory sweatshops in New York City, most of which were at that time concentrated in Chinatown. Today there are at least 100 in Northern Manhattan, 500 in the South Bronx, and hundreds more in Flushing, Astoria, and Corona, Queens, and in sections of Brooklyn, which are worse than the Chinatown shops. Citywide there are now at least 3,000 garment factory sweatshops in existence, according to ILGWU. . . .

There are two major reasons why this is such a growth industry:

- The number of illegal (i.e., undocumented) aliens in the City has continued its rapid growth. These latest immigrants arrive in the City in dire straits. If they can sew, they are easily recruited by shop operators to work long hours at low pay, in conditions they cannot complain about for fear of being turned over to immigration authorities. . . .

-Lessening foreign competition. While wages in Taiwan and other countries sewing garments for American manufacturers are still low, they are nonetheless rising at a steady rate. Additionally, transportation costs have skyrocketed making it even less attractive to send work overseas.

During the past ten years, there has been geographic expansion of the sweatshop industry out of Chinatown to the point where sweatshops now operate wherever concentrations of undocumented aliens exist. Within Chinatown, the shops have recently spread east to Allen and Chrystie Streets and north into Little Italy. In Northern Manhattan, they have opened along Broadway and Amsterdam Avenues between 157th and 180th Streets. Since my report was released in late 1979, there has been a phenomenal growth in Korean-run shops now found along Northern Boulevard and adjacent side streets in Long Island City, as well as Greek and Korean shops in Corona, Astoria, and Jackson Heights, Queens.

Truckers, Sweatshops and Organized Crime

The extent of the importance and control of trucking firms in the sweatshop industry is graphically demonstrated by the fact that most sweatshops now are actually financed and set up by the trucking companies. The trucker provides the start-up loan, may arrange for the leasing of the sewing and steam-pressing machines (which are really the only equipment needed), and will often even arrange for the lease and provide the sweatshop operator with orders from SA jobbers. The trucker will then deliver the material to be sewn and pressed and will pick up the finished garment and deliver it to the jobber. The trucker's dominance is such that the jobber will pay the trucker directly out of the monies for sewing the garments. These charges, computed on a per-garment basis, are far greater than normal trucking costs and enable the trucker to make an exorbitant profit.

Many of the new sweatshop operators can only exist if represented by one of the several established trucking companies. These have agreed to divide up buildings they serve, thus eliminating competition and further subjecting the operator to the trucker's control. Without going through one of the established truckers, it is nearly impossible to get work from the jobbers. This means many of the contractors are, in the words of the business, "married" to the trucker for the life of the shop. The only way to switch truckers is to go out of business and reopen elsewhere under a different name. As a result, neither the established nor newer contractors can even consider switching to a different trucker, perhaps one that charges lower rates for moving garments to Midtown. This is confirmed by my staff's discussions with over 40 Chinatown and numerous Northern Manhattan contractors. Invariably, when asked about their ability to switch trucking companies, perhaps to one with lower rates, the response was, "It cannot be done." They all said they were fearful of reprisals taking the form of "lost" or "damaged" future shipments, burglary of sewing equipment, fires set in their shops at the direction of truckers, and even beatings. Responses given to my staff included, "I'm allergic to pain," and "Our shop doesn't have fire insurance."

Through their most complete control of the sweatshop garment trucking business and consequent lack of trucking competition the trucking companies have been able to charge motor carriage rates far in excess of what is reasonable and proper. As discussed in greater detail later on, the rate for moving a women's dress from Chinatown to Midtown now stands at about 24 cents, for a pair of slacks at about 12 cents, and for a typical skirt at 15 cents. The Northern Manhattan rate for the dress is 20 cents. . . .

The trucking firm's apparently high rates are allowed to exist, in large part because there is no government monitoring of trucking done entirely within New York City limits. The ICC's rate setting and route granting authority does not apply to any trucking done within a twenty mile radius of New York City (thereby also excluding from ICC purview trucking for the many sweatshops in Northern New Jersey). One ICC official stated, "90% of the trucking in the country is, due to deregulation, not covered by ICC jurisdiction." Nor does the New York State Transportation Department, charged with regulation of motor carriers transporting property within the State have jurisdiction over carriers' routes located entirely within a municipality. Because of the dearth of government regulation, the rates for transport of garments within New York City (and to New Jersey shops) are based entirely on what the "market" will bear. . . .

That organized crime runs the garment trucking industry was reported by Wall Street Journal staffer Jonathan Kwitney in his recent in-depth book, Vicious Circles, The Mafia in the Marketplace. Said Kwitney:

> Trucking was just one of the many tools the Mob has used to control the garment industry, but in the 1970s it is probably the most important one.

Additionally, officials with the New York City Police Department's Organized Crime Monitoring Bureau told my staff they "believe most of these trucking companies are Mafia controlled, especially by the Gambino family." Following are the major trucking firms engaged in sweatshop trucking:

Consolidated Carriers Corporation

(155 West 35th Street, New York City; Incorporated March 1957):

My survey shows Consolidated controls the largest portion of the Chinatown sweatshop trucking business. . . . The survey concluded that Consolidated serves roughly one-third of the Chinatown shops. . . .

The Pennsylvania Crime Commission Report states that the Gambino family owns Consolidated Carriers Corporation and has for a long time held interests in numerous garment manufacturing companies, both in Northeastern

Pennsylvania and New York City. The Commission reports that, "Catherine Gambino (wife of New York organized crime boss Carlo Gambino) opened a garment manufacturing firm in Pennsylvania in 1948." The commission then goes on to state that Thomas Gambino, Carlo's son, began operating the Peggy Ann Dress Company in Peckville, Pennsylvania, which had been incorporated in 1947. The Pennsylvania Commission also said Thomas Gambino held an interest in Sano Textiles of New York City and was Vice-President of Linda Ann Fashions, also of New York City.

Since ICC and New York State Transportation Department jurisdiction does not cover intra-city trucking routes (and because it is unlikely anyone would file complaints for fear of reprisals in any event, according to an ICC official), those agencies' files on Consolidated do not include any recent reports or investigations of official misconduct by Consolidated. The files do report charges made in the early 1970s that Consolidated was omitting garments from its cargo manifests and that the company was illegally inserting into hauling contracts a clause limiting liability for garments to only $50 a shipment. These practices were dropped when the ICC applied administrative pressure.

. . . [There was a] November, 1972, crackdown on what the New York City Police Department termed "monopolistic parking practices" of certain trucking companies in the garment district. The Police Department said that six different trucking companies were "controlled by organized crime" and were keeping competitors out of SA by leaving empty trucks at curbside so as to take up all available loading space. The Department started a ticketing blitz against the six trucking firms, including Consolidated Carriers. Then Commissioner McCarty of the Organized Crime Control Bureau said, as reported in the New York Times (November 1, 1972) that Carlo Gambino, Sebastiano Aloi, Carmine Tramunti, and Natale Evola were behind the trucking companies that were targeted. The Department said that Gambino, Tramunti and Evola are the reputed leaders of three of the City's five organized crime families. But the ticketing campaign lasted only a few days. Sources in one of the unions representing some of Consolidated's drivers, as well as Village Voice accounts by Jack Newfield, report that former Congressman, John Murphy, called Mayor Lindsay and the Police Department on behalf of the Gambinos to complain, and that is why the ticketing stopped.

In July, 1978, Consolidated Carriers faced, for the first time, a strike by some of its drivers. It was a two-day "wildcat" strike orchestrated by Local 20408 of the United Warehouse, Industrial and Affiliate Trades Employees Union, and it succeeded in stopping sweatshop deliveries and pickups for a day and a half until it was allegedly broken up, according to Local 20408 President Matthew Eason, by "thugs hired by the Gambinos." During the picketing in front of Consolidated's West 35th Street offices, Eason was beaten with a lead pipe and another person was stabbed.

Local 20408 was not, and is still not, the primary union representing Consolidated's drivers. Rather, they have been in an organizing struggle against Local 102 of the ILGWU, the main union for garment trucking firms' drivers. (Most of Consolidated's drivers are reportedly not members of either union. Also, Consolidated reportedly has bypassed Local 102 by hiring employees from temporary employment agencies.)

Several shop owners doing business with Consolidated and interviewed for this report stated that they were established by Consolidated. A number of these owners reported that if they stopped using Consolidated, the consequences would be serious. They stated that switching to another trucker, perhaps one that might charge cheaper rates, would result in immediate reprisal, such as "losing" the next shipment of dresses, robberies of equipment and threats of beating. Commented one owner of a Canal Street shop, "These people will do anything to keep us in line."

Lucky Apparel Carriers, Inc.

(248 West 35th Street; Incorporated May 1960):

My survey indicates that Lucky Carriers services roughly one-fourth of the Chinatown shops. They do not operate in Northern Manhattan. The survey also revealed that Lucky Carriers closely cooperates with Consolidated in apportioning customers and routes. Several shop owners "married" to Consolidated reported that on some occasions their shipments are picked up by trucks belonging to Lucky Apparel. They also said that drivers working for Consolidated Carriers are at times temporarily seen driving trucks belonging to Lucky, and are later again seen driving Consolidated trucks. Additionally, two shop owners using Consolidated Carriers were suddenly informed that the following day their new carrier would be Lucky, with the same terms and conditions as had prevailed with Consolidated. According to one of the shop owners, these switches are made whenever it is more convenient in terms of routing for the two trucking companies involved. This is a practice the Police Department told my staff is also common in the refuse carting business.

Whether Lucky Apparel Carriers is owned by Consolidated Carriers is unclear, although several shopowners adamantly asserted the two firms are under the same ownership. Matthew Eason, President of Local 20408, one of the unions representing Consolidated's drivers says he believes the "two companies are the same." . . .

Interstate Dress Carriers

(247 West 35th Street):

With at least 300 trucks, Interstate is the largest garment carrier in the Northeastern United States. Much of its business consists of moving garments between Eastern Pennsylvania shops and New York City, and between the several hundred sweatshops in West New York, Weehawken, Union City, and Jersey City, New Jersey, into Manhattan. However, the firm is also active in the New York City sweatshop transport business, as its trucks have been seen in Chinatown, the South Bronx, and other locations. The firm also trucks for the garment piece goods industry located in the area of Manhattan along Broadway, between Canal and Houston Streets. . . .

IDC was at one time owned by Abraham Giddens and Jack Lieberman. A 1959 FBI report linked Giddens to Harry Strasser, identified as a known garment racketeer and who, in the Pennsylvania Crime Commission report mentioned earlier, was stated to be a business partner of Albert Anastasia, "the notorious head of Murder, Inc." As for Lieberman, the commission linked him to Russell Bufalino, who was named in the Commission report as a reputed organized crime boss. The Report states, "Bufalino allegedly had some influence over the inner workings of the company."

Jack Lieberman died in 1975, and his nephew, Sidney Lieberman, took his place as principal of IDC. (He was made Vice President. Jack Lieberman's widow, Natalie, residing in Florida, is President.) 1978 ICC files in Washington list Natalie Lieberman as President and Director of IDC with an annual salary of $72,800; Sidney Lieberman as Vice-President, annual salary of $79,800; Judith Lashen as Secretary and a Director, at $108,150 a year; Barry Pollack as Office Manager and Controller at $42,035. 1979 IDC records list Natalie Lieberman's salary as $99,400, Sidney Lieberman's as $76,689, and report Judith Lashen as "deceased." Barry Pollack is not listed at all in the 1979 files.

Sidney Lieberman has been linked in testimony in open court (by FBI agent Michael Denehy and by other FBI agents who testified), in the case of United States v. DiLapi, Ladmer, in the Eastern District of New York, to the reputed mobster Anthony "Ducks" Corallo. Agent Denehy called Corallo a don of the Luchese crime family. Reporters covering organized crime and the New York City Police Department Organized Crime Monitoring Bureau assert the Luchese family is in control of loan sharking in the garment district. In his testimony at the DiLapi sentencing hearing, Denehy stated that the Luchese family has control over "all goods moving into and out of the Manhattan garment district." Also during this hearing, the FBI agents testified (from information in their intelligence files) that Lieberman had known Corallo for more than 15 years, and that he considered him an "old friend." Lieberman told the FBI that in 1975 he had loaned Corallo $15,000, and he admitted that the "loan" had never been paid back.

SWEATSHOPS TO SHAKEDOWNS:
ORGANIZED CRIME IN NEW YORK'S GARMENT INDUSTRY

**Part III of "Return of the Sweatshop," a report by
State Senator Franz S. Leichter
(29th S.D., Manhattan)
March, 1982
Glenn von Nostitz, Counsel
Timothy Finn, Special Investigator
Michael Weber, Researcher/Investigator**

In "Return of the Sweatshop," a report I released in late 1979, the existence of several thousand illegal garment sweatshops throughout New York City was documented. The New York City Fire and Buildings Department, as well as Federal and State agencies were chastised for failing to enforce safety and wage laws in these factories, where as many as 60,000 workers, mostly undocumented aliens, produce, largely at subminimum wages, more than three-fourths of the garments manufactured in New York.

Part II of "Return of the Sweatshop," released in February 1981, revealed organized crime involvement in sweatshops through trucking companies which finance the opening of shops, arrange for work from Seventh Avenue manufacturers (termed "jobbers") and reap enormous profits through trucking overcharges. Combined with the decreasing rates jobbers are paying to sweatshop operators (termed "contractors") for each garment made, the report showed how contractors have been placed in an untenable position where they are forced by high trucking costs and low contract rates to pay bare-subsistence wages and to avoid compliance with safety and health laws. Part II also named several of the major retailers profiteering by selling sweatshop-produced garments at inordinately high mark-ups.

This Part II of "Return of the Sweatshop" presents additional disclosures about organized crime's central role in New York's garment industry and the estimated 3,000 sweatshops operating here:

-Organized crime's power and influence in the garment industry is spreading. It has solidified its traditional base in garment trucking and is expanding in the manufacturing end of the business. The Gambino and Luchese families are at the center of this mob influence. Besides controlling or heavily influencing jobbers, garment trucking firms and trucking trade associations, the Gambino family, in particular, oversees a 700 member association of contractors which negotiates with the International Ladies Garment Workers Union.

-Organized crime domination results in higher prices for consumers. A portion of the purchase price of every dress made in New York City goes directly into mob coffers through inflated trucking charges, usurious interest payments, payroll padding, kickbacks, and other illegal or quasi-legitimate practices. Very little of the retail price reaches the thousands of people making these garments for less than minimum wage in shops located in converted Queens storefronts, uptown Manhattan basements, and dilapidated Bronx lofts, nearly all of which have been set up through trucking companies.

-Jobbers can save as much using sweatshops as they would by importing garments from Hong Kong or Taiwan. In addition to these production savings, these jobbers benefit from the short New York turnaround time of three weeks from design to production compared with at least three months if goods are imported, as well as from reduced transportation costs and avoidance of paperwork and quotas involved with importing. Part II showed how contractors are "married" to their truckers; this Part III shows that jobbers, especially those using sweatshops, are also "married" to their truckers.

-Jobber-contractor-trucker combinations depending on and working closely with, although not directly under the control of, organized crime figures are also found in New York's garment industry. These combinations also engage in trucking overcharging and together with firms directly under organized crime control provide most of the work for the sweatshops. . . .

The Gambino-Luchese Garment Interests

The influx of racketeers and organized crime figures into the garment industry commenced in the early 1920s. Some of the more prominent mob figures were Arnold Rothstein and "Legs" Diamond, who supplied needed protection to both employers and unions, as well as Lepke Buchalter, Ben Levine, Joseph Ambruso, and Jacob "Gurah" Shapiro. The lieutenants for this group included James Plumeri (Jimmy Doyle) and his nephews John and Vincent Dioguardi, as well as Benedict Macri, close associate of Albert Anastasia, head of the notorious Murder, Inc.

Police intelligence reports from the 1950s state that certain organized crime figures became involved as "legitimate" businessmen in the garment district in the decades following World War II. They included Harry Strasser, Thomas "Three Fingers Brown" Luchese, Abe Chait, Joe Riccobono, Joe Rosato, Carlo Gambino, and "Guv" Guarnieri.

The Luchese family has been especially prominent in the New York and Eastern Pennsylvania garment industry. A 1958 United States Senate Report . . . concluded that Thomas "Three Fingers Brown" controlled a number of garment concerns in Northeastern Pennsylvania, including Harvic Sportswear, run by his son, Robert Luchese; Bob France Coat Company; V & L Hat Company and others. He also owned Peggy Ann Dress Company in Pecksville,

Pennsylvania, which was actually run by his son-in-law, Thomas F. Gambino (who is discussed in detail later). . . .

According to a 1980 report of the Pennsylvania Crime Commission, "A Decade of Organized Crime," and also according to a 1959 internal report of the New York Police Department, Luchese used front men such as reputed family capo Joe Rosato to set up shops for him. Internal NYPD reports from the early 1970s reveal that Rosato ran County Garment Delivery, which became Stallion Trucking and that Abe Chait, identified as a Luchese associate, owned several garment district trucking outfits (Champion Trucking was the main one) and a number of manufacturers. Additionally, articles appearing in Women's Wear Daily (August 24, 1977) disclosed that James Plumeri held interests in several major garment firms including Barton Trucking, Advance Junior Dress, Bonnie Stewart Dress, Ell-Gee Carriers, and Seam Binding Company.

The Luchese garment interests continue to the present. The center of these interests has been and still is the Second Budget Corporation. Located at 463 Seventh Avenue, Second Budget is a relatively large jobber with sales last year in excess of $40 million. It was newly incorporated in 1980 when it acquired the assets and assumed the debts of Budget Dress Corporation. The latter was founded in 1938 by Alfred Rosengarten, Robert Frank and Herbert Goldberg. Rosengarten is listed in the 1959 NYPD report and elsewhere as an associate of the Luchese organized crime family.

Current ownership of Second Budget consists of Alfred Rosengarten (President), Jerome Goldberg (Secretary) and, until his death last December, Nicholas Patti (Vice-President). Credit reports state that Second Budget is, in fact, a subsidiary of GRP Industries, believed to stand for "Gambino-Rosengarten-Patti."

Nicholas Patti is listed by at least one law enforcement agency as a soldier of the Gambino family. During the 1950s Patti owned Tasso's Restaurant (now defunct) in Queens, termed by the NYPD in their 1959 memorandum as a "well known hangout for known criminals."

Second Budget uses sweatshops located in the South Bronx, Chinatown, and Queens. Conditions in nearly all these shops are substandard and on five separate occasions in the last three years Budget has been found by the State Labor Department to be in violation of laws prohibiting illegal homework. . . . Nevertheless, Nicholas Patti was last year named by the State Labor Department to serve on a State Commission investigating the illegal homework problem, established under legislation enacted in the 1981 legislature. . . .

In the Bronx Budget uses as a contractor Janet Lynn, Inc. A 1981 National Labor Relations Board case (Region II, New York) concerning complaints against the firm included employee affidavits stating the shop had no time clock, that the boss (President, Eva Battistini) writes workers' hours on ledgers and these hours are always inaccurate, and that extensive illegal homework is done out of the shop.

Another contractor which works almost exclusively for Budget is Mary Fran Dress Company (830 Westchester Avenue, Bronx). Mary Fran is owned by Thomas Gambino (related to but not the same as Thomas F. Gambino) and Joseph Siracusano, believed to be the son of Vincent Siracusano, nephew of Thomas "Three Fingers Brown" Luchese. A jobber which occupies the same premises as Mary Fran is Penny Lane Fashion, Inc., whose President is also Joseph Siracusano.

Amy Deb, Inc., (identified in credit reports as an affiliate of Second Budget) is owned by Robert Luchese (son of Thomas "Three Fingers Brown" Luchese), Thomas F. Gambino, Alfred Rosengarten and Salvatore Russo. Amy Deb uses many of the same sweatshops as Budget Dress, and in 1980 had gross sales of approximately $15 million.

Manufacturer Sherwood Fashions, Inc., has been an important part of the Luchese garment interests. It was founded in 1959 by Luchese associate Alfred Rosengarten and attorney Amadeo Lauritano. As reported in Women's Wear Daily (August 24, 1977) and confirmed by federal government sources, its ownership in 1980 consisted of the estate of Thomas Luchese (co-administered by Thomas F. Gambino and Robert Luchese), Alfred Rosengarten, and Robert Azario. New York Police Department intelligence files list Robert Luchese as "heir with Thomas Gambino" to the Luchese garment center interests. Sherwood has been reducing the size of its operations in recent years. In the mid-1970s it had annual gross sales of about $30 million but by 1980 this had declined to about $15 million.

Almost without exception every law enforcement source relied on in this report as well as jobbers and street sources state that Thomas F. Gambino has become, in the words of one detective "the major power" in the garment district and in the words of another, "increasingly the central figure on Seventh Avenue." One long-time jobber said, "Thomas Gambino is building a virtual dynasty on Seventh Avenue."

Thomas F. Gambino is son of late don Carlo Gambino and son-in-law of Thomas "Three Fingers Brown" Luchese. He has no criminal record and has not been identified as a member of any organized crime family. However, he has numerous business relationships and contacts with persons who are organized crime figures. Besides having actual or de facto ownership of numerous jobbers, he also owns and controls a large number of trucking firms and as detailed later, is a controlling factor in important garment trucking trade associations.

The major piece of this garment center empire is Consolidated Carriers Corporation (141 West 35th Street) which Thomas F. Gambino owns with his brother Joseph. Consolidated's subsidiaries include Dynamic Delivery, GRG

Delivery (stands for "Gambino-Ruff-Gambino), JHT Leasing, Greenberg's Express, Clothing Carriers Corporation, and Trucking Personnel, Inc. Consolidated is the largest hauler of garments within New York City and, according to one trucking industry source, in the United States. . . . Consolidated is directly in control of many sweatshops.

Federal law enforcement sources also state that Thomas F. Gambino and Sidney Lieberman (referred to later) own a controlling interest in Astro Carriers (213 West 35th Street) which provides trucking services to garment shops in Northern Manhattan and the Bronx, and that he also exercises control over Major Dependable Delivery Company (321 West 35th Street).

Confidential federal reports state that Thomas F. Gambino shares control, with Sidney Lieberman, of the following garment district firms:

Terry Shaw, 213 West 35th Street (may be defunct)
Huggable Togs, 463 Seventh Avenue
Ellen Stacey, 463 Seventh Avenue

Federal and local authorities and jobbers interviewed for this report also believe that Thomas F. Gambino exercises control over Miss Jamie, a jobber located at 463 Seventh Avenue in which Carl Gambino, Jr. (Carlo Gambino's grandson and nephew of Thomas F. Gambino) and Sol Shaw are the shareholders. . . .

Although Thomas F. Gambino has denied any organized crime associations, this is disputed by law enforcement agencies, including the Pennsylvania Crime Commission . . . "Thomas Gambino is closely associated with Paul Castellano, Aniello Dellacroce, and Joe N. Gallo." (Castellano is boss of the Gambino family, Dellacroce the underboss and Gallo the consigliere, or counselor). Boss Paul Castellano, in fact, has been observed at the offices of Consolidated Carriers Corporation. . . .

Federal authorities (supported in some instances by street sources and internal NYPD reports) believe that identified members of the Gambino organized crime family have actual or de facto ownership of the following firms:

Christine Dress (was owned by Joe Riccobono, and may now be defunct)
G&I Dress Company, Brooklyn (Paul Castellano, owner)
Sanjo Dress, 1400 Broadway, Manhattan
C&D Coat Company, 138 West 25th Street (family member Mario Traina, owner)
A.B.J. Outerwear (member Daniel Fatico, owner).

The current head of the Luchese crime family is Anthony "Tony Ducks" Corallo. According to numerous law enforcement and other sources, Corallo has assumed many of the garment district functions of the late Thomas Luchese and he strengthened his position in the family after the 1976 murder of capo Andimo Pappadio (referred to later). He has reportedly had some influence over Interstate Dress Carriers, a large trucker (according to Interstate Commerce Commission annual filings, with over 700 employees) which hauls garments throughout the Eastern United States. IDC's Vice-President, Sidney Lieberman (mentioned earlier as owning firms with Thomas F. Gambino) was closely linked by an FBI agent in open court testimony with Anthony Corallo; Lieberman had lent Corallo sums of money and admitted he was a close personal friend of Corallo (Eastern District of New York, United States v. DiLapi, Ladmer, et al., 1980).

A former prosecutor familiar with the Luchese family stated that some of the money the Luchese family obtains from illegal drug operations is "buried" in ostensibly legitimate businesses, including garment shops.

Confidential Federal reports state that "Jimmy Brown" Luchese, Thomas Luchese's brother, owns Duo Garment Delivery . . . Salvatore Corallo, brother of Anthony Corallo, is Duo's Secretary-Treasurer, according to State Unemployment Insurance Division records and incorporation papers on file at the State Department. Duo Garment Delivery has the sole trucking contract for Second Budget Corporation. . . .

Salvatore Corallo is also the controlling shareholder of Merit Dress Delivery, Inc. Merit's officers and other shareholders are Bert Goldman, Joel Goldman, and Lawrence Goldman. Their father, Charles Goldman, along with David Katz and Edward Friedman and George Fleischman founded Merit Dress Delivery in 1939. Even though Charles Goldman passed leadership of Merit over to his son, Bert, over the years a number of organized crime figures and associates have had direct influence in the company. According to accounts in Women's Wear Daily (August 22, 1977), Luchese capo Joe Rosato held an ownership interest in Merit, and later sold his share to Burton Chait, son of Abe Chait (who is discussed later).

Bert Goldman is currently in Federal prison for his recent conviction for embezzlement and filing of false and fraudulent income tax returns. Goldman took $300,000 of Merit assets over a three-year period which he used for personal expenses, including new wardrobes, airplane tickets, Steuben glass, a redwood deck for his home, and other amenities (United States v. Goldman, Southern District of New York, 81 Crim. 0396). Goldman was caught by an Interstate Commerce Commission audit of Merit's books.

Merit also has the following affiliates: 159th Street Realty Co., United Wire Hanger (one of the largest hanger supply houses in the garment industry), Merit Express Co., and Uniplant, Inc. Bert Goldman is also President of Star Garment Delivery Company, which operates out of the Merit terminal on West 36th Street and out of Paterson, New Jersey. B. Goldman Trucking also operates from Merit's yards. Merit is the largest garment trucker to New England and services the numerous and proliferating Rhode Island sweatshops.

Another jobber with Luchese family involvement is Dawn Joy Fashions of 501 Seventh Avenue. Dawn Joy uses contract shops in Northern Manhattan, Chinatown, and Queens. According to internal police reports from the 1970s it was heavily influenced by Salvatore Graffignino, a member of the Luchese family (believed to be a capo) who meets regularly with Thomas F. Gambino. According to federal authorities, Graffagnino still controlled Dawn Joy as of one year ago.

According to records of the State Unemployment Insurance Division, a principal of Dawn Joy is Sheldon Silverman. He is also listed by the Unemployment Insurance Division as an officer of Royal Green, Ltd., a jobber located at 463 Seventh Avenue that has used Northern Manhattan sweatshops.

Other firms Salvatore Graffignino owns or has de facto ownership of . . . include LT One Cutting (247 West 35th, President: Herbert Diamond), Eiffel Classics (263 West 36th) and Lieberman and Resitsky Trucking (213 West 35th). President of the latter is Sidney Lieberman, mentioned elsewhere in this report as a close associate of Anthony Corallo and Vice-President of Interstate Dress Carriers.

. . . [I]dentified members of the Luchese crime family have actual or de facto ownerships in the following firms:

> Leroy Fashions (238 Gates Ave., Brooklyn, controlled by family member Peter De Palermo)
>
> J&P Trucking (Bronx, family member Vincent Luchese controls)
>
> Linda Trimmings (256 West 38th Street, family associate T. Paolucci controls)
>
> Borgia Fashions, Inc. (Manhattan, soldier Angelo Urgitano has controlled--may be defunct).

Thomas Dioguardi, on several law enforcement lists as a member of the Luchese family, runs Dom Rose Mills of 313 West 37th Street, a supplier of fabrics to jobbers. He also owns, at the same address, De Vico Textiles, Gold Rose Fabrics, Knitcrest Knitting Mills, and S&S Textiles. He is the brother of John "Johnny Dio" Dioguardi, a now-deceased garment district businessman who was convicted of racketeering. . . .

Luchese associate Abe Chait was, according to former prosecutor Steve Frankel and articles appearing in Women's Wear Daily (August 22, 1977) a very powerful figure in garment district trucking in the 1950s. His main holding was Champion Trucking, visited by Anthony "Tony Ducks" Corallo almost daily according to the newspaper account. Chait also held interests in Barnett's Express, Burton Transportation, Faultless Trucking, and others.

Reputed Luchese capo Andimo Pappadio, who was murdered in 1976, owned the firms Farrell Modes and Pilgrim Dress and, according to federal documents was a "silent partner" in Tempo Fashions and Syd Fashions. According to business records on file in the New York County Clerk's office the two other partners in Temp were Sidney Bender and Milton Reibman. Court records reveal they were convicted of skimming cash from the firm Tempo Fashions in 1975.

Andimo Pappadio's wife, Eleanor Rose Pappadio, became a partner in the garment district hauler Ideal Trucking Company (255 West 36th Street) in January, 1966, investigation of business records and court papers reveals. She succeeded Marily Chait, wife of the then deceased Abe Chait. Also in 1966, Mariano Macaluso became a partner in Ideal Trucking. Macaluso is listed by law enforcement agencies (federal, state, and local) as a soldier in the Luchese crime family.

According to business records on file at the New York County Clerk's office and according to files of the New York State Unemployment Insurance Division, Fred Pappadio, a brother of Andimo Pappadio, became a partner of Ideal Trucking in 1975 and another brother, Michael, became a partner in 1977. . . . In 1978 Michael Pappadio dropped out of the firm but his wife Frances, and son Michael Jr., became partners . . .

Andimo Pappadio also had an interest, with Mariano Macaluso, in Garment Carriers Corporation (307 West 37th Street). From 1967 to 1975 the partners for Garment Carriers Corporation were identical with Ideal Trucking. Real estate records on file at the New York County Clerk's Office show that a Marco Macaluso is President of SMTF, Inc., which purchased the building at 307 West 37th Street in 1978 for $250,000.

In the 1975 case United States v. DeLorenzo, et al. (EDNY, 75 Crim. 472), Michael Pappadio was convicted of using for tax evasion two garment center firms, M.B.H. Sales and Bidio Management. Also convicted in that case were Alphonse Esposito and Mateo DeLorenzo, the latter a member of the Genovese crime family. The basis of the case was that Pappadio had falsely listed Esposito and DeLorenzo as salaried employees of M.B.H.

Records introduced at the trial showed that Pappadio had interests or ownership in at least thirteen garment industry firms. Among these were She-She (also known as House of She), Women's World, Haymarket Juniors, Pin-Up, Lady Dye Shop, Marjo Manufacturing, Miss Robbins, Patricia Manufacturing, and Daro Sales. He owned most of these firms with Irwin Bishins [who] testified that he met Michael Pappadio in the 1950s when Pappadio was manager of the Pennsylvania Contractors Association, an anti-ILGWU organization in Northeastern Pennsylvania, and had started M.B.H. with him in the early 1960s as a belt-maker before it was changed into a cutting room. . . .

The Bufalino, Genovese and Colombo Families

According to the Pennsylvania Crime Commission the Bufalino organized crime family of Northeastern Pennsylvania has held and still holds some garment manufacturing interests in New York State and Pennsylvania. The Commission states that boss Russell Bufalino was associated with two garment district firms, Bonnie Stewart Dress Company and Fairfrox. Bufalino or other members of his family also control Endicott Dress Company in Endicott, New York, Tri-Cities Dress Company and Binghamton Dress Company, both of Binghamton, New York, and Owego Textile in Owego, New York. According to the Commission, the latter is controlled by Anthony "Guv" Guarnieri, identified as a Bufalino capo. The Commission believes that Guarnieri is going to assume control of the old Magadinno crime family in the Northern and Western part of New York State.

Bufalino himself was indicted for attempted murder on December 21, 1980. The indictment charges him with conspiring with James "The Weasel" Fratiano to murder Jack Napoli to prevent Napoli from testifying at Bufalino's 1978 extortion trial.

Russell Bufalino was employed at Fairfrox from 1972 to 1978. Fairfrox filed for dissolution in March, 1979, shortly after Bufalino was convicted and incarcerated for extortion.

According to the Pennsylvania Crime Commission, Russell Bufalino was closely associated with the late trucking executive Jack Lieberman, President of Interstate Dress Carriers (IDC, mentioned earlier in connection with the Luchese family). The Commission states that "Bufalino allegedly had some influence over the internal workings of the company" and that, moreover, "in the early 1950s, Albert Anastasia, . . . was reputed to have an interest in IDC." . . .

The Bufalino family's garment district role seems to be waning. The family controlled numerous Northeastern Pennsylvania contract shops which worked for Seventh Avenue jobbers, but most of these have now folded in the face of competition from the lower-wage and closer New York City sweatshops.

As for the Genovese family, John "Gentlemen John" Masiello, a capo in that family, was associated with the manufacturer Jade Fashions, according to the New York City Police Department. Other local law enforcement agencies indicate that James "Jimmy the Gent" Burke controls a number of sweatshops in the South Ozone and Richmond Hill areas of Queens.

Joseph "Joe Stretch" Stracci, associated with the Genovese family is described in Women's Wear Daily (September 2, 1977), by a former prosecutor and by street sources as one of the major "money men" in the garment industry. "Money men" provide financial support in a seasonal, often cash-needy industry. . . . Stracci, . . . in the past, has held interests in Zim-Stra Originals (a coat maker), and according to wiretaps of New Jersey Mafia boss Sam

DeCalvacante, Stracci has also had an interest in Silverline Express Co., a major garment trucker to Northeastern Pennsylvania.

Other "money men" include Michael Pappadio and "Izzy" Kamhi, according to published reports and street sources. The Kamhi family (sometimes spelled "Camhi") owns a number of truckers, cutters, and jobbers, although it was impossible to discern any direct connections between the Kamhis and organized crime. . . .

The Colombo family has principally been involved in the garment district through the person of Vincent Aloi, a capo in that family (according to most law enforcement lists), who has been particularly influential in garment trucking. As detailed later, the family also has influence at the Master Truckmen of America and at the Greater Blouse, Skirt and Undergarment Association. As reported in the press in recent years, the Colombo family has come largely under the control of the Gambino family, and member Carmine Persico is generally considered to exercise oversight over the Colombo operations.

According to Federal authorities, Vincent Aloi exercises control over the following garment trucking companies: Trucking Service, Inc. (247 West 37th Street), Roxy Delivery (535 Eighth Avenue), K&K Garment Delivery (260 West 37th Street), United Marlboro (260 West 37th Street) and Hudson Valley Trucking (same address as Roxy).

Vincent Aloi was recently released from federal prison after serving a nine year sentence for racketeering. There are reports that he is resuming his earlier activities and influence in the garment district.

Trucking Revisited

The garment industry in New York consists of jobbers, contractors and truckers. Jobbers buy the fabrics, design the goods and sell them to retailers. Contractors actually make the garments. But the truckers are most important. They haul the fabrics into and the garments out of Manhattan as well as between jobbers and contractors. Without them nothing moves. . . .

Jobbers wishing to move goods must deal with one of the established truckers, and getting out of a trucking contract can prove troublesome, even if the jobber merely wants to transfer to another of the established trucking operations. As one executive put it: "If I'm unhappy with something Consolidated has done, I'll call (Thomas F.) Gambino and he'll usually take care of it. If there's a big problem, he might have some other trucker take over the route. But then I'll have to buy my way out of the rest of the contract. Switching isn't easy." One former prosecutor said that in some instances, only on condition of making substantial extra payments to the present trucker. In unusual cases, "a few extra people might have to be put on your payroll."

Few jobbers try switching, and even fewer try using a more independent trucker. As the former prosecutor quoted above commented: "If you're with Consolidated or one of the others, you're protected. You don't have to worry about hijackings. They provide security. If you break off, however, then you're in real trouble." And as another source explained: "They don't need to use force. If you try to go out on your own you get frozen out. Nobody--no contractors, no cutters, no truckers--will deal with you and you will end up going out of business very fast."

Control is such that even if the usual trucker is unable to make a pickup from a contract shop and the jobber uses another trucker, the jobber has to pay both. One jobber explained that in rare instances when Consolidated cannot take a load he'll call "this small outfit, just a couple of trucks" to handle it. He said "Tom (Gambino) understands." But, he added, he has to pay Consolidated just the same.

Jobbers wishing to use sweatshops are even more beholden to the trucking companies. . . . [M]ost of the sweatshops are set up and financed by the trucking companies, who arrange for work to be done. There are very few contractors who work independent of the trucker to [whom] they are "married." Therefore if a jobber needs a certain number of dresses made he will call the trucker, who will then guide the work into one of his "married" shops. . . .

Garment truckers have coordinated their operations through five closely related trucking associations. In the 1970s the most important of these was the Master Truckmen of America (MTA) at 1450 Broadway. Operation Cleveland, a joint United States-New York City probe of garment trucking conducted in 1973 (and the last substantial investigation or prosecutorial effort in the area) demonstrated how the MTA not only was restraining competition by assigning all the trucking routes but was also exacting percentage fees (usually 10%) from every sale or transfer of a garment trucking firm. In Operation Cleveland, undercover agents, upon purchasing the two-truck Gerro Trucking were immediately approached by the MTA and forced to pay as a fee ten percent of the sale price. If Gerro's new owners had refused, they would have faced a strike by Local 102 of the ILGWU and other sanctions. (Local 102 represents garment truck drivers and helpers.) The imminent strike was called off when the payment was made. Frank Wolf, then head of the MTA, was convicted of income tax evasion as a result of the payoff. Grand jury testimony reveals that Wolf was involved in another scheme where he was paid substantial sums each month for allowing WTC Air Freight to transport garments between New York and California.

The MTA is now headed by Herbert Gershon. Former Wolf prosecutor Steve Frankel believes that Gershon "has little real power" and that other elements are in control. Other law enforcement sources report that Fred Pappadio and Michael Pappadio exert some influence there but that the MTA is principally under the control of Vincent Aloi and Thomas F. Gambino. According to testimony at Frank Wolf's trial, Aloi was his "boss." Harvey Brody, Aloi's business partner in Roxy Delivery, is on MTA's Executive Board. . . .

Among other trucking trade groups are the Garment Trucking Association of New Jersey, Associated Dress Carriers of Brooklyn and Queens, the New York and New England Dress Carriers, Inc., and the Cloak and Suit Truckers Association. The first three organizations occupy the same offices in Room 2302 of 450 Seventh Avenue, and the latter is housed with the MTA at 1450 Broadway.

Executive Director of the New Jersey Garment Trucking Association is Sidney Lieberman (identified . . . as Vice President of Interstate Dress Carriers, . . . as being closely linked to Anthony "Tony Ducks" Corallo, and . . . as a business partner of Thomas F. Gambino). Executive Director of the Brooklyn-Queens Association is Jack Lieberman, . . . although federal authorities believe that Thomas F. Gambino is the controlling factor there. President of the New York and New England Dress Carriers is Michael Vuolo (who has been identified as a former official of the International Longshoreman's Association), who is also owner of AAA Garment Delivery, a major sweatshop hauler. Federal investigations reveal that Michael Pappadio is, in fact, the controlling factor in that organization.

All five organizations together negotiate a single trucking employee contract with Local 102 of the ILGWU. . . . Local 102 has close connections to organized crime figures and associates. . . .

A "Contractors" Association

In Chinatown and along Manhattan's West Side in the 20s, the Gambino crime family has ensured labor domination and supplemented its control of sweatshops through the Greater Blouse, Skirt and Undergarment Association, located at 225 West 34th Street. Ostensibly, Greater Blouse is an association representing the interests of about 700 unionized contractors (including at least 420 in Chinatown), negotiating on their behalf every three years with Local 23-25 of the ILGWU, entering agreements with other trade associations, and existing generally to resolve labor problems. Member contractors run the gamut from horrendous sweatshops to shops satisfying most safety and wage laws.

Business representative of Greater Blouse and by all accounts the person "in charge" of the organization is Joseph Nicholas Gallo, listed by law enforcement agencies as the consigliere (or counselor) and a third in command of the Gambino organized crime family. Executive Director of Greater Blouse is James Clemenza, listed by law enforcement agencies as a soldier in the Colombo family, using the aliases "Jimmy Brown" and "Jimmy Milo." The Greater Blouse Association's office has been listed in NYPD internal reports as a "possible organized crime location," i.e., meeting place.

Recent internal federal reports state that Gallo's illegal interests include, among others, "labor racketeering" and that he is "considered to be of some influence in Chinatown." Other law enforcement files list him as controlling local 812 of the International Brotherhood of Teamsters and as having been "very close" to late don Carlo Gambino. Federal authorities assert Gallo has been associated with Steinberger Trucking, in which Arthur Riccomonte, an owner of Art-Ed Trucking (a garment trucker) is a principal. Gallo is also associated with F& R Sewing Machine Company of 213 West 35th Street.

Yik D. Lai oversees Chinatown operations for Greater Blouse Association. He is a business representative of the Association and he also owns some Chinatown property. He is President of A-Plus Realty, owner of 17 Allen Street (at the corner with Canal Street which houses numerous sub-standard sweatshops that are members of the Greater Blouse Association). Another officer of Greater Blouse is T.S. Wong. He is also Vice-President of A-Plus and owns a number of Chinatown contract shops.

Numerous contractors interviewed for this report complained bitterly about the Greater Blouse Association. Said one contractor: "We have to join, and we have to pay out $50 a month dues. If we don't join, we don't get any work." Another contractor commented that when he applied for membership in the Greater Blouse Association, he had to pay $250, and when he wanted to ask questions, he was told, "just sign it."

In 1976 the Chinese Garment Makers Association. . . brought a lawsuit in State Supreme Court to challenge what the CGMA termed a "secret agreement" between Greater Blouse's officers and the National Skirt and Sportswear Association (representing numerous Seventh Avenue jobbers who provide work to the Chinatown shops). This agreement provided for the jobbers to pay the required 7 and 1/8 percent payroll tax directly into a special account kept by Greater Blouse rather than directly to the contractors as previously done. The payroll tax would then be paid to the contractors on a quarterly basis, after "administrative expenses" were deducted.

The plaintiffs complained that the agreement would cause the perpetually cash-short members financial problems, forcing some out of business. They also complained that since the percentage would be deducted from the gross proceeds of a contractor (including trucking charges, overhead, profit, and other costs) rather than from only the contract price, the amount deducted under the agreement would be greater than under the previous system. They estimated the total to be diverted as in excess of $30 million a year.

Plaintiffs based their challenge on their assertion the Association was run in an undemocratic manner. They alleged members had never seen the

Association's by-laws (which had been changed to allow the directors to enter agreements binding the Association. At the time only two of twenty-three directors were Chinese.) They also said that members' requests for financial reports of the Association were repeatedly denied. However, the court decided against the CGMA, ruling that the challenged method of electing the directors did not violate state law. . . .

Loan-Sharking: Another Form of Control

While trucking is central to organized crime's domination of New York garment making, also having an impact on the operation of the garment industry is widespread loan-sharking.

Garment manufacturing is an industry where cash needs are large and often sudden. The necessary funds to pay suppliers and employees often cannot be raised from conventional sources, but can be obtained from all-too-willing loan sharks who, in return for their favors, extract large weekly interest rates. . . . If the jobber is unable to come up with the "vig" it is not uncommon to settle with the loan shark by having "no show" jobs placed on the payroll and, in some instances, by having mob figures and associates direct the manufacturer's day-to-day operations. This may result in the use of particular contractors and truckers. . . .

Law enforcement sources say it is common for garment district loan sharks to run "legitimate" businesses. For example, in June, 1976, Louis "Gene" Rucci, who married Carlo Gambino's niece, was given a three-year sentence for usury. Rucci ostensibly was a legitimate businessman, for 25 years operating Cathy's Infant Wear, a contractor employing sixty persons in the Bay Ridge section of Brooklyn. In his probation report Rucci is quoted as explaining that, "My relationship by marriage to certain organized crime figures led to my involvement in usury as a sideline to my formal and legitimate employment." He said he was active in garment district loan-sharking and said, as recorded in the probation report, that he saw nothing unusual in his loan-sharking activities. He described them as a sort of "moonlighting." Rucci received an extra three months on his sentence for failing to cooperate in an investigation of Gambino bosses Paul Castellano and Joe N. Gallo. He stated that: "Cooperation could possibly result in danger to myself and loved ones."

Another example of garment district loan-sharking was the case of Vincent "Jimmy East" Ciraulo (a member of the Luchese family) and Thomas Ragusa. They were indicted in 1978 for running a million-dollar-a-year loan shark operation preying on garment district manufacturers. Ciraulo and Ragusa operated out of the Yerevan Social Club, also known as the Blue Moon Social Club at Lexington Avenue and 28th Street. The court papers said they roughed up some jobbers who did not pay on time. Ragusa and Ciraulo each received three years in prison and three years probation after entering a guilty plea just before going to trial.

Andimo Pappadio, a Luchese capo mentioned several times in this report, was considered by law enforcement and other sources to be one of the garment district's main loansharks. He was shot to death in 1976 because of his loan-shark activities, according to one prosecutor.

In 1979 midtown witnessed the murder of Barry Chang, owner of a string of contract shops and a person the police department says was heavily involved in loan-sharking. Chang worked with a number of garment district jobbers and with Consolidated Carriers Corporation. The owner of a contract shop at 47 Division Street in Chinatown, for example, stated that Barry Chang lent him $27,000 and that "there was no interest." Chang was shot near Macy's on West 35th Street, opposite Consolidated's offices. On his body was a promissory note made out to Thomas F. Gambino for $5,000, according to NYPD files.

Conclusions

Most of the actual manufacture of garments in New York City is carried out in contract shops, a large portion of which clearly come under the classic definition of "sweat-shop." These sweatshops and many of the jobbers supplying them with work are under the de facto control of domination of traditional organized crime families.

At first glance the garment industry in New York appears entirely legitimate. The actual level of violence in the industry is low and, partly for this reason, organized crime domination and influence has escaped serious public scrutiny. The reality is that organized crime is exacting its toll by exploiting sweatshop workers desperate to find employment and by engaging in a host of other illegal or quasi-legal activities such as restraint of trade and resulting overcharges, provision of no-interest "loans" that end up with the lender dominating the debtor's business, and outright extortion and loan-sharking. These activities lead directly to higher costs to consumers.

5

An Investigation Concerning Racketeer Activities in Connection with the Air Freight Industry in the New York Metropolitan Area

A Report by the New York State Commission of Investigation, 1968.

I. Introduction

. . . The Commission conducts a continuing inquiry into organized crime and racketeering. During 1966, the Commission received information from several sources which caused it to focus its attention on the air cargo industry in the metropolitan area of New York City. This information . . . indicated that various illegal activities were taking place in consequence of a relationship between an association of truck owners operating in the air freight industry and a teamster union local which had exclusive jurisdiction in the air freight industry. The particular area of this activity involved Kennedy International Airport.

These reports were investigated by the Commission's staff. Further information was gathered from other agencies with whom a continuing liaison was maintained. This initial survey indicated that what was rumored appeared to be true. Known racket figures and members of the national crime syndicate were discovered to be in controlling positions in both the truckmen's association and the teamster union local. . . .

II. The General Situation

The metropolitan area of New York is serviced both for passengers and air cargo by three major airports. These are the John F. Kennedy International Airport, and the Newark and LaGuardia Airports. Along with other facilities, these three airports and the one at Teterboro, New Jersey, are operated by The

Port of New York Authority (hereinafter referred to as the Authority). The Authority was created by a Compact between the States of New York and New Jersey in 1921. It has as its general functions, the "better coordination of the terminal, transportation and other facilities of commerce" and the promotion and development of trade and commerce in, about and through the port of New York. This encompasses an area of an approximately twenty-five mile radius from the Statue of Liberty which is known as the Port District.

With regard to the air terminals under its jurisdiction, it has the responsibility for purchasing, constructing, leasing and operating them. Newark Airport, located in the State of New Jersey, has been operated by the Authority since March of 1948. It has been in existence since 1928. It is leased from the City of Newark and includes some 2,300 acres in its physical plant. In 1966, cargo volume handled at Newark Airport represented some 120,084 tons. Operations began at Teterboro Airport in 1917 and it was purchased by the Authority in 1949. Teterboro, operating as a general aviation facility, did not handle any cargo tonnage in 1966. LaGuardia Airport has been operated by the Authority since 1949, although functioning since 1939, and occupies a site of some 575 acres in the County of Queens. In 1966, LaGuardia had reported air cargo tonnage of 21,465 tons.

The John F. Kennedy International Airport (hereinafter called JFK) is located in Queens County in the City of New York on a site of 4,900 acres and is leased from the City. It has been operated by the Authority since 1947. The following statistics and figures will convey some idea of the magnitude of the JFK complex. The Authority itself has approximately 770 employees at JFK and some 37,500 other persons are employed by the airlines and related industries located at the airport. Further, uncounted thousands of employees of the many service companies required to maintain this complex, closely approximating a city of its own, have daily access to the airport. In addition, for 1966, the Authority recorded seventeen million passengers* moving through the air terminals at JFK. These employees and passengers are served in this "self-contained city" by a 525 room hotel, post office, a bank, a tri-faith chapel and various food preparation centers. JFK also contains what is known as Terminal City, which consists of the International Arrivals Building, numerous unit terminals and parking facilities for approximately 10,000 automobiles. George Howard, an economist employed by the Aviation Department of the Authority, made the following comparison to convey the size and value of JFK Airport:

---

*This figure is broken down by the Authority as follows: eleven million domestic passengers and six million overseas passengers.

. . . the Port's investment in all facilities represents some 606 million dollars, and out of that John F. Kennedy International Airport represents almost 400 million dollars. And that is due to go to some 500 million dollars in the next few years.

The reason for this 100 million dollar expansion was of interest to this Commission since the bulk of the funds allotted were earmarked for the expansion of the Air Cargo Center.

A. *The Air Cargo Center*

Historically, the growth of the air cargo business at JFK can be traced by the corresponding growth of the Air Cargo Center. When the Center was first put into operation in 1956 it covered an area of approximately eighty-nine acres. That year JFK handled 65,600 tons of cargo.* In 1966, the Center had expanded to 13 cargo buildings plus 2 cargo service buildings with a total of more than one million square feet of work space and occupied a total of 159 acres. The cargo handled that year had grown to 477,000 tons. At the present time, the Air Cargo Center at JFK constitutes the largest such facility, and moves the largest tonnage in the world. The Authority's projections, in its master planning for future growth, call for a further enlargement of the existing 159 acres to an acreage total three times that figure. . . .

The air cargo industry has established a pattern of growth which calls for a doubling in volume each five year period. And the end is not in sight. . . .

Value of Cargo. The growth in the cargo tonnage just described was also paced by the growth in the dollar value of the cargo carried. Testimony at the Public Hearing indicated that the value of the air cargo moving through JFK in 1962 approximated 2.8 billion dollars. Three years later, in 1965, this figure had gone up to 4.7 billion dollars, and in 1966 this figure was about 5.5 billion dollars. It was estimated, conservatively, that the amount for 1967 was 6.3 billion dollars. It is well known that air cargo, generally, is of a higher value than cargo which is shipped by other means. High value cargoes demand the speed and rapid handling inherent in air-shipping. This high value factor has created law enforcement problems. . . .

---

*This figure represents revenue cargo and includes both domestic and overseas shipments.

E. Air Freight Trucking

The entire tonnage of air cargo arriving at and being shipped from JFK annually are ultimately dependent on surface modes of transportation. To keep pace with the growth of the air cargo industry there has been a corresponding development in the New York City area and elsewhere in what is termed the air freight trucking field. The air freight truckmen's function is to pick up freight (air cargo) from a shipper and deliver it to the air line terminal. For incoming cargo the process is reversed.

Essentially there are three systems in existence in moving air freight. An air freight forwarding firm may be used to ship freight. The forwarder picks up the cargo, arranges for its air transit and then through its agents in different parts of the county, delivers the cargo to its ultimate destination. In the second case, the shipper may contact an airline himself and thereupon, the airline arranges to have a contract carrier pick up or deliver the freight. Finally, a shipper may contact what is known as a local drayage agent who will either pick up or deliver the freight pursuant to the shipper's instructions and the shipper selects and arranges for the air transit on his own. Regardless of the method chosen, the common denominator in each is the truck and the driver.

In the instance where a shipper contacts an airline directly and then the airline dispatches a truck for the pick-up, a preexisting contractual relationship between the truckman and the airlines is utilized.

Air Cargo Inc. Behind this contractual relationship is a corporate organization known as Air Cargo Incorporated (ACI). This corporation was formed in 1941 by the airlines to provide them with the ground support service necessary to transport air freight. ACI is wholly owned by the domestic airlines and lists all thirty of them as its sole stockholders. It has five regional offices with its headquarters in Washington, DC. The New York region is number one in terms of tonnage and business, reflecting the leading position in the cargo field occupied by JFK. Locally, ACI has the primary function of establishing air freight pick-up and delivery services at the airports. ACI, on behalf of the airlines, bargains with the local truckmen, contracts with them for services and oversees the service aspects of the truckmen's contracts. Billing is handled on a central basis by ACI for its contract truckers. The corporation supports itself by means of an "override" which is the difference between the amount paid to the truckmen and the amount charged to the shipper.

Of prime concern to ACI is the free and uninterrupted flow of air freight in and out of the airports.

Alvin C. Schweizer, New York regional director of ACI, testified at the hearing with regard to attempts of both the union and an association of truckmen to interfere with his function of selecting and approving trucking firms to service the airlines. In 1965, the association of truckmen, the Metropolitan Import Truckmen's Association, notified ACI at contract renewal time that ACI would now be required to bargain with them as a group. This was a departure from ACI's established position and was successfully refused at that time. ACI maintained that it should be free to negotiate for ground trucking services with any competent and qualified trucker, regardless of the trucker's membership in an association. Again in 1966, ACI was faced with similar demands. On that occasion, the result was that the truckmen bargained individually with ACI but all utilized the services of the same attorney. This attorney was also the counsel to the association. . . .

It should be noted that in July of 1965, the same association notified ACI that if a certain changeover in truckers was carried out, as contemplated, by an airline, then the association would shut down the entire airport. The non-association trucker who was to have taken over the service in question resolved this problem by joining the association and, even though a New Jersey based corporation, it also signed a contract with the union having the exclusive air freight jurisdiction at JFK. . . .

During the period of 1965-1967, the union, Local 295, International Brotherhood of Teamsters, also made numerous attempts to dictate policy to ACI. . . .

III. The Association

A. *MITA (1958-1965)*

In 1958, a small group of truckmen who serviced the piers located around the metropolitan area of New York formed an association intended to protect their mutual interests. This organization, called the Metropolitan Import Truckmen's Association (MITA), was chartered by the State of New York the same year. The charter stated that the purpose of the association was to foster the development of understanding, cooperation, mutual benefit and protection of all its members. Originally, MITA had 8-10 members and it grew steadily until in 1964 its membership rolls included approximately 50 trucking companies. Its officers and members were basically hard working truckmen. Dues ranged from a low of twenty dollars a month to a high of ninety dollars and were based on the number of vehicles operated by the member company.

In its early states, MITA had no full time employees. Its officers were working truckmen and the association was successful in obtaining for its members many favorable working agreements on the piers. Regular monthly meetings were held and many industry problems were solved. During this period, it did much to improve the import truckman's lot on the waterfront. From approximately 1962 to 1967, however, the complexion of MITA underwent a gradual change. The spokesmen and leaders of MITA changed from the professional truckman to the professional racketeer. The first person to enter the picture was one John Masiello, known to law enforcement officials as a member of the national crime syndicate and who has a criminal record, having been convicted for smuggling.* He was also one of the subjects of a prior Commission investigation into loan-sharking.

Masiello had been a member of MITA since 1960 and represented the interests of a firm which he reputedly owned, Atlantic Coast Leasing Co., Inc. In 1963 he appeared on the payroll records of MITA as a "trucking consultant." A member of the Executive Board of MITA characterized his duties as "taking care of things such as labor negotiations and seeing people to help expedite the appointment system on the piers." Masiello was quick to surround himself with persons of a similar background who were also placed on the payroll of MITA. These people were classified as "trouble shooters," which would seem to be a questionable description of them.**

. . . In the later part of 1965, as a result of publicity arising from this Commission's loan shark hearing, John Masiello disassociated himself from MITA. However, prior to his leaving, he arranged for his successor. Anthony Di Lorenzo had accompanied Masiello to general membership meetings of MITA for a few months prior to Masiello's resignation. When Masiello announced his resignation, he recommended that Di Lorenzo replace him, even though Di Lorenzo*** had not been a member of MITA. Di Lorenzo was then personally hired as a trucking consultant. Among his assigned duties was the handling of labor negotiations for the truckmen. Within a few months, Di Lorenzo had formed a corporation, Anthony Di Lorenzo Associates, Inc., which corporation was then retained by MITA as its "trucking consultant." The payment specified in the contract entered into between MITA and Di Lorenzo Associates was $25,000 per year.

---

*In 1956, Masiello was convicted for smuggling watches, after an arrest by U.S. Customs authorities. At that time he was an employee of his brother's trucking firm, P.M. Trucking Co., Inc.

**Those identified at the hearing were:
(1) Morris Schoenfeld--11 arrests with 4 convictions for gambling since 1959.
(2) John D'Amico--7 arrests and 3 convictions for bookmaking since 1957.
(3) Milton Luban--3 arrests and 1 conviction for larceny since 1942.
(4) John Campenella--2 arrests and one conviction for violation of Vehicle and Traffic law since 1966.

***Anthony Di Lorenzo has been identified as a younger member of the national crime syndicate. His criminal record lists arrests and convictions for auto theft and felonious assault dating back to 1944.

Anthony Di Lorenzo's brother, Lawrence, was also on the payroll of MITA as a trouble shooter. Lawrence Di Lorenzo was a principal in a trucking company known as Pier Cargo, Inc., as well as a firm called Pier Air Cargo, Inc.* Both these firms were located at the same address in downtown Brooklyn. When the books and records of Pier Cargo Inc. and Air Cargo Inc were reviewed by a Commission accountant pursuant to subpoena, they reflected a series of loans to Pier Cargo, Inc. totalling between twenty thousand and thirty thousand dollars over a period of two years beginning in 1965. These loans were made to the corporation by Isidore Ungar.** Isadore Ungar was also on the payroll of MITA as the treasurer.

Ungar became treasurer of MITA a short while after Anthony Di Lorenzo became its consultant. The prior treasurer was notified he no longer held the position. Up to this time the members of MITA were regularly supplied with accurately prepared treasurer's statements. Testimony at private hearings indicated "there were no reports" when Ungar took over. . . .

By 1965, the take-over of MITA was virtually complete. Persons with criminal records monopolized the payroll.

An attempt was made to explain why persons with criminal records were on the payroll of MITA throughout these years. Alfred I. Richter, Executive Director of MITA, a charter member of the association and a man with thirty-two years experience in the trucking field in New York City, stated that the hiring and firing of the 'trouble shooters' was solely in the control of the "consultants." When queried as to what he meant by the consultants, he stated "Mr. Masiello and Mr. Di Lorenzo." . . .

---

*On April 14, 1967, Pier Air Cargo reported a theft to the New York City Police Department. The goods stolen were in transit from JFK to a consignee in Manhattan. The shipment contained 100 thirty-two caliber Omega pistols. One of these pistols was subsequently recovered on December 27, 1967, at 1:30 a.m. in Yonkers, NY by the Yonkers Police Department in the possession of one Joseph (Mazzie) Saccomanno, who was duly arrested therefore. The important thing to be noted here is that Saccomanno is a known associate of John Masiello, Jr. and his brother Kenneth, who are sons of John "Gentleman Johnny" Masiello. Masiello resides in Yonkers, NY.

**Ungar died of natural causes in 1967 before the public hearing. His criminal record shows arrests for threats to kill and rape and convictions for bookmaking. He was a gambler who operated out of a bar and grill on New York's lower east side. The license of the premises in question was revoked as a result of the illegal activities therein. He was not known to have had any prior experience in the trucking industry.

This then was the situation which prevailed, up to 1965, in the pier truckmen's association. Concurrent with these activities at MITA, somewhat similar organizational activities were taking place among the air freight truckmen at JFK.

B. Jet Stream Truckmen's Association (1960-1965)

The Jet Stream Truckmen's Association (Jet Stream) closely paralleled MITA in its beginnings. It was formed by a small group of truckmen and was granted a New York State charter in May of 1960. The essential difference between MITA and Jet Stream is that Jet Stream was formed to represent the mutual interests of the truckmen engaged in the air freight industry. . . . MITA . . . was originally to serve the pier truckmen. The Jet Stream charter states that it was to foster the development, understanding, cooperation and mutual benefit of all members and to secure as members trucking operators primarily engaged in ground transportation of air imports and exports for the Port of New York. At its inception, it was primarily a social organization and its dues ($10 a month) were applied to cover the costs of the monthly dinner meetings. As the volume of air cargo increased, the problems of the truckmen likewise increased and it became necessary for Jet Stream gradually to raise its dues. By the summer of 1965 they averaged $50 a month per member. They had, approximately, thirty trucking companies as members.

During the early part of 1965, informal discussions had begun between members of MITA and members of Jet Stream relating to a merger of the groups. By the spring of 1965, discussions had progressed to a stage where members of the Executive Board of MITA and others were meeting with the membership of Jet Stream at JFK. John Masiello was present at these meetings and was active in stressing the merits of a merger.

It is significant that the president of Jet Stream at the time of the merger discussions was Frank Yandolino. Yandolino was the airport manager for a trucking firm known as J.S. Wald, Inc. John Masiello was on the payroll of J.S. Wald, Inc. at this same period of time as a consultant. Yandolino knew Masiello was connected with J.S. Wald but was reluctant to be specific as to his exact role there. . . .

Yandolino also operated his own trucking firm, Tempo Trucking & Transportation, Inc. at the same time that he was on Wald's and Jet Stream's payrolls.

Witnesses were hesitant when asked to be specific about the role Masiello took in these merger discussions. Most, however, clearly recalled that he was present and that he seemed to have an interest in the proceedings. One witness recalled that Masiello approached him at a meeting and after inquiring which rental company supplied the witness' trucks, told him "You know, I rent trucks too."

C. Cargair Trucking Association, Inc. (1964-1965)

There was still another association of truckers which appeared at JFK, known as Cargair Trucking Association, Inc. (Cargair). This association was formed in 1964 by a group of air freight truckers who dealt primarily with the domestic airlines. These ACI contract carriers joined together to negotiate with the union in November 1964 and then attempted to negotiate with ACI in the summer of 1965. Membership in Cargair never exceed ten and almost all Cargair members also belonged to Jet Stream.

The president of Cargair was Vincent Dionisio. Dionisio was also a principal in Mercury Air Freight, Inc. Harry Davidoff, the secretary-treasurer of Local 295, IBT, was an extremely close friend of Dionisio's, as well as a regular visitor to Mercury. Cargair shared office space in Mercury's headquarters in Cargo Building 80 at JFK. Cargair's membership dues ($200 a month) were appreciably higher than the other associations, allowing the association to furnish its offices lavishly and to rent Cadillacs for its representatives.*

In June of 1965, Cargair merged with Jet Stream. . . .

The newly purchased furnishings were turned over to Jet Stream without any apparent reimbursement to Cargair. Jet Stream then occupied the office space formerly used by Cargair.

By August of 1965, Jet Stream had merged with MITA. The structure which remained had MITA as a single all encompassing association at its head and two subdivisions or arms, one constituting the Pier division and the other, Jet Stream, representing the airport. This, essentially, was the situation at the time the commission examined it. This was the organization which had Anthony Di Lorenzo Associates as its "trucking consultant."

D. MITA (1966-67)

The main office of MITA was located at 304 West 58th Street, in the Borough of Manhattan. This office space was occupied by two other corporations. Anthony Di Lorenzo Associates and a vehicle leasing firm, Rite-Way Leasing and Sales Co. Inc. (Rite-Way). Rite-Way was owned and operated

---

*In 1965 the Suffolk County Police Department observed the notorious John "Sonny" Franzese and Phillip Vizzari, both identified in this Commission's loanshark investigation, in a 1965 Cadillac sedan being operated by Vizzari, which was leased to Cargair. Franzese and Vizzari were observed in conversation with a known gambler in Lindenhurst, LI, and were followed [in the Cadillac] from there to JFK.

by Anthony Di Lorenzo and specialized in leasing trucks to air freight truckmen.* MITA still retained known criminals with gambling backgrounds as its "trouble shooters" or field representatives in its Pier branch. The Chairman of the Executive Board of MITA was Angelo J. Ponte. Mr. Ponte was a principal in a waste paper firm known as West Street Trucking Corp., Inc., with offices in New York City and Jersey City, NJ. He was a principal in numerous other corporations as well.** None of the corporations with which he was connected were members of MITA, however. Both Anthony Di Lorenzo and his uncle, Matteo De Lorenzo,*** had been employed in various capacities over the years by Mr. Ponte. Anthony Di Lorenzo considered him a social friend.

Commission investigators determined that Anthony Di Lorenzo regularly operated an automobile listed in the name of West Street Trucking and registered in the State of New Jersey. As Chairman of the Board of MITA, Mr. Ponte was supplied with a new Cadillac automobile for his exclusive use. This was not the case with any of the proceeding Chairmen. . . .

It will be remembered that meetings of the Board of Directors were few and far between during this period. One witness could not recall a single meeting between 1965 and 1967.

At JFK, MITA has a branch office for its Jet Stream division. Salvatore Cirami became the president of Jet Stream after the merger. He owned and operated Air Freight Haulage, Inc. and had been previously active in both Cargair and Jet Stream. Not to be outdone, the field representatives of Jet Stream also had extensive criminal records.**** These field representatives

---

*John Masiello also operated a vehicle leasing firm, ANR Leasing Inc.

**One of these, Ponte's Steak House, on the lower west side of Manhattan, was the scene of a late evening meeting of some of the witnesses at the Commission's public hearing. The meeting involved Anthony Di Lorenzo, his uncle Matteo and one Joseph Curcio, a known associate of Anthony "Ducks" Corallo and John "Dio" Dioguardi. The meeting took place shortly after Curcio and Matteo Di Lorenzo were subpoenaed to testified at private hearings of the Commission.

***The brother of Anthony's father, slight difference in the spelling of surname.

****Henry Bono, alias Chubby, whose criminal record included convictions for rape and narcotics and an arrest for criminally receiving stolen property; Phillip Giaccone, convicted of disorderly conduct after an arrest for felonious

(continued...)

were supplied with leased Cadillac automobiles even though their duties were minimal and all operating costs were paid by MITA. . . .

E. Air Freight Haulage Co., Inc.

Salvatore Cirami was the president of the Jet Stream division at the time of its merger with MITA and continued in that capacity thereafter. Early in the investigation, reports reached the Commission that Cirami had had a dispute with Anthony Di Lorenzo for an unknown reason. It was also reported that on one occasion when he attempted to attend a Jet Stream meeting he had been physically barred from entering by Di Lorenzo. The picture which unfolded during the investigation ultimately proved to have many ramifications. Cirami was shown to have links with John "Dio" Dioguardi, as well as being the beneficiary of what could be classified as a "sweetheart" contract with Local 295. Additionally, he was found to have paid substantial salaries to two well known racket figures who were carried on his payroll as salesmen.

Cirami owned and operated Air Freight Haulage Co., Inc. from an office on Rockaway Blvd. in Queens, New York. He had been active in the air freight field for twenty years. At the time of the public hearing, Air Freight Haulage had ten to fifteen vehicles picking up and delivering cargo. The firm was, and had been, an ACI contract carrier for many years. Cirami testified that he operated ten to fifteen vehicles with seven or eight employees through the use of what he called independent contractors. These so called independent contractors were paid a salary depending on the contractual arrangement entered into between them and Cirami. These drivers were required to pay their own taxes, social security and unemployment. This arrangement was not as clear to all his drivers as Cirami would have the Commission understand. One of his former drivers applied for unemployment benefits when he left Air Freight Haulage, and after a hearing, was determined by a referee to be an employee, and awarded $200.

Cirami had a union contract with Local 295 but only half his drivers were union members. The standard teamsters contract at JFK called for a driver to join the union within thirty days of his hiring. The benefit to Cirami was apparent in his being able to operate with non-union drivers. It meant a savings to him of approximately $75 per month per nonunion employee. This would be the cost to him for each employee's union benefits. It also meant that he did not

---

****(...continued)
assault and rape and arrested for possession of a gun, gambling and possession of bookmaking records. Both Bono and Giaccone were owners of Independent Air Freight, Inc., along with Nicholas Accardi, in whose automobile John Franzese and Phil Vizzari were observed.

have to pay for various fringe benefits accruing to union members. Cirami explained that he was allowed to operate under this arrangement because officials of Local 295 were not aware of the situation. As a matter of fact this "sweetheart" contract was common knowledge throughout the airport.

1. Matteo De Lorenzo. Even if Cirami was not paying all his drivers the union scale, he was paying substantial salaries to two persons well known to law enforcement officers. The books and records of Air Freight Haulage Co., Inc. showed that from July 1965 to May 1966, Matteo De Lorenzo was on the payroll as a salesman at a salary of $175 a week; plus expenses and the use of an automobile. As previously stated, Matteo De Lorenzo is the uncle of Anthony Di Lorenzo. He was hired by Cirami after Anthony Di Lorenzo had approached Cirami at a Jet Stream division meeting and informed him that his uncle needed a job. This was all the urging and recommendation Cirami needed. He also was the first salesman ever employed by Cirami.

Matteo De Lorenzo's background was a varied one but it hardly qualified him for the position of air freight salesman. His criminal record was extensive and dated back to 1928. It included convictions for robbery, possession of guns, and theft from interstate shipment (his only prior trucking experience). In his career, he had been incarcerated in the House of Refuge, Sing Sing, and the Federal Penitentiary at Atlanta. In Atlanta, he met Phillip Masiello, who later introduced him to his brother John Masiello. He was related by marriage to the notorious Cosmo 'Gus' Frasca, known by law enforcement officials as a caporegime in the national crime syndicate. Matteo de Lorenzo also frequented the bar operated by MITA's treasurer, Isidore Ungar.

De Lorenzo had no definite hours of work set out by Cirami nor did he have a desk, office space or a telephone at Air Freight Haulage. However, he managed to get to the office on pay days. His alleged duties consisted of generating new business for Cirami.

Cirami was unable to recall whether De Lorenzo had produced any business as a salesman.

Q. . . . Can you tell me the name of one particular customer that he brought
to you in the ten months that he was working for you? . . .
A. There was some activity but I don't remember.
Q. Can you give me one customer?
A. I can't remember at this time--I don't remember.

2. Joseph Curcio. Joseph Curcio's background was as unsavory as was De Lorenzo's. His criminal background included arrests and convictions for contempt of court, illegal possession and transportation of alcohol, gambling, felonious assault and conspiracy. Among his associates were Anthony "Ducks"

Corallo, John "Dio" Dioguardi, Harry Davidoff, and incidentally, Joseph Valachi.*
Curcio's career had been union oriented. Curcio and Davidoff had both been officers of Local 649 of the notorious United Automobile Workers AFL in the early 1950s. This organization should not be confused with the present United Auto Workers headed by Walter Reuther.

The aforementioned United Automobile Workers was discovered to have been formed and to have operated under the direction and control of John "Dio" Dioguardi and Anthony Corallo. When John Dioguardi went to jail for a violation of the New York State income tax laws,** Joseph Curcio succeeded him as New York Regional Director of the UAW-AFL. Curcio remained an officer of Local 649 as well. In late 1955, Local 649 UAW-AFL became Local 269 International Brotherhood of Teamsters.

Curcio kept up his associations with all these people even after leaving the Teamsters union. He then operated a printing business which included among its customers Air Freight Haulage and Local 295.*** Cirami knew him previously from the garment center of New York and as a social friend.

Curcio was on the payroll of Air Freight Haulage from April through September of 1966 as a salesman. His salary was $175-$200 per week and he submitted expense vouchers "from time to time." His activities were summed up simply by Cirami at the public hearing:

> COMMISSIONER GRUMET: . . . Did he do anything for that money?
> THE WITNESS: He contacted people.
> COMMISSIONER GRUMET: What did he do?
> THE WITNESS: To move freight with us; but it just didn't fit into our regular routine and after a period of five months I saw there was nothing significant forthcoming and I couldn't afford it, so I just laid him off.

---

*Curcio and Valachi were cellmates in Atlanta Penitentiary.

**On his release, Dio formed a labor relations firm, Equitable Research Associates, which . . . "represented management firms and in many cases assisted them in avoiding unionization." Salvatore Cirami retained Equitable Research Associates for $500 at a time when he was having labor difficulty with Local 808, International Brotherhood of Teamsters, (which local preceded Local 295 in the air freight field).

***Curcio's son is a printing agent or "jobber" for Jard Products, a novelty firm owned and operated by John Dioguardi. Jard did business with Cargair, MITA and numerous other air freight firms.

. . . In the summer of 1966, Cirami broke away from the Jet Stream division and negotiated a renewal of his Air Cargo Inc. contract alone. The Jet Stream members had a prior agreement to negotiate as a united group. Cirami, as the president of Jet Stream, was aware of this. Cirami had, on occasion, designated Curcio to represent Air Freight Haulage at their association meetings so that Curcio was known to the other owners. Cirami attempted to attend the first regular meeting of Jet Stream held after he signed his contract with ACI. He felt that he needed Curcio to accompany him although this was not his usual practice. Cirami was physically barred from entering that meeting by Anthony Di Lorenzo, even though as president, Cirami would have normally conducted the meeting. . . .

It was apparent that the real control of the association was now firmly vested in the hands of its "consultant," Anthony Di Lorenzo.

IV. The Union--Local 295, International Brotherhood of Teamsters

A. Background

In 1951, law enforcement agencies who were assigned to organized crime investigations noted that John "Dio" Dioguardi* was becoming active in the affairs of a local union which was organizing members in the New York metropolitan area. This union was identified as Local 102, United Automobile Workers-AFL. By June 1951 Dio held the title of business manager of this local. He immediately exercised his authority and control by hiring organizers for Local 102. One of the first organizers hired was Joseph Curcio. When this take-over became apparent . . . the then president of the Local . . . protested Dio's power and control. When his protests were unheeded, he resigned as president.

Following Local 102's lead, a number of charters for local unions were issued by the International UAW in the New York area. John Dio became the Regional Director for the UAW and the UAW prospered.

---

*John Dioguardi, hereinafter referred to as "Dio," is identified by law enforcement officers as being a captain in the Thomas Luchese family of the national crime syndicate. His arrest record dates back to 1932 and continues to the present day. It includes convictions for extortion, fraud, and state and federal tax violations. He has long been identified as a major racketeer specializing in union matters. . . .

In 1958, the McClellan Committee investigating this takeover, summed this up in the following paragraph:

The locals thus chartered had a common denominator--their leadership was made up of men with lengthy and unsavory police records who had previously made their living in such rackets as bookmaking, narcotics and prostitution. A study of these UAW-AFL locals showed that Dio and those with whom he formed alliances brought 40 men into the labor movement in positions of trust and responsibility--men who, among them, had been arrested a total of 178 times and convicted on 77 of these occasions for crimes ranging from theft, violation of the Harrison Narcotics Act, extortion, conspiracy, bookmaking, use of stench bombs, felonious assault, robbery, possession of unregistered stills, burglary, violation of the gun laws, being an accessory to murder, forgery, possession of stolen mail, and disorderly conduct.

Among the men named in the aforesaid investigation were Joseph Curcio, Harry Davidoff, John McNamara and Milton Holt. (Each one of these men showed up again ten years later in this Commission's investigation of the air freight industry).

Dio was replaced by Joseph Curcio as the Regional Director of the UAW after Dio's conviction and sentence to prison in 1954. Dio was prosecuted and convicted by the New York County District Attorney's office for a violation of the State Income tax laws. Specifically, he failed to report a payoff of $11,500 from a Pennsylvania dress firm for keeping that firm non-union. His influence and control continued, however, regardless of his lack of a title, on his release from prison at the expiration of his sentence. It was at this point that Dio began operating as a labor consultant through Equitable Research Associates.

Throughout the period prior to 1956, Dio maintained a close relationship or alliance with another notorious labor racketeer, Anthony "Tony Ducks" Corallo. Corallo, like Dio, was identified as being connected with the Thomas Luchese family in the national crime syndicate. He also was a captain, but unlike Dio, was considered a candidate to succeed to the head of the family following the demise of Thomas "Three-finger Brown" Luchese.* Corallo's criminal record includes a series of arrests beginning in 1929 and includes convictions for narcotics, conspiracy and consorting. . . . Corallo had strong links to the International Brotherhood of Teamsters (IBT) at this time. It was known that the teamsters were becoming interested in Dio's organizing of the taxi industry in New York in 1955, and attempts were made to draw Dio into the teamsters.

---

*Corallo's recent arrest along with a prominent New York City official and the attendant publicity according thereto is deemed by some to have doomed his promotional chances.

128

Corallo's influence was pivotal here. James Hoffa was shown to have had numerous contacts with Dio and Corallo at this time. It was in furtherance of Hoffa's plans to take over the IBT (eventually successful) that the next step was taken. In November 1955 Hoffa arranged for the chartering of seven new teamster locals in the New York area.* Five of these new teamster locals were found to be transferred from Dio's UAW operation. Officials from UAW Locals 649, 240, 224, 227 and 228 became officials in IBT Locals 248, 269, 362 and 651. Curcio went from UAW Local 649 to teamster local 269, and became secretary-treasurer, and Davidoff went from UAW local 649 to teamster local 258, and became secretary-treasurer. Nothing was changed but the International affiliation in many instances. Corallo's teamster local 875, which predated the newly chartered locals, became teamster Local 275.

John McNamara,** identified at this time as being a supporter of the Hoffa faction in the IBT, and Hoffa's "man to see" in the New York area, arranged for the issuance of one of these charters for his own purposes. McNamara had been the president of Local 808 IBT prior to this and he arranged, without the knowledge or consent of the members involved, to transfer Local 808 members into his newly chartered local 295.*** Local 295's charter gave it exclusive jurisdiction over, and the power to organize, the air freight trucking industry in the New York metropolitan area.

. . . Within two years of the granting of these charters, Dio, McNamara, Davidoff and Milton Holt had been indicted for crimes including perjury, extortion and bribery, arising out of the misuse of their official and unofficial union positions.

This is the origin of the local union which . . . became the dominant union at JFK.

B. Growth of Local 295

Local 295 operated from an office in the Bronx, New York, after its formation. John McNamara was president and around 1960 Harry Davidoff became its secretary-treasurer. Davidoff came to Local 295 from Local 258, where he had also been secretary-treasurer. Davidoff has a criminal record dating back to 1933, including convictions for burglary, conspiracy to extort and

---

*The numerical voting power of these seven locals would have been enough to elect Hoffa's candidate as the president of Joint Council 16. Joint Council 16 is the governing body of the teamsters in the New York area.

**Subsequently convicted of contempt of court.

***The employees of Air Freight Haulage were included in this transfer.

gambling, and arrests for felonious assault (knife), possession of a gun, grand larceny, robbery, extortion and vagrancy. . . .

During the period from 1960 to 1966, Local 295 continued to grow and add more members to its rolls until in 1966 it included approximately 1200-1500 members. This was accomplished both by organizing the newly established trucking firms and by acquiring members from other union locals through the medium of the "turnover." The way the "turnover" operated was explained by a trucker whose company had previously held a contract for ten years with Local 804, IBT.* In 1960, he received a notice in the mail from Local 804 explaining that in the future Local 295 would service his existing union contract. The employees of his trucking company went so far as to complain to James Hoffa personally about this action but nothing was ever done to rescind it.

Local 804 never formally protested this action to its governing body, Joint Council 16, although it was reported that they were not anxious to lose these members. In no instance of a "turnover" did the Commission find any evidence of a formal protest being made to the Joint Council. McNamara and Davidoff were allowed to work out whatever arrangements they felt necessary without any interference from the governing bodies of the union. . . .

By 1965, Local 295 was the dominant union in the air freight industry in New York. It had contracts with all the leading air freight truckers and the members of the union included drivers, helpers, warehousemen and clerical employees.

Local 295 now operated out of its own newly constructed building in Queens, New York, located just outside JFK. . . .

During the period of 1960-1966, Davidoff never considered himself subordinate to John McNamara. Davidoff had many times stated that "he was running the show." According to one knowledgeable witness, who on one occasion sought to appeal a decision made by Davidoff, he was told by Davidoff "Don't bother going to John--I'm running the show." . . . McNamara's influence was on the wane.

"Hand and Glove" Relationship. With control of the dominant union and the truckman's association at JFK in the hands of criminal elements, . . . the air freight industry would soon find itself caught between the hammer and the anvil. . . .

---

*As recently as March of 1966, Local 804, IBT turned its members at Wings & Wheels, Inc., a JFK based forwarder, over to Local 295.

V. The Union and the Association--Interplay

A. Emery Air Freight, Inc.

. . . Emery Air Freight, Inc. operated as an air freight forwarder at JFK. It is the largest such forwarder in the nation. Emery employed approximately 250 persons in the metropolitan area and operated about fifty vehicles. With the exception of certain sales and supervisory personnel, the remaining employees, including the clerical help, were members of Local 295.

1. Work Stoppages. Emery Air Freight's relations with Local 295 was characterized as "poor" over the years. Thomas Granzow, the company's former Station Manager at JFK, prepared a list for the Commission which detailed Emery's local labor difficulties over a three year period from 1965-1967. The list contained a total of eight work stoppages or walkouts during that period, only one described by the witnesses as having some justification. The others were called "wildcat work stoppages" and were based on a variety of unjustified issues. . . . This problem was so troublesome that the management of Emery, on at least one occasion, felt it was necessary to complain to James Hoffa about these stoppages. Regardless of the lack of justification for the stoppages, they continued uninterrupted. A stoppage of work in a large trucking company is a very serious and costly matter.

Mr. Granzow testified:

Q. . . . Why was Emery, which was completely unionized with local 295, the subject of a continuing series of work stoppages over the years?

A. For two reasons, sir: One is that Emery was the leader in the industry and had probably the greatest group of members in Local 295. So that anything we submitted to the rest of the industry normally would submit to. The second is that others did not have to work interruptions because they knuckled under more easily than Emery did.

. . .

2. Hiring Procedures. Under the terms of its contract with Local 295, Emery was required to notify the union when it had a position available for a union member. This was called an "opening." The union would be given an opportunity to refer a member in need of a job to the firm with the opening. What happened to this salutary system was that favoritism would creep in and only certain members would be referred to the better openings. It also gave the union an opportunity to place members in strategic locations. In the past, Emery had been ordered by Davidoff to hire certain people. Emery, according to Mr. Granzow, instituted a system of checking these referrals from Davidoff for prior criminal records or a general security clearance. On more than one occasion, the union's referral failed to pass this background check. In spite of this failure, Emery still was required to hire the individual employee.

3. Messenger Service. In the air freight industry, parcels or shipments weighing less than twenty-five (25) pounds can be shipped by what is known as a messenger service. This is a local practice which has grown up at JFK.

Emery used a messenger service delivery from JFK in two ways. In one instance, Emery would deliver freight on its own trucks directly to the midtown terminal of the messenger service, and then the service would break the shipments down and deliver them. The other method called for the messenger service to pick the parcels up at Emery's facility at JFK.

Emery had begun this messenger form of delivery using a concern called Fleet Messenger, which was a subsidiary of Radio Corporation of America. Within a few years, Fleet Messenger had been replaced by another messenger firm, Telstar. This change took place in 1963, after Davidoff called Emery and told them to stop using Fleet and start using Telstar. Although no particular reason was given by Davidoff when he ordered this change, Telstar's president, who was John Cerrito, and Harry Davidoff were known to be friends and many persons at JFK believed them to be connected in this firm. Cerrito also leased four trucks from Rite-Way, Anthony Di Lorenzo's company.

4. The Newark Shuttle. Emery Air Freight, Inc. operated a freight terminal at the Newark Airport. This terminal was staffed by warehousemen and clerical personnel, the latter being members of Local 295. Emery's trucking in New Jersey was handled through subcontractors. Emery's prime subcontractor at Newark was a firm owned by one Howard Wofsy, Air Freight Trucking Service, Inc. Emery also carried on another trucking operation, through subcontractors again, involving the transportation of air freight between JFK and Newark in tractor-trailer trucks. The rapid expansion of JFK had made it more practical in some instances to trans-ship air freight from Newark.

In the latter part of 1965, Emery negotiated with Wofsy to have Wofsy's company become their exclusive shuttle trucker from Newark to JFK and to operate as their pickup and delivery agent in New Jersey. Wofsy was willing to accept this relationship and Emery detailed the requirements in terms of equipment and personnel. Although there was some dispute as to what actually transpired in the furtherance of this arrangement, the facts will be presented, as found by the Commission.

In the course of these negotiations, Emery wanted some assurances from Wofsy that this trucking arrangement would not result in any labor strife with Local 295. Mindful of its experiences at JFK with Local 295, Emery was concerned about the further unionization by Local 295 of their operations at Newark. Emery also raised the question as to whether Wofsy would even be allowed to operate at JFK by Local 295. Wofsy at this time held a contract for its employees with a New Jersey teamster local, Local 478.

Three witnesses who were present at these negotiations, testified at private hearings that Wofsy was questioned by Emery with regard to labor peace or "lack of complications between the two locals." At the public hearing, Wofsy denied ever discussing with Emery the guaranteeing of labor peace. Mr. Thomas Granzow, who at the time in question was Assistant to the Regional Manager of Emery, which region included Newark, testified that Wofsy had told him the following:

A.   . . . [H]e had a big problem. Harry Davidoff told him he wasn't going to be able to operate this trucking service in Manhattan or to JFK airport, as he had intended to, . . . even though the employees of this trucking company were members of a union. Mr. Davidoff had solicited a sum of money from him in order to allow him to operate this company without interference of any type and that sum was $5000.

Granzow further pointed out that Wofsy would stand to lose if he did not knuckle under to Davidoff's demands.

A.   . . . [N]umber one, the company, the small company which he had acquired in New York would probably go down the drain and he would lose his investment in the same. This was obvious. Number two, to whatever extent his trucks out of New York serviced Emery, JFK, he would probably be prohibited from that activity in the future. Number three, Emery's employees at Newark, clerical employees, belonged to the same Local 295. And we perceived that it was at least possible that economic sanctions against Emery at Newark might result. . . .

Granzow also related his attempts to have Wofsy report this incident to the appropriate law enforcement agencies. Initially, he testified, Wofsy agreed to do so but later the same day he declined. . . .
. . . Wofsy did sign an exclusive contract in February 1966 with Emery to operate the shuttle run between Newark and JFK. He operated the shuttle without any known trouble from Local 295.
Examining further into Wofsy and his New York trucking operations, the Commission uncovered . . . the relationship between Wofsy and Harry Davidoff. . . .

B. Howard Wofsy

Howard Wofsy has operated Air Freight Trucking Service, Inc. in New Jersey for approximately eighteen years. As of the time of the Commission's hearing, Air Freight Trucking's operation consisted of pickup and delivery of freight in New Jersey for airlines and forwarders; running an import freight operation from JFK; and handling a general local pickup and delivery service. The company was authorized by the Interstate Commerce Commission to operate in five counties in New Jersey and the five boroughs of New York. It also handled freight to and from the piers in New Jersey, Brooklyn, Staten Island and Manhattan. This sizeable operation required the use of seventy-five to eighty trucks which were rented from Wofsy's own leasing firm, Airport Truck Rental, Inc. Wofsy and his wife were the only principals in Air Freight Trucking. Earl, his brother, received a percentage of the profit from the company but was not a partner.

Air Freight Trucking had a union contract with Local 478, International Brotherhood of Teamsters* since December 1953.

Despite Wofsy's many years of experience in the trucking industry and the substantial nature of his operation in New Jersey, it is amazing to note the machinations in which he became involved in order that he could do some trucking business at JFK.

1. Air Freight Transportation Service, Inc. Air Freight Transportation Service, Inc. was formed by Wofsy to handle the import portion of his operation in the New York area. The stockholders, originally, were Wofsy, his wife and his brother Earl. During the same period of time, Wofsy loaned certain sums of money to a concern known as Mallary Air Freight Transportation. Wofsy put the sum loaned as "one or two thousand dollars," which was never repaid. Mallary operated as an air freight trucking company in Manhattan and maintained a depot or terminal there. This company's business at that time did not include air cargo. In spite of the loans, Mallary's financial picture did not improve, thereupon Wofsy absorbed Mallary into Air Freight Transportation Service, Inc. The former principal in Mallary was kept on as an employee and manager by Wofsy.

Air Freight Transportation Service continued to lose considerable money at this time, as had Mallary. Wofsy found himself with a lucrative trucking operation in New Jersey and a losing one in New York. How he attempted to extricate himself from one predicament and ended up in another involved several interesting ramifications.

2. Independent Air Freight, Inc. Wofsy ascribed the financial loss at Air Freight Transportation Service to absentee management, and his solution was to take in another corporation to assist him in the operation of this business. This was accomplished by merging Air Freight Transportation Service with an air freight trucking firm, Independent Air Freight, Inc. which was already operating at JFK.

The principals of Independent Air Freight proved to have a varied background. Henry Bono, Phillip Giaccone and Nicholas Accardi were each holders of one-third of the original shares of stock issued. . . .

---

*A general trucking local located in New Jersey and under the regional jurisdiction of Joint Council 73.

Loans to Independent Air Freight. Independent Air Freight was started in November 1964 by the above named principals and serviced Brooklyn with air freight pickup and deliveries. Tracing the source of the capital with which Independent Air Freight started business became somewhat of a mystery.

. . . [C]ousins of Giaccone advanced sizeable sums of money to Independent Air Freight according to Bono. Salvatore Cirami loaned Independent Air Freight $3,000 at this time as well.

Another interesting item was reflected in Independent's books in the form of an unsecured $10,000 loan made in May of 1965 by a bank, located in Newark, New Jersey. This was carried as a personal obligation of Bono's and Giaccone's. Wofsy admitted that he had introduced Bono and Giaccone to a bank officer at that bank and that he maintained accounts there personally.
. . .

Wofsy personally guaranteed this note although he had only known Bono and Giaccone for two weeks. Moreover he could not remember how they met or who introduced them. Wofsy denied that securing this loan for them was a condition to their merging with him. He also denied that he was required to accept Independent Air Freight as a partner before being allowed to operate at JFK. . . .

In the late summer of 1965, Air Freight Transportation Service Inc. and Independent Air Freight Inc. merged and were in operation. The corporation, known as Air Freight Transportation Service Inc. was now owned 50% by the Wofsy's, (husband, wife and brother) and 50% by Bono, Giaccone and Accardi, and was operating as a local drayage agent in Manhattan and Brooklyn.

4. Union Negotiation. Air Freight Transportation Service now had a union contract for its drivers as well. Wofsy had gone to Davidoff's office in the Bronx, requested a contract for his drivers and signed it without discussion. Wofsy's analysis of the situation at JFK was that Local 295 was the union to negotiate with if one was going to operate at JFK. It is worthy of note that Air Freight Transportation Service was not required by Davidoff to sign a union contract for its warehousemen or for its clerical employees and up to the time of the private hearings, they remained non-union. This represented a sizeable savings to a trucker, . . .

5. Association Negotiation. Just prior to the merger, Wofsy had been solicited to join Jet Stream. He had been approached by Vincent Dionisio, and Wofsy's partner to be, as it later developed, Phillip Giaccone. They came into his office at Newark Airport and explained "that it was good for truckers to get together to discuss the common problems that we enjoy." . . . [W]ithin a very short time he appeared at Jet Stream's office at JFK and joined. . . . Dionisio's sales talk at Newark had been effective since Wofsy agreed to pay $300 a month in dues and he also paid a $2500 initiation fee. . . .

6. When "Partners" Fall Out. The association between Wofsy and his newly acquired business associates flourished for about a year and then withered and died.

Wofsy claimed that "he was not a good partner" and he "voluntarily" withdrew from Air Freight Transportation Service in 1966. This withdrawal meant that Wofsy simply turned over his stock certificates representing 50% ownership of the Air Freight Transportation Service to Bono, Giaccone and Accardi and walked away from the corporation. The former principals in Independent Air Freight were now the legal owners of Air Freight Transportation Service. The Commission attempted to determine from Wofsy what reimbursement he received for this stock.

> THE CHAIRMAN: What did they give you in return?
> THE WITNESS: Nothing. I didn't want anything . . . the business was worth nothing.
> THE CHAIRMAN: You handed over a fifty percent interest in this business?
> THE WITNESS: Yes, it is worth nothing. . . .

The business that Wofsy thought was worth nothing in October of 1966 eventually proved valuable. In the early part of 1967, Phillip Giaccone decided to sever his relationship with Bono and Accardi. He was paid $7500 by his remaining partners for his interest. . . . [T]he Wofsy shares of Transportation minimally would have amounted to $11,250 or could have been as much as $22,500.

What is clear is that Wofsy got nothing. What is also clear is that Wofsy was now operating freely at JFK with Air Freight Trucking Service Inc., and Emery was satisfied, Davidoff was content, and the Association was receiving its dues every month from Wofsy. . . .

D. Dionisio and Davidoff

During the course of the investigation, the Commission received reports alleging acts of physical violence by Davidoff, in and around JFK. These reports also included information that Harry Davidoff was often accompanied by Vincent Dionisio, in the role of chauffeur-bodyguard.

Dionisio's background was free of any known criminal activity. It was learned that he had previously been employed as a mechanic by a bus line, operated a gas station, ran a limousine service to and from JFK and finally, became a principal in various air freight trucking firms. His role as president of Cargair has been discussed previously.

The close relationship between Davidoff and Dionisio inured to Dionisio's financial benefit. . . . [F]irms in which Dionisio had a financial interest were often the beneficiary when Davidoff forced a change of accounts. . . .

One knowledgeable witness reflected the feeling prevalent in the air freight industry that there also existed a business relationship between Davidoff and whatever firm in which Dionisio was currently active. . . .

In addition to the accounts which might have transferred as a result of union pressure, the general knowledge of Dionisio's relationship with Davidoff stood Dionisio in good stead when attempting, on his own, to get a new business.

Labor peace, in any industry, but especially in the trucking industry, is a priceless commodity. An employer who knows in advance that his trucker will not be harassed or his shipments delayed has a very definite competitive advantage. In fact, Dionisio stated publicly that "he was friendly with Harry [Davidoff]" and in a presentation to a prospective account he gave assurance that his firm would have labor peace because of his relations with Davidoff. In the tightly knit business community that existed at JFK "the word" soon got around. Dionisio often accompanied Davidoff on his daily rounds at the airport. Since Dionisio often carried a pistol, for which he was licensed,* it is possible that this was the beginning of the idea that he served as a bodyguard for Davidoff.

E. Pacific Air Freight, Inc.

Pacific Air Freight, Inc. is an air freight forwarder operating in the metropolitan area of New York, with main headquarters in Seattle, Washington. Prior to 1963, Pacific made two or three unsuccessful attempts to break into the New York trucking market. The Commission's investigation disclosed some pertinent and interesting facts as to the circumstances surrounding Pacific's successful breakthrough and it becoming one of the leading air freight forwarders in this area.**

In the spring of 1963, Gilbert Breen, a pioneer in the air freight trucking field in this area, was approached by Frank Fernandez, a vice-president of Pacific Air Freight's home office. Fernandez' purpose was to establish Pacific

---

*This permit was surrendered by Dionisio, after inquiry was made of the New York City Police Department by this Commission into his associates.

**Pacific was subsequently cited by the Civil Aeronautics Board in 1967, for numerous violations of the Federal Aviation Act of 1958, as amended. Included in the complaint were instances where it was alleged that Pacific collected higher rates than set forth in its tariff, shipped by ground when billing for air delivery and even shipped by air mail while billing for their own delivery. (See Docket 18568 before the Civil Aeronautics Board, Washington, DC).

as a viable operation on the east coast, with Breen's assistance. Thereafter, Breen began operating as Pacific's agent in the New York area through the medium of a corporation, Aero Expediters, Inc. As part of this agency agreement, Breen was to supply the sales force and the clerical staff necessary for the operation. Aero Expediters acquired a ready made sales force by hiring three persons who had previously been employed by Airborne Freight Corp. These were Robert Brazier, James Correll and Perry Florio. Brazier* had been sales manager in Airborne's New York office and Correll and Florio were two of his salesmen.

This situation continued until Gilbert Breen became a vice-president of Pacific. The next change took place when Breen gave up his vice-presidency and left Pacific altogether. During this same period, Brazier, Correll and Florio left their positions with Aero Expediters and were hired directly by Pacific. Brazier went to the Seattle office and Correll and Florio took over the sales department in the New York area. At this point Correll was in charge of Pacific's entire operation in the metropolitan area.

Pacific, even though it had severed all connections with Gilbert Breen, was still using Breen Air Freight, Inc. as its New York trucker. Matthew Breen operated this firm and it handled approximately 500,000 pounds of freight a month for Pacific. In addition to the trucking operation which they subcontracted, Pacific now had approximately 10 people in its sales force and approximately 20 people on its clerical staff.

1. Pacific and Rite-Way. By now, Pacific had grown dissatisfied with subcontracting its trucking and decided to strike out on its own. To do this, it had to have trucks and it began to make inquiries among leasing companies. The attorney for MITA, Haskell Wolf, brought Pacific and Rite-Way together. Rite-Way was principally owned by Anthony Di Lorenzo, who was now also the trucking consultant to MITA. When Pacific started operating its own trucks in April or May of 1966, it was using vehicles leased from Rite-Way. The deal was negotiated for Pacific by Brazier and Correll. The contract called for Pacific to supply its own maintenance on these vehicles. The drivers for the 16 trucks, which were first leased, came from Breen Air Freight or one of its subsidiaries. Breen was not pleased about having lost these drivers. Thereafter, within a year's time, Pacific grew disenchanted with Rite-Way. Vehicles were breaking down and maintenance and replacement costs were accruing. Somewhere in this period, Pacific renegotiated this contract with Rite-Way with the additional proviso that Rite-Way also provide maintenance. Thereupon,

---

*Corell was introduced to Brazier by his sister Eugenia Corell Napoli, who was a personal friend of Brazier's at this time. Eugenia later appeared on Aero's and Pacific's payrolls.

Rite-Way provided for the maintenance of these vehicles at a gas station which it operated near JFK* The additional cost of maintenance caused Di Lorenzo's profit margin in Rite-Way to shrink.

This arrangement soon proved unworkable and Pacific looked around for a way out of the contract. Perry Florio, then the regional manager of Pacific, contacted the Hertz Corporation and they took it from there. Their solution was to negotiate with Rite-Way for the purchase of the vehicles used by Pacific as well as buying out Rite-Way's contract. This transaction involved a sum of approximately $60,000-$70,000 being paid by Hertz to Anthony Di Lorenzo, according to one witness.

Hertz at this point was supplying Pacific approximately 21 vehicles. Rite-Way was in the process of liquidating the remainder of its business at the time of the Commission's public hearing.

2. Pacific and the Union. After Breen's former drivers, who had been Local 295 members, came over to Pacific, Local 295 and Pacific signed a contract. At the time of the hearing, approximately 40 drivers and warehousemen were covered by the contract. This contract did not include clerical employees. This factor, in itself, can result in sizeable savings to a company. Furthermore, non-union employees can be used more flexibly and "motivated for the company's benefit much more readily." There was no pattern to Davidoff's organizing of clericals, except as has been pointed out here. The clerical employees of Dionisio, known favorite, were never organized. Those of Emery were. . . .

3. Pacific and the Association. Haskell Wolf, the attorney for MITA, initially approached James Correll with a request that Pacific join MITA. Pacific occupied office space in Cargo Building 80 down the hall from MITA. Wolf's initial proposal left Correll with the impression that the association could assist Pacific in some of its pressing legal problems at JFK. When Correll inquired as to the cost, Wolf told him that Pacific would be required to pay $1000 a month dues and $5000 in initiation fees. Correll protested the amount of the initiation fee and was told Pacific could spread the payment out over an extended period of time. Correll's reason for authorizing this expenditure and his attitude towards the association are set forth below.

Q. Did you ever find out who the Association directors were?
A. No, I did not.
Q. Did you ever attend any of the Association meetings?

---

*Frank LaBell, owner of Commodity Haulage and local agent for Jet Air Freight, lent Anthony Di Lorenzo $2600, and personally guaranteed the lease for this gas station. Jet Air Freight also leased its vehicles from Rite-Way.

A. No.

Q. Did anyone . . . from Pacific ever attend any meetings at your direction?

A. No . . . The thing that I was ultimately afraid of was that we would make some sort of tactical blunder and the volume we were in at that particular time, if *we would get into a bind on a union negotiation*, it could cost us a fortune . . . for all practical purposes, we were refinancing our growth and it was crucial to keep New York going. (emphasis added)

In order to avoid costly union problems Pacific was willing to pay approximately $800 more a month in dues than any other association member, except one, and at least twice the initiation fees. It is clear that Correll was purchasing some sort of insurance for Pacific regardless of the cost. Pacific could not afford to lose out again in the New York market. . . .

4. The Napolis. While James Correll was employed by Aero Expediters as a salesman, payroll records for 1963 of Aero indicated that his sister Eugenia Correll Napoli was also on salary as a sales representative. She was paid $150-$175 per week. Eugenia Napoli's experience up to this time, included working for the telephone company in Wilkes Barre, PA, modeling, an airline stewardess and being in the chorus at the Copacabana in New York. Prior to appearing on the payroll of Aero Expediters, Eugenia was known to law enforcement agents in New York and Florida as a companion of the late Paul "Paulie Ham" Correale.* She was on Aero's payroll at the time when Pacific took over Aero Expediter. She thereafter left Pacific to travel with her husband, James "Jimmy Napp" Napoli to Las Vegas in 1964.

After leaving Pacific, Eugenia leased an apartment in New York's Greenwich Village. In her signed application for the apartment, she represented that she was a vice-president of Aero Expediters, Inc., an owner thereof, and received a salary of $25,000 per year. The rent they paid for two years on this apartment was $288 a month.

In 1966, Eugenia Napoli was again carried on the payroll of Pacific as a sale representative for four or five months at a salary of $175 per week. Once again, she was hired by her brother. Eugenia's employment at this time closely coincided with her husband's incarceration in the Federal Penitentiary under a conviction for an income tax violation.

From 1963 to the date of the private hearing, October 13, 1967, she had no other gainful employment. Nor did her husband, James Napoli, to the knowledge of the Commission. He had not been employed since they met. In

---

*Identified by law enforcement officers as a member of the national crime syndicate, "Paulie Ham" was identified as being a soldier in the Luchese family. He also was known to have played a major role in the gambling syndicates operating in New York City.

response to an inquiry as to how her husband supported her, Eugenia said: "
. . . Well, he is a gambler. "

James "Jimmy Napp" Napoli lives in a town house on the east side of
Manhattan. It is known that he paid $53,000 for the purchase of the four-story
building on East 31st Street. After extensive renovation costing more than
$100,000 which included the installation of a private elevator, he, his wife
Eugenia and their family moved in during 1967. There is a nurse for the two
children and additional help comes in two or three times a week. James Napoli
operates a 1966 Cadillac for which he paid cash and rents garage space for it.
All bills are paid in cash or by money order. . . .

Napoli was described at the Commission's hearing as being a "super-banker"
in the numbers or policy racket operations conducted in the New York-New
Jersey area. As a super-banker, Napoli would receive policy bets that a regular
banker would not be able to handle. He operated as a lay-off agent for smaller
operations. . . .

VII. J.S. Wald, Inc.

J.S. Wald, Inc. was a long established, highly respected trucking firm
operating in and around New York City. At the time of the investigation, it was
being operated by two vice-presidents, Paul M. Wald, a son of the deceased
founder and his brother-in-law, Robert Roth. J.S. Wald's drivers were covered
by a union contract with Local 807 IBT.* Robert Roth had been employed by
J.S. Wald for the nine years preceding the hearing. Law enforcement agents
had long known of a link between John Masiello and J.S. Wald. A major extent
of this information was developed by the Commission.

A. Chess Trucking, Inc.
John Masiello had been employed by his brother Phillip's trucking firm,
P.M. Trucking Co. at the time John was arrested and convicted of smuggling
on the waterfront in New York. As a result of this conviction, P.M. Trucking
Co. went out of business and J.S. Wald Co. through J.S. Wald, Sr., the then
president, purchased some of their physical assets and vehicles.

In 1961, John Masiello sold Wald the accounts and good will of a bankrupt
and dormant trucking firm, Chess Trucking Inc. Masiello was in control of
Chess Trucking as a result of loans which he had made to that Company. The
contact was drawn up by Masiello and called for the sale of the good will of

---

*Wald was never required to transfer its members from local 807 to local
295.

Chess Trucking to Wald. It appeared merely to be an attempt on Masiello's part to salvage something from Chess and also to use Chess as a wedge to infiltrate another business. Implicit in this arrangement was the understanding that Masiello was to advance J.S. Wald some money as well.

The terms of the Chess Trucking sale called for John Masiello to deliver 75-100 trucking accounts previously held by Chess Trucking to J.S. Wald for a total payment of $164,700. J.S. Wald paid Masiello $80,000 in cash on the signing of this agreement and the balance, $84,700, was represented by notes to Masiello, to be paid over a five year period. Of the 75-100 accounts purchased by J.S. Wald, they were only able to retain two.

The original cost of $164,700 paid over a five year period, ended up costing J.S. Wald $300,000 before these notes were retired. This figure included interest payments made over that period.

A significant provision of the contract of sale between Chess Trucking and J.S. Wald required J.S. Wald to hire Masiello as a consultant for the same period of time that the notes were outstanding, 1961-1966, at a salary of $10,000 a year. This entire arrangement was negotiated by Paul Wald* for J.S. Wald. Masiello did no work on a regular basis for Wald, had no office and was never called on by Roth for any advice. It was clearly a device aimed at giving Masiello what looked like a legitimate source of income. By 1966, these so-called consulting services of Masiello cost J.S. Wald a total of $50,000. The ultimate cost to J.S. Wald of the two accounts acquired from Chess Trucking totaled $350,000.

During this period, J.S. Wald also rented vehicles, as needed, from Masiello's leasing firm, A.N.R. Vehicle Leasing, Inc. The company also borrowed sums of money from Masiello on numerous occasions.

B. Setmar Holding Corp.

One bad experience apparently was not enough for J.S. Wald. The Commission ascertained that in 1966, J.S. Wald entered into a contract with Setmar Holding Corp. under which Wald was to pay $49,500 for the good will and accounts of another dormant bankrupt trucking company called Anden-Formac Inc.

This turned out to be a repetition of the Chess deal. Setmar Holding Corporation was organized and operated by John Masiello. Anden Trucking Co. was the trucking branch and Formac Warehouse Inc. was the warehouse branch which constituted Anden-Formac Inc.

---

*He later became Chairman of the Board of MITA, at the same time Masiello was a consultant to MITA.

Anden Trucking Company's background was also well known to law enforcement officials. The prior owner of Anden, which at one time operated twenty-five to thirty vehicles in and around the Brooklyn piers, was an inveterate horse player who was forced by his gambling losses to borrow money to keep his company alive. It was never established from whom he borrowed, but within a short time, he had acquired three partners in his business.* The next step was that the owner of Anden Trucking was put on the payroll by his partners, who then became his bosses. Finally, he was dismissed by them, leaving them in control of what had been his business.

Formac Warehouse was a corporation which operated a bonded warehouse and which ultimately also came under the control of the Notaros. This combined operation failed under the dubious management skills of the Notaros and became dormant.

Masiello, through Setmar Holding Corp. sold to J.S. Wald Co. approximately 50 accounts which Anden Trucking had previously serviced. In addition, Ignatz Bonacorsi, pursuant to this arrangement, became a vice president of J.S. Wald. He was taken on to service these particular accounts. Instead of serving them, he left J.S. Wald and took all those 50 accounts with him.

This deal cost J.S. Wald $49,500 plus Bonacorsi's salary and did not produce any revenue for J.S. Wald. . . .

In 1967, J.S. Wald filed a petition in bankruptcy in the United States District Court, Southern District of New York. Among the creditors who were listed in the Court records were Elizabeth Masiello, wife of John, in the amount of $13,500. Although this debt was listed in her name, it represented money owed to her husband, John Masiello.

A.N.R. Truck Leasing Corp., John Masiello's operation, was listed in the amount of $4,400.

Setmar Holding Corp., discussed above, was a creditor in the amount of $33,075. . . .

IX. Recommendations

As we said in the Commission's opening statement at the public hearing, the attempt by racketeers and criminal elements to gain control of the air freight industry in New York must be stopped. . . . [W]e urge that the International

---

*Ignatz Bonacorsi, Lou Notaro and Joseph Notaro. The latter two are nephews of the late Joseph "Little Joe" Notaro, who was identified . . . as being a "capo" in the Bonanno family of the national crime syndicate.

Brotherhood of the Teamsters' Union examine all the facts regarding the conduct of Harry Davidoff, the secretary-treasurer and dominant figure of Local 295. Appropriate action should be taken to rid this Local of all undesirable individuals who are inimical to the labor movement and to take proper measures to invalidate any coercive or illegal agreements which may have been made under Davidoff's direction.

6

Waterfront Corruption

Report Made by the Permanent Subcommittee on Investigations of the Committee on Governmental Affairs United States Senate, March 27, 1984.

Six days of hearings in February of 1981 by the Senate Permanent Subcommittee on Investigations showed that corrupt practices were commonplace on the Atlantic and Gulf Coast waterfronts.

The hearings were conducted under authority granted the Governmental Affairs Committee and its duly authorized subcommittees by Rule XXV of the standing Rules of the Senate and by Senate Resolution 361, which was agreed to on March 5, 1980.

Section 3 of Senate Resolution 361 authorized the Subcommittee to conduct investigations of labor racketeering and organized criminal activities and to identify the individuals involved. . . .

Citing criminal activity within the International Longshoremen's Association and the American shipping industry, witnesses at the hearings described the struggle for economic survival in ports that are riddled with kickbacks and illegal payoffs to union officials.

Witnesses testified that payoffs were a part of virtually every aspect of the commercial life of a port. Payoffs insured the award of work contracts and continued contracts already awarded. Payoffs were made to insure labor peace and allow management to avoid future strikes. Payoffs were made to control a racket in workmen's compensation claims. Payoffs were made to expand business activity into new ports and to enable companies to circumvent ILA work requirements.

Organized crime was found to have great influence in the operation of the ILA and many shipping companies. Some shipping firms, because of fear or a willingness to participate in highly profitable schemes, have learned how to prosper in the corrupt waterfront environment. They treat payoffs as a cost of doing business.

The free enterprise system has been thrown off balance. Contracts were not awarded on the basis of merit. The low bid did not beat the competition. Profitability was not based on efficiency and hard work but rather on bribery, extortion and questionable connections. The combination of these corrupt practices was a recipe for inflationary costs and economic decline.

Much of the corruption on the waterfront stemmed from the control organized crime exercises over the ILA, a condition that has existed for at least 30 years.

In the mid-1950s, reports of widespread corruption in the ILA led to a Congressional investigation into labor racketeering on the docks. The Senate Select Committee on Investigation of Improper Activities in the Labor or Management Field, an extension of the Senate Permanent Subcommittee on Investigation, looked into the problem of ILA involvement in waterfront corruption.

In August of 1957, the Select Committee, chaired by Senator John McClellan of Arkansas, called as witnesses Captain William V. Bradley, president of the ILA, and Thomas (Teddy) Gleason, General Organizer and the union's third ranking official.

Pointing to the ILA's record of tolerating corruption practices within its leadership ranks, Senator John F. Kennedy of Massachusetts pressed Bradley and Gleason on what constructive steps they were taking to control questionable and illegal conduct by union officials.

Senator Kennedy noted, for example, that, according to the New York State Crime Commission, 30 percent of the officials of ILA longshore locals had police records.

Bradley and Gleason responded in general terms, saying in effect, that they were not running a police department and that they didn't expect to move any more vigorously against ridding their union of corrupt officials.

Twenty-four years later, in February of 1981, Gleason, who had been president of the ILA since 1963, was still defending his union against charges that it was controlled by organized criminals. . . .

Gleason was wrong. . . . He failed to refute the charge that his union is controlled by organized crime. . . .

A document handed to Gleason at the hearings, Subcommittee exhibit No. 2, was a chart showing the names of senior ILA officials who had been convicted of felonies in the federal government's investigation of waterfront labor-management corruption.

Known by the acronym, UNIRAC, for union racketeering, the investigation and subsequent prosecutions resulted in convictions of more than 20 of the ILA's most prominent leaders.

Equally damaging to the ILA and Gleason's claims that the union is free of organized crime's dominance was evidence showing that several of the ILA leaders were members or associates of traditional La Cosa Nostra or Mafia families.

Confronted with the chart showing the ILA officials' convictions, Gleason would not address adequately the fact that his union's leadership had so many felonious criminals in its ranks.

It could not have escaped Gleason's attention that Anthony Scotto, president of the ILA's largest local, No. 1814 in Brooklyn, was convicted of racketeering, demanding and accepting payoffs and federal income tax fraud.

It could not have escaped Gleason's attention that Scotto, as international Vice President and General Organizer, was a nationally prominent labor leader, a man with substantial political influence and the ILA leader mentioned frequently as likely to succeed Gleason as president.

Nor could it have escaped Gleason's attention that Scotto was identified in 1969 as being a member of the Carlo Gambino crime family and that as recently as 1979 court-authorized electronic surveillance and police observation established that Scotto was summoned to a Brooklyn bar by Michael Clemente, a crime family gangster of considerable notoriety, so that the two of them, Scotto and Clemente, could discuss the very government investigation that would eventually send them both to prison.

With Scotto, there were other ILA international vice presidents who were convicted of labor racketeering--George Barone and William Boyle of Miami, Anthony Anastasio of New York, Vincent Colucci of New Jersey and William Landon of Jacksonville, Florida. Barone, Anastasio and Colucci have been identified by the Department of Justice as being members of organized crime families while Boyle has been identified as an associate.

Fred R. Field, Jr., the former General Organizer of the ILA; Carol Gardner, an international assistant general organizer; and Thomas Buzzanca, an international organizer, were convicted of labor racketeering. Buzzanca has been identified by the Justice Department as being a member of a crime family and Field was identified as an associate.

Barone, Buzzanca, Colucci and Landon were presidents of ILA locals. Anastasia was an executive vice president of an ILA local. Another convicted officer, James Vanderwyde, was coordinator for the Atlantic Coast District of the ILA and an officer in a Miami ILA local.

These were some of the better known ILA officials convicted of labor racketeering. There were others in smaller ports--seven in Wilmington, North Carolina; two in Charleston, South Carolina; and one each in Mobile, Alabama; San Juan, Puerto Rico; Houston, Texas; Boston, Massachusetts; Jacksonville, Florida; New Orleans, Louisiana; Tampa, Florida; Southport, North Carolina; and Port Allen, Louisiana.

An even more damaging development that came out of the government's inquiry was the fact that the senior members of the waterfront conspiracy-- Scotto, Field, Barone, Buzzanca, Colucci, Gardner, Boyle, Vanderwyde--were found to be controlled by gangsters outside the union. To varying degrees, they were doing the bidding of organized crime figures whose conduct had been brought to the attention of law enforcement for many years.

Evidence showed that Colucci, Gardner and Buzzanca took direction from a Genovese crime family operative in New Jersey, Tino Fiumara. Barone, Boyle and Vanderwyde were found to be under the direction of another Genovese family figure, Anthony Salerno.

Anthony Scotto, who the Justice Department said 12 years ago was a Gambino family member . . . also owed some allegiance to the Genovese gang. Scotto's acquiescence to Mike Clemente's summons was a display of the loyalties of a man who enjoyed the friendship and trust of important political leaders. Scotto had many connections in the respectable world, yet he still had to meet his obligations to the organized crime figures who got him his ILA job. . . .

Teddy Gleason's testimony before the Subcommittee was not in keeping with a labor leader whose first commitment is to his members and to the principles of trade unionism. The evidence is overwhelming that criminals have a strong voice in his union. He should have acknowledged that such a problem exists and he should have indicated what steps he is taking to correct it. The most obvious action he can take is to exercise the clause in the ILA constitution which enables the union to remove from office officials who are found to be unfit for their positions.

The Congress also has a responsibility. It should strengthen existing laws to allow government to do more to clean up corruption when it exists in unions such as the ILA. . . .

Longshore and other waterfront workers should be protected fully against the cost of job-related injuries. However, there should be a mechanism installed in the compensation claims process to assure that the insurance system is not exploited illegally.

The Federal Longshoremen's and Harbor Workers' Act makes it too easy for longshoremen to feign or exaggerate injuries. The burden of proof is placed on the employer, who must demonstrate that the claimant's injury is non-existent or is not as serious as he and his doctor say it is.

As seen in the Subcommittee's hearings, one company with operations on the Brooklyn pier saw its annual workmen's compensation claims jump from $230,000 to $1.4 million in two years. The only way the company could bring down the claims was to begin paying off ILA Local President Anthony Scotto $5,000 a month. Costs then returned to a more reasonable level. The Subcommittee received testimony indicating that another company suffered such high workmen's compensation claims that it went bankrupt because of them.

The onslaught of fraudulent claims resulted, in part, from the abuse of those provisions of the Federal Longshoremen's and Harbor Workers' Act which allow the injured employee a "free" choice of treating physician. The Act should be amended to require that employees select treating physicians from a list of authorized physicians compiled by the Department of Labor from names submitted by employers. Workmen's compensation, as envisioned by Congress, is designed to insure employees against the possibility that they would be unable to work and earn a livelihood because of an injury at work. By striving to protect the legitimate concerns of the worker who is injured on the job, the Congress created an invitation for the unscrupulous to create yet another waterfront racket. By providing for a listing of authorized physicians, the rights of the workers will continue to be protected while the potential for fraud will be reduced.

In addition to its findings in the legislative area, the Subcommittee makes the following additional findings:

(1) With respect to the waterfront, the Subcommittee believes in the need for state, local and regional commissions and regulations to fend off the abuses documented in the hearings. The New York--New Jersey Waterfront Commission has been in existence for nearly 30 years. It has not stopped corruption completely in the Port of New York. But it does exercise many valuable law enforcement and regulatory services. As one Federal prosecutor put it, the commission has not solved every problem, but things would be much worse without it.

The Subcommittee noted that hoodlums were expelled from the Port of New York by the commission in the 1960s. But, because there were not such regulatory government components in the gulf coast ports, these crime figures were able to go to Miami, Savannah, Norfolk and other Southern ports and resume their criminal conduct under the guise of trade unionism. . . .

(2) The Subcommittee's hearings . . . also demonstrated the value and necessity of vigorous, imaginative law enforcement by state and local police. Nowhere was the effectiveness of state investigative work better displayed than in the two-and-one-half year undercover operation run by the New Jersey State Police in the Newark area.

Known as Project Alpha, the investigation consisted of state police officers, in an undercover capacity, operating a trucking company that gradually fell under mob control. Assisted by the FBI and funded in part by a $1 million grant from the Law Enforcement Assistance Administration, Project Alpha demonstrated the many illegal pursuits of the Genovese and Bruno crime families in the Newark area.

As a result of the inquiry, state and federal charges were brought against 34 persons for a variety of crimes including possession of stolen property, unlawful sale of handguns, conspiracy for possession of stolen property, possession of counterfeit New Jersey Certificates of Titles, possession of counterfeit checks, loansharking, possession of counterfeit New Jersey drivers licenses and interstate transportation of stolen property.

Important as the criminal prosecutions stemming from Project Alpha were, also valuable was the new information law enforcement officials were able to learn about the internal workings of the crime families, how mob members work with one another in certain circumstances and how they compete in others. . . .

(3) Although some employers were victims of economic extortion and fear of organized crime, other firms became willing participants, eager to pay off to gain a competitive edge in the marketplace. . . . The business executives on the waterfront who pay off should be prosecuted. Those who don't pay off should be protected by their trade associations and by State and Federal laws.

(4) Information developed in the waterfront corruption hearings, coupled with information that came out of the Subcommittee's examination of the government's investigation of the Teamsters Central States Pension Fund, demonstrated that the U.S. Department of Labor has not taken an effective role in combating corruption in national unions.

. . . The Labor Department has primary jurisdiction in this area but has not met its obligations. It has neither created an adequate presence in the field; nor has it shown a willingness to build cases against allegedly corrupt union officials.

An example of the Labor Department's erroneous attitude was seen in the waterfront corruption hearings. A workmen's compensation claims racket had sprung up in the early 1970s on the Brooklyn docks. According to testimony received at the hearings, the Labor Department was aware that there was a problem but did nothing to stop it. On the other hand, the department continued to insist upon the strictest interpretation of the law which put the entire burden of proof on the employer to demonstrate that a longshoremen's claim was fabricated or exaggerated. The Labor Department should have taken steps to require more proof of genuine injury. That was the proper solution to the problem. When the Labor Department refused to take corrective action, one of the employers faced with increasingly costly compensation claims solved the problem in his own way. He began paying off a labor leader $5,000 a month. His claims returned to a more reasonable level.

It is the responsibility of the Labor Department to protect union leaders and honest officials. The department has personnel on the scene where labor racketeering first surfaces. They have access to information that no other federal agency has. No other federal component is vested with the authority and the tools to detect, investigate and dispose of properly information indicating corrupt and questionable practices in the labor-management field. . . .

IV. Miami Waterfront Became a Major Crime Area

Organized Crime Took Over Miami Waterfront
In 1972, the Metropolitan Dade County Department of Public Safety received information indicating that Miami's Dodge Island Seaport had been infiltrated by organized crime.

The Subcommittee received testimony on this subject from George R. Havens, Chief Investigator for the State's Attorney Office for the 11th Judicial Circuit of Florida.
Havens summed up the state's investigative findings this way:

> Our information established that virtually every commodity affecting the transportation industry on the Dodge Island Seaport was under the control and domination of a small group of highly sophisticated and organized criminals.

Tracing the origins of the organized crime group that controlled Dodge Island, state investigators learned that many of the group's members were affiliated with the International Longshoremen's Association, particularly with ILA locals in New York.
When these men were barred from working on the Port of New York by the New York-New Jersey Waterfront Commission, they moved to Florida and began to organize ILA locals on the Miami docks. These organization efforts began in the mid-1960s, Havens said.

ILA Organizers Had Criminal Backgrounds
The principal union organizers the ILA sent to Florida in the mid-1960s were George Barone, Douglas Rago, James Vanderwyde, William Boyle and Fred R. Field, Jr. The staff of the Investigations Subcommittee assembled background information on these men from arrest records, independent investigation and interviews with law enforcement officials.
George Barone, born on December 16, 1923 in Brooklyn, New York, has been identified by law enforcement authorities as being closely associated with the Genovese organized crime family of New York and Florida.
Barone became involved in the waterfront industry in the 1950s as an organizer for the ILA. . . .
In 1955, Douglas Rago and James Vanderwyde, both felons with extensive criminal records, organized ILA Local 1826 in Brooklyn. The local was to represent laborers known as Chenangoes, workmen who loaded and unloaded railroad cars. This category of waterfront worker was not required to register with the waterfront commission. The Waterfront Commission Act prohibited felons from being union officers or agents but the ban did not apply to Local

1826. Barone became president of the local as well as president of a similarly formed local, No. 205, also outside the reach of the Waterfront Commission Act prohibition. Both locals had several persons with criminal records as officers.

From 1959 to 1961, the waterfront commission held hearings on criminal activity on the New York docks. These hearings indicated that a criminal element continued to exercise substantial influence at the Port of New York.

Barone was called before the commission but refused to testify. . . . Douglas Rago, also invoked the fifth amendment privilege at the waterfront hearings. . . .

Douglas Rago, born on September 2, 1932, is reportedly a member of the Genovese crime family. His criminal record includes arrests for failure to register for the selective service, armed robbery, attempt to kill police officers, assault and armed robbery, perjury, bookmaking and fraud. He has been imprisoned in the past at both New Jersey State Prison at Rahway and Sing Sing.

Rago began working as a longshoreman in New York in 1948. He became an ILA organizer and secretary-treasurer of Local 1826. A waterfront commission report of March 23, 1956, referred to Rago as a vicious criminal and longtime associate of John Scanlon, a reputed organized criminal who was murdered in 1958.

William Boyle, born on August 16, 1916, has an arrest record that dates back to 1933 and includes arrests and convictions for burglary, petty larceny and liquor smuggling.

Law enforcement authorities developed information indicating that Boyle was a "bag man" who collected payoffs from waterfront executives in Atlantic and Gulf Coast ports. . . .

James Vanderwyde, Sr. was associated with an organized crime group in the 1940s that was involved in criminal activities on the New York docks. Membership in the group was largely of persons of Irish descent. Later Vanderwyde became an associate of Italian organized crime groups.

With Douglas Rago, Vanderwyde was one of the organizers of ILA Local 1826. Vanderwyde became the business agent of Local 1826. Vanderwyde's previous convictions included petty larceny in connection with a burglary, possession of a pistol, assault and robbery. He was sentenced to two and one-half years to five on the assault charge and five to ten years on the robbery conviction. Vanderwyde had a reputation for being a "strong arm enforcer" for the ILA.

In June of 1960, Vanderwyde was called before the waterfront commission. He invoked his fifth amendment privilege.

State and Federal law enforcement agencies called Fred R. Field, Jr. an associate of organized criminals, particularly the Genovese family. Field reportedly worked with many organized criminals including George Barone, the late Benny Astorino, the late Albert Anastasia, Douglas Rago, William Boyle and Anthony Salerno. Field held many ILA positions and later became General Organizer of the International.

Law enforcement authorities said that in 1966 Field and Astorino traveled to Miami to work out arrangements to extend the ILA's jurisdiction into Miami. Police believed that Gulf Coast maritime executives learned from Field and Astorino that they would be expected to make payoffs to ILA officials in return for labor peace.

George Wagner Blended into Criminal Environment of Docks

George Wagner, who had worked on the Brooklyn docks following World War II, was a participant in a major stock fraud scheme controlled by Carmine Lombardozzi, a notorious organized crime figure.

Convicted for his role in the fraud, Wagner received a sentence of 5 years' probation. He was convicted again in 1960 for selling fraudulent securities and received a 1-year prison sentence. In 1962, Wagner was sentenced to 2 years for grand larceny.

Now relocated and protected under the Justice Department's Witness Security Program, Wagner testified before the Subcommittee on his experiences in the late 1960s and early 1970s as a shipping executive on the Miami waterfront.

Having spent many years in the stolen and counterfeit securities racket, Wagner said, he became acquainted with several organized crime figures. These friendships enabled him to blend in easily with crime figures on the Miami waterfront.

Wagner said:

> Throughout my career of selling fraudulent securities I regularly associated with members of the mob or Mafia. I traveled in what was called a "hoodlum fraternity," drinking and eating in places frequented by the mob. I learned about individuals' affiliations with the various mob "families" as well as their criminal specialties--which is counterfeiting, stolen securities, narcotics, guns, burglaries and union shakedowns.
>
> I learned much about George Barone, Doug Rago, and Jay Vanderwyde. Initially, these men were engaged in burglaries and bank robberies. They then were put into union jobs with the ship cleaners local union and then the International Longshoremen's Association in New York. Each local was run by the mob and employed people such as Vanderwyde for "heavy" work. Vanderwyde was known as a "shooter" and reputedly shot and killed two people who incurred the displeasure of mob bosses.

Wagner said that William Boyle formed ILA Local 1922 in Miami. Wagner was named acting port shop stewart for Local 1922, handling the daily "shape up" or assignment of workmen to the various stevedore companies. In 1967, Wagner became general manager of Marine Terminals, Inc., but he continued to manage the daily "shape" for Local 1922. This placed him in the unusual position of being a fulltime management executive and an ILA operative.

William Boyle, George Barone and James Vanderwyde encouraged Wagner to accept the job with Marine Terminals. They discussed the assignment with A.P. Chester and Jacob Sklaire of Chester, Blackburn & Roder, the shipping firm that owned Marine Terminals.

ILA officials in Miami conducted a kind of background check on Wagner before he was allowed to go to work for Marine Terminals. They wanted to establish his credentials as a reliable mob consort.

Wagner believed that one of the most convincing testimonies to his own credibility as a trustworthy person was information Barone received indicating that he had gone to prison and remained silent while most of his partners in crime got off. . . .

In his new post with Marine Terminals, Wagner said, he was expected to pay off Cleveland Turner, president of ILA Miami Local No. 1416, James Vanderwyde and William Boyle. But A.P. Chester, president of the company, told him he need not pay off George Barone. "Mr. Sklaire takes care of George Barone," Chester explained, according to Wagner. . . .

At Barone's direction, Wagner rented heavy equipment and received kickbacks from the rental firm. Wagner said he entered Marine Terminals into contracts with other businesses and allowed the businesses to inflate their bills, with the understanding that the padded invoices would enable the enterprises to kick back to Barone and other ILA officers. The payoffs would be channelled back though Wagner.

In some transactions, Wagner said, an initial payment of $10,000 cash to Barone was required and monthly payments of $1,000 were then made over the life of the contract.

When Marine Terminals' parent company, Chester, Blackburn & Roder, set up a freight consolidation firm, Wagner won permission from George Barone to allow the new enterprise to operate without union employees. The company, Caribbean Freightways, paid substantially lower wages to its workers. As a result, the firm earned higher profits, Wagner said, explaining that Barone was paid a commission on all containerized shipments which Caribbean Freightways handled.

Twin Terminals Services, Inc., of Miami also benefited from making a deal with George Barone, Wagner testified. . . . Twin Terminals was a freight consolidator, operating out of an airport warehouse.

. . . Barone allowed . . . Twin [Terminals] to circumvent union regulations requiring that containers be unloaded and reloaded before being shipped out, Wagner said. Known as the "strip and stuff" rule, this requirement stipulated that union workers would not handle containers loaded by non-union help within a 50-mile radius of the docks. When non-union employees loaded the containers, the ILA required that its members unload and reload--or "strip and stuff"--the containers before transferring them to the ship.

By avoiding the unload-reload, or "strip and stuff," requirement, Twin Express was able to operate with half as many employees and with less pilferage since the goods were never removed from the containers, Wagner said, adding that shipping documents were doctored and the seal on the container was broken and falsified to give the impression the "strip and stuff" procedure had been adhered to. . . .

. . . Some ILA work gangs were more efficient than others. Some gangs, which consist of 12 to 14 men, were known to steal, others had reputations for drinking on the job, but some were known to move quickly and get their work done competently and honestly. It was the competent gangs that shippers wanted and, for a price paid to an ILA leader, they could hire them, Wagner said, pointing out that those shippers who didn't pay off often had to make do with inefficient work gangs.

Because of his special relationship with Cleveland Turner, president of ILA Local 1416, Wagner said, he had no trouble scheduling sufficient numbers of men and sufficiently competent gangs to load and unload the ships of Marine Terminals' clients.

Wagner recalled another situation in which George Barone's conduct as a union leader seemed to be at odds with official ILA policy. There was an ILA strike in 1971, Wagner said, but George Barone worked out an arrangement with shippers in some smaller ports like Key West, Fort Pierce and Laudania and ILA workers stayed on the job there. Wagner said the shippers paid off Barone for his special treatment. . . .

Wagner said Thomas (Teddy) Gleason, the ILA president, was aware of the strike breaking activities that were taking place in Florida by ILA workers with Barone's approval. Wagner said he decided that Teddy Gleason was controlled by the mobsters. Barone, Rago, Boyle and others certainly conducted themselves "as if they owned Gleason," Wagner said.

Barone, Boyle and James Vanderwyde frequently told their story of how Captain William V. Bradley, ILA president in the 1950s, gave up his job under threats from organized criminals. . . .

From his executive position inside Marine Terminals, Inc., Wagner was of great value to mob figures. He took advantage of his opportunities, Wagner said, describing his activities as resulting in huge payoffs to organized criminals and to himself.

Asked to estimate the amount of money he earned for the mob and himself, Wagner said he earned many times more than $200,000.

Payoffs to ILA officers did not always take the form of cash. Wagner said that for several years he bought groceries and meats for William Boyle's family. Wagner said he paid the cost of catering the wedding reception for Cleveland Turner's daughter.

Barone, Boyle, Rago and Vanderwyde were the principal recipients of payoffs from Marine Terminals, ... But these four men were not candid with each other as to the amount of money they were receiving. They often seemed anxious to short change one another . . . .

Instead of devoting himself to his duties as vice president of Miami Local 1922, Douglas Rago rarely showed up at the office, Wagner said, recalling that Boyle told him that Rago spent most of his time at the track where he frequently would bet as much as $10,000 in one day. . . .

On four occasions, Wagner said, he drove William Boyle to the airport to meet James Cashin, an ILA officer from New York. Wagner said that Boyle told him Cashin was bringing money skimmed from Las Vegas casinos. Boyle told him that five New York crime families received skimmed monies from the casinos in return for limiting their activities in Las Vegas.

Wagner said Cashin gave Boyle a briefcase on each of the four trips to Miami. . . . Boyle and Wagner then went to the Local 1922 offices where Boyle counted the money which was in $100 bills. . . . Wagner said Boyle took the money to Rago, who then handled its distribution.

In sum, Wagner said, everything he saw and knew about Douglas Rago confirmed for him his belief that Rago was a made member of the Genovese gang, that Rago was "a power to be reckoned with as far as New York went, he was the guy that, under Salerno, controlled Miami, the dock area that is." . . .

During the period of payoffs, Wagner testified, Marine Terminals prospered. He said that by November of 1974 the company was in such healthy financial condition that A.P. Chester and Jacob Sklaire decided they no longer required the services of a mob representative on the payroll. In addition, Wagner said, Barone had become dissatisfied with him. Wagner was fired, although he did receive what he called a "substantial severance."

As a shipping executive and as a person highly experienced in white collar crime, Wagner had built for himself several profitable kickback and payoff schemes of his own, the proceeds from which he did not share with the mob. Barone resented anyone having this kind of independence, Wagner said, and Barone's resentment, as much as anything else, resulted in his dismissal. . . .

Wagner was bitter and felt Barone and the others had betrayed him. He felt that because he had arranged for them to receive large payoffs over several years that they owed him something in return. He vowed to tell law enforcement about the mob's control of the Miami docks. . . .

V. UNIRAC Was Massive Waterfront Inquiry

Local Authorities Called for Federal Help

George R. Havens, chief investigator for Miami in the task force inquiry at the Dodge Island Seaport, told the Subcommittee that in 1973 a valuable informant began assisting on the case. He was Joseph Teitelbaum, a shipping company executive who turned over strong evidence demonstrating the extent of waterfront corruption.

Teitelbaum, who had been in the shipping industry for more than two decades, revealed to authorities that in the early 1960s he had been approached by Fred R. Field, Jr., ILA General Organizer. Field informed Teitelbaum that the ILA was going to take over Dodge Island and that "those businesses that cooperated with union officials would prosper and those that did not would go out of business," Havens said.

Just as Field had predicted, uncooperative companies did suffer. They were vandalized and had labor problems until they agreed to make kickbacks and payoffs. The illicit payments were the price of labor peace, Teitelbaum said.
. . .

The U.S. Department of Justice was contacted. With the task force cooperating fully, principal responsibility for the waterfront inquiry shifted in 1975 to the Federal Bureau of Investigation and the Organized Crime and Racketeering Section of the Justice Department.

FBI Began Investigations in 1975

In 1975, the FBI began its investigation of the Atlantic and gulf coast maritime industry. The Bureau named the investigation UNIRAC, for union racketeering, but the acronym was a misnomer. Not all the corruption discovered was caused by dishonest union leaders. Also identified was a system of kickbacks among businessmen and illegal payoffs to union officials by businessmen who found it more advantageous to cooperate with corrupt union officials than with law enforcement.

According to FBI Director William H. Webster, UNIRAC was the most successful labor racketeering investigation ever conducted by the Bureau. As of February of 1981, the UNIRAC investigation had resulted in 129 indictments and 110 convictions. Among those indicted were 52 union officials, nine of whom were organized crime members or associates. Of the remaining, 77 defendants, who included industry officials and their corporations, 20 were organized crime members or associates. Several defendants were awaiting trial.

Testifying before the Subcommittee, Webster said the inquiry was unique in that it covered an entire industry. . . . The FBI directed its attention toward the major companies, labor unions and organized crime groups engaging in patterns of racketeering activity throughout the maritime industry. . . .

Evidence Revealed Extensive Corrupt Practices

Webster said the undercover activities obtained direct evidence against persons who had demanded and received hundreds of thousands of dollars from the waterfront industry as a condition of doing business.

There were also evidence developed of repeated demands and receipts by high ranking ILA officials of thousands of dollars of free labor and materials for their homes. ILA officials and organized crime figures boasted that they regularly received confidential information from law enforcement agencies such as the New York-New Jersey Waterfront Commission. . . .

Webster said the Bureau found evidence indicating that some steamship company officials extorted money from contractors. . . .

From October of 1975 to January of 1977, a 16-month period, Teitelbaum's payments to ILA leaders were documented by the FBI. These payments--made by Teitelbaum or by three FBI undercover agents working for Teitalbaum's companies--were in cash or in merchandise and totalled about $46,000.

The "Rippling" Effect of Waterfront Corruption

The Subcommittee received testimony indicating that certain shipping companies . . . in some instances . . . shared in the corruption. In one case, the maritime officials took kickbacks and payoffs from their own companies and diverted attention from themselves by concealing the illicit payments in inflated costs or by saying the money went to corrupt union leaders in exchange for labor peace.

The scheme was set in motion in the fall of 1975 when . . . Teitelbaum wanted to bid on what seemed to him to be a promising container service contract with the Zim American Israeli Shipping Company of New York and Haifa, Israel. Zim was to ship Ford cars for the Ford Export Corporation of Newark, New Jersey from the east coast to Japan.

Teitelbaum, who had begun to cooperate with the FBI in reporting corrupt practices on the docks, learned that there was only one way he could win the Zim contract--and that was to first work out a payoff arrangement with George Barone, the President of ILA Local 1922 in Miami.

Teitelbaum was told by Barone to plan to carry out the terms of the contract with Zim not in Miami, which was Teitelbaum's base of operations, but in Savannah, Georgia. Then Barone gave Teitelbaum the exact terms of the continuing kickbacks he would be required to make.

Teitelbaum said the payoff would begin with a $15,000 lump-sum payment. Following the one time only lump sum payment, he would make continuing kickbacks of $12 per container shipped; 50 cents per ton of break bulk cargo; and one percent of the ship's entire manifest.

Shortly after Barone gave him the kickback formula, the same quotations on the same contract were given him by a man named Anthony Morelli, a trucking executive with organized crime ties.

But Teitelbaum had no way of knowing the complex network of differing interests that came together to constitute the elaborate kickback scheme he was being called up to finance in the Zim contract. The FBI, however, did unravel this complicated conspiracy. . . .

. . . [T]he Zim contract--and the complex plotting that surrounded it--were a "microcosm of the shipping industry and a perfect example of the far-reaching effects of waterfront corruption."

The FBI's investigation of the Zim contract . . . revealed:

A substantial kickback being paid to a union official who promised to obtain business for a shipping company at a certain port;

Fraudulent billings and inflated costs to absorb the kickback;

The manner in which labor racketeers paid off company officials who responded by giving the racketeers special treatment;

Shipping companies' practice of absorbing the cost of illicit payments by inflating bills and passing the added expense on to the consumer;

The fact that shipping companies not wishing to make kickbacks were precluded from competing in a free marketplace; and

The failure by company officials and other participants in the scheme to keep accurate records and pay taxes on their incomes.

Shipping companies are perfectly willing to accept union payoffs as a cost of doing business and only the exposure of their own employees (in the) scheme generated any reaction. This clearly demonstrates . . . the acceptance and pervasiveness of payoff and kickback schemes on the waterfront.

. . . Zim American Israeli Shipping Company was represented in the negotiations with Teitelbaum and Morelli by Captain Reuven Ilan, vice president for operations; Robert Partos, director of interline operations; and Chaim Neumann, vice president for marketing.

Also figuring prominently in the scheme was Michael Colletti, general manager of the Ford Export Company. Anthony Morelli, owner of All Port Service, Inc., of Newark, worked closely with Ilan, Partos, Neumann, Colletti and George Barone in order to perpetrate the kickback fraud. . . .

. . . [T]he ties between Teitelbaum, Barone, and Morelli were only part of the conspiracy in the Zim payoffs. Also revealed in the FBI's inquiry was the fact that Zim officers were . . . also part of a plot to siphon funds from their own company.

Robert Partos and Chain Neumann of Zim admitted to the FBI that they were paid off by Morelli. [Another principal said that] Captain Ilan, had returned to Israel when the inquiry got close to him, Partos and Neumann concealed the kickbacks they were receiving by inflating invoices, arranging improper discounts and destroying billing documents. In these pursuits, Ilan, Neumann and Partos worked in alliance with Michael Colletti of Ford Export. . . .

ILA Gulf Coast Leaders Convicted

On September 1, 1979, in federal court in Miami, George Barone, William Boyle and James Vanderwyde were convicted of crimes related to their conduct as IlA leaders on the waterfront in Gulf Coast ports.

Barone was convicted of racketeering, extortion, demanding and receiving prohibited payments and federal tax fraud. At the time of his conviction, he was listed as president of Miami ILA Local 1922; as business manager of ILA Local 1804-1, New York; organizer in the Atlantic Coast District; and the international second vice president. His positions with the ILA gave him a combined salary of $117,000 a year.

William Boyle, whose ILA offices included being an international vice president, a member of the executive board of the South Atlantic and Gulf Coast District, and secretary-treasurer of Miami Local 1922, was convicted of racketeering, extortion, receiving kickbacks as administrator of an employee benefit plan, demanding and receiving prohibited payments, and federal tax fraud.

James Vanderwyde, coordinator of the ILA's Atlantic Coast District and office manager of Local 1922, was found guilty of racketeering, extortion and demanding and receiving prohibited payments.

Cleveland Turner, president of ILA Miami Local 1416, was convicted on September 1, 1979, of racketeering and demanding and accepting prohibited payments. Also on that day, Fred R. Field, Jr., who had held the position of General Organizer of the ILA, was found guilty of racketeering, extortion and demanding and receiving prohibited payments. Landon L. Williams [sic], president of ILA Local 1408 in Jacksonville, Florida, was convicted of racketeering and demanding and receiving prohibited payments. Williams also served as international vice president of the ILA and as a member of the executive board of the South Atlantic and Gulf Coast District.

From November of 1977 to September of 1980, seventeen other ILA officers and leaders from Gulf Coast locals were convicted in UNIRAC prosecutions.

Douglas Rago, vice president of ILA Local 1922 in Miami, was not indicted in the UNIRAC inquiry. . . .

Permanent Reforms Were Not Won in Gulf Coast Ports

Even though Barone, Boyle and Vanderwyde and 19 other ILA leaders in Gulf Coast ports were convicted of labor racketeering in the UNIRAC prosecutions, a genuine clean-up of corruption on the waterfront had not occurred. This was the view of George R. Havens, chief investigator in the state's attorney's office in Miami.

Havens said the Dodge Island Seaport operated today in much the same fashion it did before the UNIRAC inquiry. In addition, he said, Federal investigative resources, which had focused on waterfront corruption for four years in UNIRAC, were now dispersed throughout the country and there was no Federal law enforcement arm continuing to examine the issue of crime on the docks.

Law enforcement should know which ILA leaders were in a position to replace Barone and his corrupt colleagues. But, Havens, said, Federal, State and local authorities did not seem to have such information; nor were they trying to obtain it.

Similarly, the U.S. Department of Labor had shown little interest in bringing about reform of the collective bargaining process on the Gulf Coast ports, Havens said.

Meanwhile, the Gulf Coast docks were returning to the domination of organized crime figures. . . .

VI. Widespread Corruption Found on East Coast Docks

Prosecutor Cited "Pervasive Nature" of Waterfront Crime

The waterfront corruption that was found to be prevalent in Miami and other Gulf Coast ports was also revealed to be widespread along the waterfront in New York City and New Jersey.

Robert B. Fiske, the United States Attorney for the Southern District of New York from 1976 to 1980, told the Subcommittee of the "pervasive nature of the corruption and payoff schemes" that existed on the east coast docks.

Summing up the east coast version of the UNIRAC case, Fiske testified that labor leaders and management were found to be participants in corrupt practices. Payoffs were made to labor officials to achieve efficient work from longshoremen and to hold down workmen's compensation claims. Business also paid off union representatives for their help in winning new contracts.

The investigation revealed the commonplace use of kickbacks by mid-level shipping company executives to obtain new business. Additionally, organized crime figures were found to be playing a significant role in controlling and influencing business activities on the waterfront.

Fiske said that in the prosecutions brought by his office, more than 20 separate companies or their respective executives were convicted of crimes relating to payoff or commercial fraud schemes.

In addition, more than 10 elected ILA officials were convicted of racketeering offenses relating to payoff schemes. Included among the convicted ILA officials were the presidents of 5 ILA locals in the New York metropolitan area. The investigation in New York led to successful investigations in the ports of Norfolk, Virginia, and Philadelphia.

Anthony Scotto, High Ranking ILA Leader, Was Convicted

On November 15, 1979, Anthony Scotto, was convicted of taking $200,000 in a pattern of illegal payoffs. Scotto, the president of Brooklyn ILA Local 1814 and the General Organizer of the ILA, was one of the most influential labor leaders in New York State.

Sentenced on January 22, 1980, Scotto was given a 5-year term in prison and a $75,000 fine. He was incarcerated in the federal penitentiary in Danbury, Connecticut in July of 1981.

Fiske . . . told the Subcommittee that the evidence at trial showed that from 1975 through 1979 Scotto and Anthony Anastasia, an ILA international vice president and executive vice president of Brooklyn Local 1814, used their positions to demand illegal labor payoffs exceeding $300,000 from at least six separate waterfront businesses employing ILA labor.

Three businessmen--Walter D. O'Hearn, William (Sonny) Montella and Nicholas Seregos--who employed ILA labor testified at the trial about payoffs they had been required to make.

Fiske said the businessmen's testimony, the tape recordings and other evidence revealed that Scotto and Anastasia received more than 40 separate cash payments--some as high as $15,000--as kickbacks or commissions and as Christmas bonuses.

Scotto Was Nationally Prominent Political Figure

Anthony Scotto, who was the grandson of a Brooklyn longshoreman and the son of a sanitation department employee, began working on the docks when he was a teenager. In June of 1957, he married Marion Anastasio, the daughter of Anthony (Tough Tony) Anastasio, who was the head of Brooklyn ILA Local 1814, the largest of all the ILA locals. Tough Tony Anastasio was believed by law enforcement authorities to be a capo in the organized crime family headed at the time by his brother, Albert Anastasia[o], and later led by Carlo Gambino. . . .

Anthony Anastasio appointed Scotto to a series of union jobs. When his father-in-law died in March of 1963, Scotto was named to succeed him. Shortly thereafter, Scotto was made a vice president of the ILA.

Scotto became prominent in politics. He was a delegate to the Democratic National Conventions in 1972 and 1976. When, in 1969, New York Mayor John Lindsay failed to win the Republican primary, Scotto was one of the principal sponsors of the Mayor's successful efforts to win reelection as the candidate of an Independent party and the Liberal Party. In 1974, when Congressman Hugh L. Carey of Brooklyn ran successfully for Governor, Scotto was a fund raiser for him and remarked that "I was told that I accounted for almost a million dollars" to be contributed to the Carey campaign.

A New York Times profile of Anthony Scotto had this to say about him:

> To his admirers, (Scotto) is a dedicated, progressive, articulate leader of the longshoremen's union, an up-from-the-docks scrapper with street savvy, a college education and a social conscience, who has cultivated powerful politicians and incurred slanderous enemies to advance the welfare of his union members, the viability of the Brooklyn waterfront and causes ranging from civil rights to cultural philanthropy.

Scotto's admirers included some of the most powerful political figures in New York. Several of them testified on his behalf as character witnesses in his criminal trial of labor racketeering. Character witnesses in criminal trials are used by defense attorneys to indicate that a defendant is a reputable person. They do not testify about the facts in the case but instead answer standard questions about the defendant's reputation for honesty and integrity. This method of criminal defense was employed in the Scotto trial. . . .

. . . Fiske said Scotto's success in extracting payoffs stemmed from his ability to combine three roles--labor leader, political leader and member of an organized crime family.

Fiske said Scotto wielded great political power. Scotto acknowledged in his trial that he had selected several commissioners of the Department of Ports and Terminals, the component of New York City government which manages the waterfront. Controlling the Commissioner, Scotto was "able to affect the disposition of public lands in and around the waterfront" and obtain advance information on the city's plans to develop the area, Fiske said.

At the trial, prosecutors played a tape recording of Scotto conversing with a former Commissioner of Ports and Terminals, Louis Mastriani. Scotto learned about a particular real estate development in the Bronx and "at the same time delivered an envelope containing a thing of value to the Commissioner for his assistance in another matter," Fiske said. . . .

Pointing out Scotto's power as a labor leader went beyond the Brooklyn waterfront. Fiske said that in 1978 Scotto's personal attorney was appointed to the New York-New Jersey Waterfront Commission. Included within the Commission's power is law enforcement and subpoena power over the ILA. Opposition to the appointment emerged and Governor Carey withdrew it.

Scotto's position on the docks was strengthened by his affiliation with organized crime, Fiske said, citing a 1969 assertion by the Department of Justice that Scotto was a capo in the Carlo Gambino crime family of New York. . . .

Devorkin Described Scotto as Organized Crime Member

The government believed that organized crime families had divided the Port of New York into three sections--New Jersey, Manhattan and Brooklyn. The Gambino family operated on the Brooklyn docks. The Genovese family operated in Manhattan and New Jersey.

The government's view was given to the Subcommittee by Michael Devorkin, a former Assistant United States Attorney in the Southern District of New York. He was accompanied in his testimony by Louis J. Freeh, a Special Agent with the FBI. Devorkin was a prosecutor in the UNIRAC case and Freeh was an investigator.

In 1959, after Anthony Anastasio died, Scotto, by now president of Brooklyn Local 1814, went to Carlo Gambino and Michael Clemente and said that out of respect for his wife's family, Gambino should admit Scotto into his crime group as a replacement for Anthony Anastasio. Clemente, as a high ranking member of the Genovese gang, was asked to give the action his blessing. Devorkin said the request was granted. Scotto was made a "button" in the Gambino family, committing his allegiance to that organization but, at the same time, assuring Clemente that he would cooperate with the Genovese group. Later Scotto was promoted to capo in the Gambino family. This was the same family his father-in-law had been a capo in. His wife's late uncle, Albert Anastasia, had headed the family until his gangland slaying. Carlo Gambino then became head of the family.

Gambino was, in the 1960s and early 1970s, one of the most influential organized crime figures in the nation. Devorkin said Scotto met secretly with Gambino. But seeing Gambino and other known mob figures became more complicated for Scotto as he became more and more visible as a political figure. This offended some mob leaders who felt he had forgotten his own roots and was neglecting his responsibilities to the people who gave him his high position. In taped conversations, for example, Mike Clemente, a powerful mob figure in the Port of New York, complained about the fact that Scotto had become so important politically that he was no longer sufficiently accessible to mob leaders like himself. . . .

Clemente, who was in his 70s and enjoyed reminiscing about his many years on the waterfront, was recorded on September 12, 1978 telling William (Sonny) Montella how Scotto became a mob member. Clemente said that when Albert Anastasia was murdered and Albert's brother, Anthony Anastasio, had died, Scotto came to him and asked to be made a member of a crime family. Scotto, Clemente said, was concerned that he would be rejected for membership in a crime family. Clemente told Scotto that if he conducted himself properly, he would be accepted into a crime family. Clemente seemed amused by Scotto's emergence as a political personage while, at the same time, being a made member, or "wise guy," in a crime family. . . .

In another taped conversation with Montella--this one on November 21, 1978--Clemente expressed disappointment with Scotto because Scotto was not devoting enough time to looking out for the interests of organized crime figures. Clemente recalled that he went against the wishes of his own family, the Genovese group, when he promoted Scotto to become the General Organizer of the ILA. . . .

McGrath Services Paid Off Scotto

The Subcommittee investigated allegations that the Longshoremen's and Harbor Workers' Act was being illegally exploited in a scheme participated in by employees, labor leaders, lawyers, doctors and organized crime figures.

The statute provides workmen's compensation to longshoremen who are injured on the job. The compensation is in the form of wage substitution payments from the employer or his insurance company.

Until 1972, the law required that employees applying for compensation had to use doctors selected from a panel nominated by employers and approved by the U.S. Department of Labor.

However, in 1972, the statute was amended and employees--or claimants-- were allowed to choose their own physician. Shortly after the implementation of the new law, shipping companies began to note a marked increase in claims.

One such maritime enterprise was the McGrath Services Corporation of New York. McGrath is a stevedoring company engaged in loading and unloading vessels and operating terminal facilities on Atlantic, gulf and Pacific coasts. The firm employed about 400 persons. According to its president, Walter D. O'Hearn, early in 1974 company officials realized that costs of longshoremen's workmen's compensation claims in Brooklyn at pier 13 were "exploding."

Testifying before the Subcommittee, O'Hearn said compensation costs in 1972 were $230,000. In 1973, they rose to $616,000. In 1974, they were $1.4 million. O'Hearn testified:

My associates and I were disturbed by these developments and we investigated them. It didn't take very long to find out what was going on.

Once claimants were allowed to select their own physicians, a racket developed. O'Hearn said participants in the scheme were dishonest longshoremen who feigned or exaggerated injuries, the lawyers who processed the claims with the Labor Department, doctors who fraudulently certified to the accuracy of the false claims and "most likely, organized crime figures who set the whole thing up."

Workers were complaining of nonvisible, soft tissue injuries that were impossible to disprove. Company executives noticed that the workmen who suffered these injuries lived in diverse geographical areas but they tended to seek advice from the same lawyers and treatment from the same doctors.

The Labor Department, which has the responsibility for enforcing the Longshoremen's and Harbor Workers' Act, required compliance with section 20 of the statute, that provision giving an automatic presumption of validity to employee claims filed, O'Hearn said.

O'Hearn pointed out that the worker does not have to prove that he was injured. He need only find a doctor to treat him. The burden of proof rests with the employer, who must demonstrate that the worker suffered no injury.

O'Hearn remembered one longshoreman who showed up on the pier wearing patent leather shoes and announced five minutes into his shift that, "I hurt myself." He filed a claim and the claim was ruled valid, O'Hearn said.

The racket seemed to be foolproof because of the apparent complicity of the doctors. O'Hearn said executives could not hope to win challenging the doctors' medical findings. Yet, he added, if a solution to the problem were not found, the company could have been bankrupted by it.

O'Hearn said his firm was a self-insurer and that in 1974 it self-insured the first $50,000 of each workman's compensation claim. The Federal Government requires that the self-insurer have the $50,000 on deposit with the Department of Labor for each worker covered. Liabilities beyond $50,000 were covered by conventional excess insurance, O'Hearn said.

In addition to the direct costs of the claims, McGrath Services Corporation also had to meet other growing expenses. The excess insurance coverage rose from $400,000 to $2.5 million in two years. McGrath Services was required to deposit an additional $2 million in securities with the Labor Department over a two-year period, O'Hearn said, adding that the economic situation caused by the workmen's compensation problem was desperate. Unless the problems were solved, the company had no future.

O'Hearn said McGrath Services officials tried to combat the workmen's compensation racket. They appointed an experienced waterfront superintendent to intensify company safety efforts. But there was an immediate attempt to scare the new man off the job. His wife received threatening phone calls and he was threatened as well. Then someone set fire to his car.

Next, McGrath Services increased the number of personnel committed to safety precautions. A cash incentive program was initiated in which employees with claim-free records would be awarded cash bonuses. When that approach failed, the company turned to the government.

Hearing O'Hearn's charges that the rising workmen's compensation costs were the result of a flourishing waterfront claim racket, the Labor Department's regional deputy commissioner replied that he "knew something was going on" but added there wasn't anything the department could do about it. The deputy commissioner said the department did not have enough money to set up a system of treatment of claimants by impartial physicians, O'Hearn testified.

Another officer of McGrath Services, Robert Nicol, asked the New York-New Jersey Waterfront Commission for help. That produced no results. Nor did a request for assistance at the King's County Medical Association.

O'Hearn, using his own industry organization, the National Association of Stevedores, tried to have the Longshoremen's and Harbor Workers' Act amended again, this time changing the statute in such a way as to remove the opportunity for collusion between the allegedly injured workman and his doctor. Legislation was introduced in Congress but it did not pass.

O'Hearn said he then went to Anthony Scotto, the president of Brooklyn ILA Local 1814, an international vice president. From March to October of 1974, O'Hearn said, he and Scotto met six times to discuss the problem.

Believing Scotto to be "astute and politically powerful," O'Hearn warned him that McGrath Services and other shipping companies would close down their operations in Brooklyn unless the compensation scheme was brought under control. O'Hearn said Scotto's response was to say that he knew of no such racket and that he had no ability to assist the beleaguered McGrath Services Corporation in cutting its insurance costs.

Apparently, O'Hearn had not used the right approach with Scotto. One of O'Hearn's colleagues, David Rosen, explained that what was needed was someone with experience in labor negotiations to deal with Scotto, someone who had "street" smarts, someone like himself. Rosen met with Scotto. To Rosen's way of looking at it, he had solved the problem. But Rosen's solution led O'Hearn to question his colleague's judgment and integrity.

O'Hearn explained that Rosen had become a shareholder of McGrath Services and served on its board of directors. This had come about through a 1973 purchase of McGrath stock by a New York City newspaper distribution company, the Metropolitan News Company.

After his meeting with Scotto, Rosen reported to O'Hearn that Scotto believed the phony claims could be stopped--but at a price. The price was $5,000 a month and a Christmas bonus. Rosen supported the idea of paying off

Scotto and, to demonstrate his commitment to the concept, he had already made the first payment.

O'Hearn, whose grandfather had started the firm, had been with the company for 30 years and did not like the arrangement Rosen had gotten the corporation into. On the other hand, there was no realistic way out. Rosen had made clear what would happen if he reneged on the commitment to continue to pay off Scotto. The choice he faced was to pay off or suffer the consequences.

Afraid to go to police for fear of losing their company or their lives, McGrath Services officials decided to go ahead with the payoffs to Scotto. However, it was agreed that O'Hearn would make future payoffs. From the summer of 1975 through September of 1978, O'Hearn made 18 cash payments to Scotto totalling $210,000.

Once Scotto began receiving the money, he moved quickly and effectively to reduce workmen's compensation costs, O'Hearn said. Scotto was able to have a state law and federal regulation changed that had prevented injured longshoremen from being treated for work-related injuries in an ILA-sponsored clinic in Brooklyn. By the summer of 1976, the clinic was allowed to treat work-associated injuries, O'Hearn said, explaining:

> All of a sudden claimants started utilizing the clinic rather than the doctors who had been part and parcel of the conspiracy. . . .

McGrath executives saw workmen's compensation costs decline dramatically at the Brooklyn pier. Where annual costs had risen from $230,000 in 1972 to $1.4 million in 1974, the figures began a downward trend in 1975 with an $883,000 total that year, and with $302,000 in 1976, $345,000 in 1977 and $375,000 in 1978. . . .

In order to keep their company afloat during the years of severe workmen's compensation costs and then to make the $210,000 in payoffs to Anthony Scotto, O'Hearn and his partners--Heiman Gross, Robert Nicol and Edward Wallach-- and their wives incurred considerable personal debt. O'Hearn said the indebtedness, including a $100,000 loan from Nicol's father, made even more unsettling a situation in which they feared for their own economic security and for their personal safety. He had no words to describe the "fears, anxieties and constant forebodings" which had plagued their lives for six years, O'Hearn said.

As for Rosen, the more O'Hearn and his partners saw of him, the more determined they were to severe his ties with their firm. Increasingly, they came to learn of his association with organized crime figures--and not lower level organized criminals but rather persons high up in mob affairs. Rosen, for example, acknowledged that he met frequently with Pennsylvania crime figure Russell Bufalino.

O'Hearn feared that as the company came more and more to rely on Scotto for its economic survival, the role of Rosen in the enterprise would be strengthened until finally Rosen took over. That was why, O'Hearn explained, company executives wanted him, not Rosen, to make the payments to Scotto.

Eventually, O'Hearn was able to negotiate Rosen's resignation as an officer and member of the board of directors of McGrath Services. But Rosen remained a substantial shareholder.

The workmen's compensation racket brought McGrath Services to the edge of bankruptcy, O'Hearn said. But the company did survive. Not all Brooklyn shipping firms were as fortunate. Other companies were also hard hit by the high costs. Pittston Stevedoring Company, went out of business. A long established firm in the Port of New York, Pittston closed its doors because it could not obtain insurance covering injuries to its workmen. . . .

VII. Influence of Clemente, Fiumara and Other Crime Figures Seen

Montella Tapes Revealed Widespread Dimensions of Corruption

A crucial electronic surveillance operation was based on the activities of William (Sonny) Montella, general manager of Quin Marine Services, Inc., a marine carpentry, lashing and container repair firm with main offices in Brooklyn. Marine carpenters and lashers, most of whom in the Port of New York are ILA members, secured cargo previously loaded on board ships.

According to former Assistant U.S. Attorney Michael Devorkin, who led that aspect of the prosecutions that used the Montella tapes, the Justice Department believed corruption on the waterfront to be so commonplace that a successful inquiry could be mounted only if sufficient numbers of cooperating witnesses could be found. One such potential cooperating witness was believed to be Sonny Montella. . . .

From late 1977 through March of 1978, court-authorized wiretaps on Montella's office phones revealed that Montella and several of his aides were making monthly payments to Scotto and another ILA leader, Thomas Buzzanca, president of Locals 1804 and 1804-1, whose members were lashers, maintenance men and container repairmen employed in Manhattan and New Jersey.

It was also learned that Montella was making payments to Mike Clemente. Discovery of the payoffs to Clemente was an important breakthrough in the case. It meant that the investigation had implicated not only Anthony Scotto, but also Clemente, the most important organized crime leader on the Manhattan and New Jersey waterfronts. . . .

Mike Clemente Wielded Influence in Manhattan and New Jersey

Former Federal prosecutor Devorkin said Clemente . . . was the senior member of the gang which worked to control the Manhattan and New Jersey waterfront. Basing his operations on the Manhattan docks, Clemente had considerable influence on both the ILA and shipping firms using the Port of New York. Clemente extorted funds from maritime firms. He also used his power to win special treatment for favored businesses. For example, Clemente was able to collect more than $1.2 million from the Netumar Steamship Line in exchange for preferred treatment for the company.

In the 1940s and early 1950s, Clemente was the leader of ILA Local 856 in Manhattan. Devorkin said public hearings on waterfront crime in the 1950s provided evidence of Clemente's associations with Mafia bosses Albert Anastasia, Vito Genovese and Joseph Profaci. There were telephone calls that showed Albert Anastasia had asked Clemente to get a job on the docks for his brother, Anthony. It was also revealed that Profaci, Carlo Gambino and another mob figure, John (Johnny Dio) Dioguardi, had attended the wedding of Clemente's daughter in 1951.

In 1953, Clemente was convicted of extortion and perjury in connection with payoffs he received from a waterfront firm. Because of the conviction, and the resulting five-year prison sentence, Clemente resigned as head of Local 856.

While Clemente was in prison, Profaci and Genovese provided financial support to Clemente's family. Upon release from prison, Clemente received an additional offering. It was a "substantial sum of money" from the John W. McGrath Company as a form of tribute to, "in effect, make up for the fact that Mr. McGrath had been one of the principal witnesses against him at the state trial."

Clemente returned to the waterfront, but not in any official capacity. He never again held a position in the ILA. Nor did he go to work for a maritime company. But he did wield significant authority in waterfront affairs.

Companies licensed by the New York-New Jersey Waterfront Commission were effectively barred from contact with Clemente because they feared a loss of their own license if caught dealing with a person of his character. Devorkin termed Fred R. Field, Jr., as Clemente's "prodigy." Field succeeded Clemente as head of Local 856. Devorkin added:

> Through Field, other ILA members, and his organized crime affiliations, Clemente effectively maintained his control over the Manhattan waterfront and various ILA and waterfront activities.
> Clemente exercised control over union members and company supervisors and executives who worked principally on the Manhattan piers. He also exercised control over various ILA leaders on the local and international level, including Teddy Gleason, the ILA president, Anthony Scotto, George Barone, Fred Field and Thomas Buzzanca.

Clemente also controlled certain ILA activities and shipping companies in New Jersey, Devorkin said.

Tino Fiumara Was Genovese Gang Operative in New Jersey

Mike Clemente, based on the Manhattan docks, delegated authority for the New Jersey waterfront to Tino Fiumara. Working under Fiumara's direction were Michael Copolla, Carol Gardner and Thomas Buzzanca. Fiumara, who listed his occupation as a parttime salesman in an auto repair shop,and Copolla, a "self-employed haberdasher," had no formal connection with the ILA. Colucci, Gardner and Buzzanca were ILA officials. Buzzanca, president of an ILA local with members in Brooklyn and New Jersey, was also required to coordinate his affairs with Anthony Scotto, ILA boss of the Brooklyn docks.

Fiumara, in his late 30s, had at an early age demonstrated his value to Frank (Funzi) Tieri, who was then head of the Genovese family. Devorkin said Fiumara had maintained his close ties with Tieri and had been assigned by the Genovese family to oversee all waterfront activities in northern New Jersey.

Fiumara had a reputation for ruthlessness and was widely feared by shipping executives as well as his own colleagues such as Buzzanca, Gardner and Colucci. . . .

Vincent Colucci's devotion to Fiumara was unique. Devorkin said that reliable informants had reported to the government that Fiumara personally murdered Colucci's two brothers. Yet Colucci still embraced Fiumara as his leader.

Devorkin said information developed by government investigators indicated that Fiumara had been associated with the late Peter LaPlaca, a capo in the Genovese crime family, and a friend of Clemente. . . .

Summary of the Clemente Prosecution

On May 2, 1980, a jury in the Southern District of New York convicted seven defendants in *United States v. Clemente, et al.*, on 160 counts involving federal charges of racketeering, racketeering conspiracy, extortion, illegal labor payments, tax evasion and perjury.

The defendants were sentenced as follows: Michael Clemente, 20 years; Tino Fiumara, 25 years; Thomas Buzzanca, 10 years; Vincent Colucci, 5 1/2 years; Carol Gardner, 10 years; Michael Copolla, 13 years; and Gerald Swanton, 5 years.

The indictment charged that the defendants ran a criminal enterprise which controlled businesses and unions in the Port of New York.

The gang extorted or demanded more than $1.5 million from four businessmen who testified at the trial. Based on their testimony and other evidence, Devorkin said, "it is fair to conclude that millions of dollars of other payoffs were received."

Controlled by Clemente from Manhattan and Fiumara from New Jersey, the gang utilized the "classic scheme of extortion," victimizing steamship lines and other waterfront business activities servicing the Port of New York. . . .

Five waterfront businessmen testified about the extortion racket and how they made $1.5 million in payoffs from 1974 through 1978. Three businessmen . . . testified that they paid more than $300,000 in cash to avoid economic injury threatened by Clemente gang members.

Two other businessmen . . . testified that they paid Clemente $1.2 million to obtain economic benefits for their company, the Netumar Line. The testimony of these witnesses was supported by electronic surveillance and other evidence. . . .

Devorkin described Clemente as Fiumara's "senior partner." Although Fiumara had an "iron grip" over New Jersey waterfront activities and New Jersey ILA locals, he still recognized Clemente as his superior in mob affairs. When, for example, Montella complained to him about the rough manner in which Carol Gardner and Vincent Colucci collected payoffs, Clemente moved quickly to have Thomas Buzzanca take over the collection duties.

Clemente exercised similar influence over Anthony Scotto. In late November of 1977, Clemente received a document from someone he identified to Montella as "his guy," a probable reference to Genovese gang boss Frank Tieri or underboss Anthony Salerno. The document, provided the mob by a source inside the Waterfront Commission, asserted that federal authorities using electronic surveillance had established that Sonny Montella was making illegal payments to Buzzanca, Gardner, and Colucci.

According to Devorkin, Clemente showed the document to Montella and raised the possibility that an informant inside his company, Quin Marine Services, Inc., had betrayed him. Clemente also suspected Joseph Lacqua, Anthony Scotto's cousin and the owner of a Brooklyn lumber company. He vowed that if Lacqua were found to be the informant "we'll break his (obscenity)." . . .

Clemente's unprecedented power over the ILA was similar to Fiumara's. As Devorkin pointed out, their influence was all the more remarkable when contrasted with the fact that neither man held an official position with the union. Yet they never hesitated to speak for the union in working out their illegal transactions.

One illustration of this was seen in a taped conversation in which Fiumara's assistant, Michael Copolla, talked about a deal he and his boss, "T," had made with Irving Held, a major stevedore who shipped bananas into New York and New Jersey.

Copolla, who, like Fiumara, had no official link to the ILA, said, "T's got the banana king," meaning Fiumara had persuaded--or coerced--Held to follow his directions. In return, Copolla said, the ILA was going to help Held cut costs. Copolla explained that Fiumara had arranged for smaller ILA work gangs to unload the banana boats. This would result in savings for Held.

Irving Held, who was found to have ties to Genovese boss Frank Tieri, was later convicted and sentenced to one year in prison on Taft-Hartley violations for having arranged loans to Carol Gardner.

Clemente's feeling that Scotto had not done enough to return the favors done him was revealed in a conversation with Montella. Clemente had a grandson who was finishing law school and needed a summer job. Clemente wanted Scotto to use his influence with a friend at the National Labor Relations Board to get the grandson a temporary position at the NLRB. Scotto apparently did not make an effort to help and the young lawyer didn't get the job. Clemente was annoyed at Scotto's inability or unwillingness to be of assistance. . . .

While Clemente had serious misgivings about Scotto, he seemed to have none about Fiumara. The New Jersey mob figure had no political ambitions. Unlike Scotto, Fiumara gave Clemente the "satisfaction" he felt he deserved. Fiumara was more of a waterfront gangster in the traditional sense. He was not the defendant who would receive many character endorsements from socially and politically prominent people. But his lack of character witnesses in no sense diminished his influence on the waterfront. In fact, Devorkin told the Subcommittee that the Clemente trial revealed only a small portion of the depth of Fiumara's port activities.

Devorkin said Fiumara's organized crime activities and control over the New Jersey docks were further corroborated by information provided the government by Ralph Picardo, a reliable witness who had testified several times for the government.

Picardo worked on illegal schemes for Sal Briguglio and Anthony (Tony Pro) Provenzano, who were Genovese gang members who ran a Teamsters Union local in New Jersey. Devorkin said both Briguglio and Provenzano disliked Fiumara but told Picardo they had to tolerate him because he was with Frank Tieri, Genovese family boss. Devorkin said another reliable witness had reported seeing Fiumara attend regular meetings with Tieri to discuss family business.

Picardo, who was partly responsible for receiving labor payments in the port from the Seatrain Company, was told by his associates that Fiumara also received payoffs from Seatrain as the price of labor peace with the ILA. Picardo told authorities that he agreed with Seatrain to work out with Fiumara a method for making future ILA labor peace payments. Such an agreement was reached.

Picardo, Briguglio and Provenzano also had an arrangement with Fiumara in which Fiumara did not demand payoffs from shipping lines which were already doing business with Picardo. Fiumara told Picardo that if he had any problems with a particular steamship line he should take it up with him or with his aid, Michael Copolla, Devorkin said. . . .

7

Criminal Infiltration of the Toxic and Solid Waste Disposal Industries in New York State

A Preliminary Report by Maurice D. Hinchey, Chairman, to The New York State Assembly Standing Committee on Environmental Conservation and The New York State Legislature, September 13, 1984.

Introduction

As the State and Federal government have tightened controls on the handling of poisonous industrial wastes, the business of illegal toxic waste disposal has flourished, in some cases bringing huge profits to underworld figures. The increased costs of proper disposal, budget cuts in regulatory programs and loopholes in the law have created a breeding ground for illegal dumpers. Certain entrepreneurs who have recognized the potential for substantial profit have exercised great imagination in finding ways to disguise their illicit activities as reputable businesses. Chemical wastes have been mixed with household garbage and dumped in municipal landfills; they have been masked in sludge and spread on the land. Combustible solvents have been added to waste oil and sold to commercial establishments, schools, hospitals and apartments buildings, for use as fuel oil.

Chemical contamination of our land and water supplies has become extensive and in many instances this contamination is irreversible. Major water bodies like the Hudson and Niagara Rivers are now grossly polluted with poisonous substances. Groundwater supplies across the State are threatened by hundreds of leaking chemical dumps. Municipal and private drinking water supplies have been poisoned. And clean-up costs for abandoned toxic waste sites keep skyrocketing. With each passing day the condition of our environment deteriorates because we have failed to end the improper disposal of hazardous wastes.

While a complex regulatory system has been developed to manage hazardous wastes, refuse and septic waste disposal have been treated as separate regulatory tasks. It has become evident, however, that all of these industries are related and gaps in the regulation of garbage disposal have harbored companies engaged in the lucrative practice of illegal toxic waste disposal.

Several years ago the State made an attempt to expose the criminal element in the waste disposal industries--particularly the role of organized crime. These efforts were largely unsuccessful. Indictments were dismissed, a major investigation was aborted, and results of the legislative hearings that followed were unsatisfactory. Important questions remain unanswered and the fundamental problems in the system persist. Weaknesses in the law that encourage criminal activity have not been eliminated. Hazardous and solid waste programs within the New York State Department of Environmental Conservation (DEC) are severely underfunded. And individuals who have flaunted the law and shown a callous disregard for public safety continue to operate waste disposal business with the approval of the State.

The purpose of this report is twofold. First, to illustrate how the criminal element infiltrates the waste disposal industry in New York State and in doing so to raise questions on relevant legal and regulatory issues on which the Committee will seek comment at public hearings scheduled for later this month. Second, to demonstrate through this document and the subsequent hearings the need to renew the State's investigative efforts to identify and prosecute those individuals and corporations whose business includes the improper and illegal disposal of hazardous chemical wastes.

Background

The relationship between municipal and hazardous waste disposal became clear when the Committee conducted hearings in the Spring of 1983 on the problems of solid waste management. New York State Department of Environmental Conservation staff testified that most of the State's 526 municipal landfills operate in violation of DEC regulations. The vast majority of sites are unlined and located in areas where wastes can easily migrate and contaminate water supplies. Few inspections have been made since 1981 when federal funds for the program were eliminated. Some sites have no gates and are accessible twenty-four hours a day, inviting the illegal disposal of toxic wastes. Without supervision these landfills are destined to become tomorrow's toxic dumps; two hundred and forty two municipal landfills have already been included in the Department's registry of inactive hazardous waste sites.*

The presence of toxic waste in municipal landfills can be traced in part to the under-regulation of private garbage haulers. Because there is no statewide permit program for these carters they operate as "free agents" outside the system that regulates hazardous waste. This break in the regulatory scheme provides numerous opportunities for criminals trafficking in toxic waste.

Dirk Ottens, a Detective Sergeant with the New Jersey State Police, testifying before the U.S. Congressional Committee on Interstate and Foreign Commerce in 1980, described one method by which toxic wastes are dumped in sanitary landfills. Roll-offs are used. A roll-off is an open top container, resembling the body of a dump truck with an average capacity of 20 cubic yards. The roll-offs, he said, are lined with plastic. Sand is placed at the base in the corners and then covered with absorbent solid waste material. Drums of hazardous waste material are then emptied into it. The roll-off is hoisted onto the chassis truck and taken to a sanitary landfill where the toxics are disposed of as solid waste. According to Ottens, approximately 60 drums containing hazardous or liquid waste can be disposed in one roll-off unit.**

As far back as 1957 the U.S. Senate Select Committee on Improper Activities in the Labor and Management Field, under the leadership of Senator John L. McClellan, carefully documented organized crime's infiltration of the private sanitation industry in New York State. Carters associated with organized crime were exposed for their use of "property rights" to monopolize the industry and drive up the price of garbage collection.***

The "property rights" system is an illegal device created by organized crime to eliminate competition within the garbage industry. The system grants haulers associated with the underworld the exclusive right to pick up garbage from a

---

*New York State Assembly Standing Committee on Environmental Conservation, Toxic Substance Control in New York State: A Failed Effort, March 16, 1984, pp. 7-9.

**U.S. Congress, House of Representatives, Committee on Interstate and Foreign Commerce, Involvement of Organized Crime in the Hazardous Waste Disposal Industry and the Operations of the Federal-State Toxic Waste Strike Force in New Jersey, 96th Congress, 2d Session, December 16, 1980, p. 63.

***U.S. Congress, Senate, Select Committee on Improper Activities in the Labor Management Field, Investigation of Improper Activities in the Labor or Management Field, Private Carting Industry (New York and Los Angeles, California), 85th Congress, April 29, November 12, 13, 14, 15, and 16, 1957.

particular location or "stop." This privilege lasts for a hauler's lifetime and is recognized and enforced by members of organized crime "families." Honest businessmen who are unaware of these secret arrangements between haulers are often muscled out of the industry unless they pay a heavy price for permission to operate.

When the owner of a stop is willing to sell it, the value of the stop--or the monthly income the hauler derives from it--is multiplied by some pre-established factor to arrive at the full cost of the stop to the buyer. In New York City where the property rights system has been in effect for more than 25 years and is deeply entrenched, the factor reaches 50, 55 or 60 to 1. In other words, if a hauler collects $1,000 per month from a customer--the cost to the buyer of purchasing that stop would be $50,000-60,000.*

The Senate investigation, headed by the Committee's Chief Counsel, Robert F. Kennedy, revealed that organized crime had a "stranglehold" on the private carting industry in New York State and that disputes over property rights were settled then, as they are now, through threats and physical intimidation, property damage and economic reprisals. . . .

Law enforcement officials and past associates of organized crime who have testified before the New York State Legislature and U.S. Congress confirm the fact that . . . organized crime still exerts a powerful influence over the garbage industry in New York State. Furthermore, there is evidence to demonstrate that organized crime is also involved in the illegal disposal of hazardous wastes.**

---

*Ibid.; Steven J. Madonna, Chief, Environmental Prosecution Section, New Jersey Division of Criminal Justice, Organized Crime in the Hazardous Waste Disposal Industry (Testimony before U.S. Senate, Committee on Governmental Affairs, 98th Congress, 2d Session), February 1, 1984, pp. 10-12.

**U.S. Congress, Senate, Committee on Governmental Affairs, Profile of Organized Crime: Mid-Atlantic Region, 98th Congress, 2d Session, July 17, 1984, p. 29, pp. 37-44; Steven J. Madonna, Deputy Attorney General, New Jersey Division of Criminal Justice, Organized Crime in the Hazardous Waste Disposal Industry, submitted to the U.S. Senate Committee on Governmental Affairs, February 1, 1984; New York State Senate Select Committee on Crime, In the Matter of Public Hearing on Organized Crime and Toxic Waste, May 28, 1980, May 29, 1980, July 8, 1980; Herbert Johnson, Director, Mid-Hudson Demonstration Program on Hazardous Waste, testimony before the New York State Assembly Standing Committee on Environmental Conservation, March 13, 1981, pp. 7-8; U.S. Congress, House of Representatives, Committee on Interstate and Foreign Commerce, House of Representatives, Involvement of Organized Crime in the Hazardous Waste Disposal Industry, 96th Congress, 2d

In the late 1970s a renewed effort was made to crack down on organized crime in the waste disposal industries. The investigation, conducted by the New York State Organized Crime Task Force (OCTF), focused much of its attention on illegal activities in the Mid-Hudson Valley--specifically Rockland and Orange Counties.

According to testimony by law enforcement officials before a New York State Senate Committee, the Rockland County investigation revealed that the operators of the Town of Ramapo landfill, Carmine Franco and Anthony Rizzo, were associates of organized crime. The investigation reportedly "uncovered massive unlawful dumping of garbage and other material from Northern New Jersey and Westchester." John Fine, then OCTF investigator in charge of the inquiry, stated that "police surveillances were dangerous." He said, "A sheriff's car was cut off the road. A police officer was surrounded in New Jersey and . . . menaced with a shotgun. A town environmental employee was threatened . . . his family was threatened." Fine also reported that the investigation produced evidence that town officials, town employees, garbagemen and Franco were involved together in "payoffs" and the illegal use of town property. Fine charged that "corruption just permeated the Town of Ramapo."[*]

Both Fine and a lieutenant with the Rockland County Sheriff's Department, Stanley Greenberg, charged that then Rockland County District Attorney, Kenneth Gribetz, had been uncooperative in the investigation and reluctant to give his approval to empanel a special grand jury. However, in 1979, a grand jury was convened in Rockland County. Fine testified that Gribetz had urged him to postpone the indictments until after elections in the fall of that year. Fine also claimed that his superior, Ralph Smith, the Task Force Director, had "ordered that there . . . be no indictments before election day."[**] Nine indictments were handed down by the Rockland County grand jury but were later dismissed. Fine said he was informed that Gribetz had "told a certain person that the criminal cases in Rockland County Court . . . (were) going to be thrown out."[***]

Session, December 16, 1980, May 28, 1981.

[*]New York State Senate, Select Committee on Crime, July 8, 1980, pp. 474-479, 489.

[**]Ibid., May 29, 1980, pp. 19-26, 479-487.

[***]Ibid., July 8, 1980, p. 488; New York State, Senate Select Committee on Crime, May 29, 1980, p. 29; "Fire Crime Force Chief Says His Life's in Danger," Gannett-Westchester newspapers, p. 6; "Investigator Vows to Press

Two years later Franco was indicted in New Jersey as the President of the New Jersey Trade Waste Association, an organization of garbage haulers, reportedly dominated by organized crime. The Association was charged with monopolizing the sanitation industry in the north and central counties of New Jersey. Anthony Rizzo was also indicted in that case. Both Franco and Rizzo were named with others for their roles in a conspiracy to prevent competition in the industry through the use of threats and violence.*

The Town of Ramapo landfill is now on the State's inventory of hazardous waste sites. A leachate plume which emanates from the site contains heavy metals, toluene and xylene and is a continuing threat to the Ramapo well field, which supplies drinking water to the Village of Suffern. Among the chemicals identified which exceed State groundwater standards are: mercury, chromium, arsenic, cadmium, selenium, and others. The landfill is located on one of the major water supply aquifers in the state.**

Orange County was also the site of a major investigative effort by the OCTF into organized crime involvement in the garbage industry and the illegal disposal of toxic wastes. In July 1979 the OCTF made a request to then Governor, Hugh Carey, asking that a special grand jury be convened in Orange County. Fine said a memorandum was sent to the Governor by OCTF which detailed the involvement of underworld figures in landfill operations and illegal toxic waste disposal. Although then Orange County District Attorney, David Ritter, strongly supported the move, Governor Carey did not approve the request. Fine charged that he had been told there was a "fix in" to halt the Orange County investigation. He said he had reported this warning to Smith and Attorney General William Dowling but Smith formally closed the investigation in Orange County.*** At what appeared to be its peak, the investigation in Orange County was abruptly terminated. The case was buried and no further attempts have been made to resurrect it.

Dump Inquiry," The Journal-News, July 3, 1980, pp. 1A and 14A.

*Superior Court of New Jersey, Law Division-Somerset County, Indictment No. SGJ 66-80-8, State of New Jersey vs. New Jersey Trade Waste Association, et al., June 26, 1981.

**New York State Assembly, Toxic Substance Control in New York State, p. 14.

***New York State Senate, Select Committee on Crime, July 8, 1980, pp. 538-552.

In the last several months the Assembly Environmental Conservation Committee has investigated the claims made by Mr. Fine that "persons associated with organized crime have taken over carting companies, landfills and toxic waste concerns in Orange County."* The Committee staff has conducted record searches, interviewed public officials, and reviewed hearing transcripts from the 1950s to the present.

There is no question that the OCTF investigation under Fine unearthed a wealth of information concerning the activities of organized crime in Orange County and throughout the Mid and Lower Hudson Valley. . . .

The case study that follows highlights the tragic flaws in the legal and regulatory system that allow criminals to thrive in the solid and hazardous waste disposal industries in New York State. All County Environmental Service Corporation, deals with a company whose principals have concurrently formed other corporations to dispose of solid waste, to collect and transport septic wastes and to transport and treat hazardous wastes. It is part of a web of related corporations and business associates, each with a record of gross violations of environmental law. There is also evidence to suggest that two of the principals of All County have been associated with organized crime. This case study demonstrates the enormous potential for disreputable individuals involved in different aspects of the waste disposal industry to use their related businesses to camouflage illicit toxic waste disposal activities. . . .

All County Environmental Service Corporation

In his testimony before the Senate Select Committee Fine named a number of business concerns which he linked to organized crime figures and illegal hazardous waste disposal. One of those companies was All County Environmental Service Corporation ("All County"), a transporter of septic and hazardous wastes as well as a hazardous waste facility.*** Although the company was shut down in New Jersey and it is no longer in operation, its principals continue to do business in New York State under other corporate names.

The Assembly Environmental Conservation Committee staff has studied All County's history of operations through documents obtained from the NYSDEC, the New Jersey Department of Environmental Protection (NJDEP), the New Jersey Attorney General's Office and town and county records. What follows

---

*New York State, Senate Select Committee on Crime, July 7, 1980, p. 518.

**Ibid., p. 529.

182

is a picture of a company with a history of violating environmental laws, ties to organized crime, and a network of business associates who have been involved in illegal hazardous waste disposal practices. The All County case demonstrates the ways in which disreputable waste disposal businesses survive and regenerate themselves under different corporate names. It should also highlight the faults in the legal and regulatory system that shelter them from prosecution and punishment for their illegal actions.

For almost a decade John and Frank Coppola in concern with Robert and Joseph Mongelli owned and operated All County Environmental Service Corporation to collect and transport septic and hazardous wastes. The company's headquarters were located in Warwick, New York.* The Mongellis also owned a number of garbage disposal companies--I.S.A. of New Jersey, Inc.,** Tri-State Carting, Inc.,*** Grace Disposal and Leasing, Ltd.,**** Orange County Sanitation, Inc.,***** and Round Lake Sanitation Corporation.****** With the exception of Grace Disposal all of these

---

*John R. Coppola, Vice President, All County Service Corporation, "Application to Dispose of Solid Waste at the Orange County Solid Waste Disposal Facilities," October 24, 1974.

**New York State, Senate Select Committee on Crime, July 7, 1980, p. 518; Robert Mongelli, I.S.A. in New Jersey, Town of Wallkill, "Application for Garbage and Refuse Permit," December 13, 1981, January 16, 1984; Joseph Mongelli, I.S.A. in New Jersey, Town of Wallkill, "Application for Garbage and Refuse Permit," 1983.

***Vic Wehnan, Environmental Conservation officer, to David Archibald, New York State Department of Environmental Conservation, Memorandum, May 12, 1980.

****Robert A. Mongelli, Grace Disposal and Leasing, Ltd., New York State Department of Environmental Conservation, "Application for the Operation of a Solid Waste Management Facility," February 18, 1978.

*****Robert Mongelli, Orange County Sanitation, Town of Wallkill, "Application for Garbage and Refuse Permit," December 22, 1980, December 17, 1981, 1983, January 16, 1984.

******Joseph Mongelli, President, Round Lake Sanitation Corporation, "Application to Dispose of Solid Waste at the Orange County Solid Waste Disposal Facilities," August 2, 1974; Robert Mongelli, Round Lake Sanitation

companies presently operate in New York State, with main offices located in Orange County.[*]

This Committee has traced the ownership and history of operations of All County and its related businesses through New York and New Jersey. This is what we found:

Links to Organized Crime

The Mongellis' father, Louis, was indicted June 25, 1981 in the State of New Jersey for his role in an organized crime scheme to monopolize the garbage industry in northern and central New Jersey. I.S.A. of New Jersey, Inc. was also named in the indictment.[**]

According to the indictment, Louis Mongelli, as President of I.S.A., participated in a conspiracy with other garbage collectors to eliminate competition within the industry. Mongelli and his fellow conspirators were charged, among other offenses, with using "threats, intimidation, physical force and other means to pressure and induce garbage collectors to join the conspiracy."[***] The New Jersey state grand jury charged that the conspirators had restrained competition in the garbage collection industry; restricted the freedom of customers to hire the collector of their choice; and "raised, fixed, maintained and stabilized" prices charged by garbage collectors at "artificially high and noncompetitive levels."[****]

The indictment against Mongelli was dismissed and he pled guilty to a disorderly persons offense. He was placed on probation for one year, fined $1,000 and required to complete 100 hours of "community service." The

---

Corporation, New York State Department of Environmental Conservation, "Application for Septic Tank Cleaner and Industrial Waste Collector Permit," July 22, 1983.

[*]Orange County Department of Public Works, "Customer Master List," April 23, 1984; New York State Department of Environmental Conservation, "Waste Transporter Permit, Tri-State Carting Corporation," September 14, 1983; Robert Mongelli, I.S.A. in New Jersey, Town of Wallkill, "Garbage and Refuse Permit," January 16, 1984.

[**]Superior Court of New Jersey, Indictment No. SGJ 66-80-8, June 26, 1981.

[***]Ibid.

[****]Ibid.

184

indictment against I.S.A. was also dismissed and a civil judgment was entered against the company in the amount of $40,000.*

The close-knit business links between Louis, Robert and Joseph Mongelli are revealed through permits, permit applications and correspondence related to Round Lake Sanitation Corporation and I.S.A. of New Jersey which at different times carry the signatures of all three individuals.**

In their testimony before the Congressional Committee on Interstate and Foreign Commerce in 1980 two detective sergeants with the New Jersey State Police, Dick Ottens and Jack Penny, also tied the Mongelli family to organized crime. The following exchange between Congressman Albert Gore, Jr., Ottens and Penney will illustrate:

> MR. GORE. During your investigations have you seen any evidence of the interrelationship between solid and chemical wastes in terms of the disposal companies or individuals? We heard testimony to this effect earlier. I'm wondering if you can corroborate it. Or haulers?
> MR. OTTENS. Yes, sir, we have. We see that with authorized chemical waste facilities, sanitary landfills, hazardous waste haulers and solid waste haulers have the same principles in some cases. Haulers of both solid and hazardous are numerous.
> MR. GORE. How did you find this out? How do you develop such a profile?
> MR. OTTENS. We begin putting a cast of characters together, if you will, of the industry, namely the haulers, and the facilities and how they interact with other subsidiaries or other corporations. We look at the background of course of that corporation. We note the principals involved, who is the business agent, lawyers, or legal counsel are, the title holders, the investigators into the

---

*Telephone conversation with Steven J. Madonna, Deputy Attorney General, Chief, Environmental Prosecution Section, Division of Criminal Justice, State of New Jersey, Trenton, NJ, September 7, 1984.

**Louis Mongelli, Round Lake Sanitation Corp., correspondence with Town of New Windsor, NY, September 2, October 5, October 21, 1970; Joseph Mongelli, President, Round Lake Sanitation Corp., "Application to Dispose of Solid Waste at the Orange County Solid Waste Disposal Facilities," August 2, 1974; Robert Mongelli, Round Lake Sanitation Corp., New York State Department of Environmental Conservation, "Application for Septic Tank Cleaner and Industrial Waste Collector Permit," July 22, 1983; Robert Mongelli, I.S.A. in New Jersey, Inc., Town of Wallkill, "Garbage and Refuse Permit," December 13, 1981, January 16, 1984; Joseph Mongelli, I.S.A. in New Jersey, Inc., Town of Wallkill, "Garbage and Refuse Permit," 1983.

company and all licenses and permits that they may have. We take this as an ongoing profile which we would maintain to determine the interaction between these companies.

MR. GORE. In the course of developing these profiles, did you find there were organized crime groups or families involved in the chemical waste industry?

MR. PENNEY. Yes.

MR. GORE. Would you identify them?

MR. PENNEY. The Genovese-Tieri family and the Simon DeCavalcante organized group.

MR. GORE. Will you explain how they became involved? . . .

MR. OTTENS. We found Mario Giganti is closely associated with that group. We found also, Mario Giganti is on the payroll of Round Lake Sanitation in New York as a solicitor. That corporation is owned by the Mongelli family.

We then found that the Mongelli family under I.S.A., obtained a contract of a large industrial corporation within the State and then gave out subcontracts to chemical waste facilities within the State for the hauling and disposing of such waste.*

Documents obtained by the Assembly Committee staff chart the illegal activities of the Mongelli family beginning in 1977.

Operators of an Illegal Hazardous Waste Disposal Site

In June of 1977 the Town of Warwick discontinued the operation of its sanitary landfill on Penaluna Road and leased it to another Mongelli company, Grace Disposal and Leasing, Ltd. of Harriman, New York.*** In July the Mongellis received a permit to operate the Sanitary landfill from the Orange County Department of Health.*** The Mongellis did not apply for a DEC

---

*U.S. Congress, House of Representatives, Committee on Interstate and Foreign Commerce, December 16, 1980, pp. 63-64.

**Charles B. Rowe, Supervisor, Town of Warwick, Correspondence to William Bentley, New York State Department of Environmental Conservation, Albany, NY, June 1, 1977.

***Russell Johnson, Commissioner, Orange County Department of Health, "Permit to Operate a Refuse Disposal Area, Grace Disposal and Leasing, Ltd.," Permit No. 1418, July 15, 1977.

permit until February 1978.* After reviewing the permit application DEC determined that the operation could possibly threaten private wells and Greenwood Lake, a source of drinking water for nearly one million people in northern New Jersey and New York. DEC required Grace Disposal to conduct soil borings, install monitoring wells and a leachate collection system.** The Mongellis refused and initiated legal proceedings against the Department and those individuals who had expressed their opposition to the permit approval, charging that Grace Disposal had been unjustly treated.***

In a deposition obtained during the court proceedings James Penaluna, whose property bordered the landfill, said he had observed I.S.A. trailers unload 55 gallon drums--as many as 30-40 drums per truckload of sludge which "appeared to be a combination of grease, oil and degreasers" at the Penaluna site. The barrels, he claimed, were flattened and covered by a machine operator who was an employee of Grace Disposal. Penaluna also stated that he had observed other industrial wastes dumped at the site. He said the truck drivers told him the waste material came from the Ford Plant in Mahwah, New Jersey.**** Other residents complained that Grace Disposal had ignored buffer zone requirements and that trucks bearing New Jersey license plates dumped at

---

*Robert A. Mongelli, Grace Disposal and Leasing, Ltd., New York State Department of Environmental Conservation, "Application for the Operation of a Solid Waste Management Facility," February 18, 1978.

**Paul D. Keller, Regional Director, Region 3, New York State Department of Environmental Conservation, Correspondence to Robert Mongelli, President, Grace Disposal and Leasing, Ltd., August 16, 1978; Richard A. Gardineer, P.E., Assistant Solid Waste Engineer, New York State Department of Environmental Conservation, Correspondence to Robert Mongelli, Grace Disposal and Leasing, Ltd., November 13, 1978; Gordon Bishop, "Chemical Wastes Dumped in N.Y. Peril Jersey Waster," Sunday Star-Ledger, April 8, 1979, Section 1, p. 1.

***U.S. District Court for the Southern District of New York, Grace Disposal and Leasing, Ltd., v. Robert F. Flacke, Commissioner of the New York State Department of Environmental Conservation; Daniel E. Louis; Richard A. Gardineer and the Town of Warwick, Summons and Complaint, June 13, 1979.

****James Penaluna, Affidavit, "Town of Warwick Against Grace Disposal and Leasing, Ltd.," Supreme Court of the State of New York, County of Orange, Index, No. 3226/79, July 10, 1979.

the landfill very early in the morning and late at night, using flares to light their way.[*]

In addition to I.S.A., DEC claims Mongelli's Round Lake Sanitation and All County also used the site.[**] During the time the Mongellis operated the Penaluna landfill, All County was headquartered in Warwick. According to an Administrative Consent Order prepared by the New Jersey Department of Environmental Protection from May 1978-June 1979, All County "transported numerous shipments of hazardous waste from various generators accompanied by manifests to a location in Warwick, New York described as an All County facility; in fact, All County never owned nor operated a waste facility in Warwick. . . ."[***] The Newark Star Ledger examined these manifests which revealed that "thousands of gallons of 'solvents' . . . 'paint and pigment residues' . . . 'dirty thinners' . . . 'still bottoms' . . . 'glue residue' and other organic, toxic compounds were picked up from industries in New Jersey and slated for disposal at Warwick."[****] The company, which was registered as a hazardous waste hauler in New Jersey, was charged by the New Jersey DEP with violating the State's hazardous waste laws by shipping these hazardous wastes with improper manifest forms.[*****] All County claimed it took the wastes to Northeast Solite Corporation in Saugerties, New York, a lightweight aggregate facility, where the wastes were incinerated in Solite's kiln.[******] It is unclear why All County did not list Solite as the receiver of these wastes. To the knowledge of the Committee, Solite has never confirmed receipt of the wastes.

---

[*]William Boyle, Ibid., July 6, 1979; James Petty, Ibid., July 9, 1979; Gordon Bishop, Sunday Star-Ledger, April 8, 1979, Section 1, p. 18.

[**]Interview with Richard Gardineer, Solid Waste Engineer, New York State Department of Environmental Conservation, February 29, 1984.

[***]State of New Jersey, Department of Environmental Protection, Administrative Consent Order, "In the Matter of All County Environmental Service Corporation," June 6, 1983, p. 1.

[****]Gordon Bishop, Sunday Star-Ledger, April 8, 1979, Section 1, p. 18.

[*****]State of New Jersey, Department of Environmental Protection, June 6, 1983, p.1.

[******]Ibid., p. 1.

188

In 1980 NYSDEC ordered the Mongellis to close the Penaluna landfill.* Grace Disposal went out of business and the site, which is 36 acres in size and 50 feet deep, is now leaching organic chemicals and the toxic metals--cadmium, lead and mercury--into a stream and wetland that feed Greenwood Lake. DEC estimates the dump may produce as much as five to six gallons of leachate per minute or approximately 7,200 gallons per day.** Although DEC has placed the landfill on its list of hazardous waste sites scheduled for State clean-up funds, competition for these monies is intense. State and federal funds may never be made available to clean up the wastes the Mongellis have left behind.

A History of Violations
On June 28, 1979 All County notified DEC that it would change its headquarters to P.O. Box G, Glenwood, New Jersey, although it would still maintain an office in Warwick and other locations in New York.*** All County also acquired two storage facilities; one at River Road, Edgewater, New Jersey, the other in Newark.**** However, the Mongellis and their partners, the Coppolas, neglected to notify the New Jersey DEP of the existence of the Edgewater facility. New Jersey DEP "discovered" the site in an inspection conducted March 27, 1980.***** By Spring 1983 the Mongellis and Coppolas had compiled a long list of hazardous waste violations in the State of New Jersey. In addition to the Warwick incident, the June 1983 New Jersey DEP Consent Order charged the Mongellis and Coppolas with these violations:

From October 1978 to November 1980 All County transported numerous shipments of special (hazardous) waste from its Edgewater site to a location in "Saugerties, New York" described on the face of the manifests as an All County facility; in fact, All County has never owned nor operated a facility in

---

*Interview with R. Gardineer, February 29, 1984.

**Ibid.

***John R. Coppola, Vice President, All County Environmental Service Corporation, Correspondence to Thomas Koch, Senior Engineering Technician, Bureau of Hazardous Waste, New York State Department of Environmental Conservation, June 28, 1979.

****State of New Jersey, Department of Environmental Protection, Administrative Consent Order, June 6, 1983, p. 1 and p. 3.

*****Ibid, p. 1.

Saugerties, New York. To the best of the Department's knowledge, these shipments were disposed at the N.E. Solite/Industrial Environmental Systems, Inc. plant on Kings Highway in Mt. Marion, New York. For failing to properly complete the manifests as a generator and for the acceptance of special (hazardous) waste from a generator who failed to properly complete the manifest, the Department (found) that All County violated N.J.A.C. 7:26-7.4(a) (now codified at N.J.A.C. 7:26-7.4(e)(i) and N.J.A.C. 7:26-7.5(a) (now codified at N.J.A.C. 7:26-7.5(g)(2).

On January 9, 1981, All County violated N.J.A.C. 7:26-3.2 by hauling waste generated by Mobil Chemical Company, Edison, New Jersey to Chem-Clear, Wayne, Pennsylvania in a vehicle not registered with the Department (New Jersey license plate no. XUC-255; New Jersey Manifest No. 011939).

On October 4, 1980, a trailer, with New Jersey license plate number 619 TAF, owned by S&W Waste, Inc., 53 Pennsylvania Avenue, Kearny, New Jersey, pulled with an All County Environmental Service Corporation tractor, driven by an All County employee, collected "20 cubic yards of combustible organic residue" at Industrial Environmental Systems, Inc., Kings Highway, P.O. Box 437, Mt. Marion, New York. Said waste was accompanied by New Jersey Manifest No. DO4938. This vehicle was stopped and seized on the New York State Thruway on October 4, 1980 by three New York Environmental Conservation officers. While the vehicle was in the custody of the New York officials, samples of the contents of the trailer were obtained. Laboratory analysis revealed that the material contained 330 ppm PCBs on a dry weight basis. On October 24, 1980, the vehicle was released and the waste was hauled by this same vehicle and accepted for disposal at S&W Waste, Inc. Condition 22 of the TOA issued to S&W Waste, Inc. specifically states that this facility "is not authorized to accept PCB waste . . . ." On May 26, 1981, the Department issued a Notice of Prosecution in the amount of $5,000 to All County for transporting special (hazardous) waste to a facility not approved to accept such waste in violation of N.J.A.C. 7:26-3.4(b) (now codified at N.J.A.C. 7:26-7.5(g)(3). To date all County has not resolved this matter.

On April 9, 1981, All County violated N.J.A.C. 7:26-3.4(b) (now codified at N.J.A.C. 7:26-7.5(g)(3) by transporting special (hazardous) waste to Road Building Construction Company, Kearny, New Jersey, which is not authorized to accept hazardous waste. . . .

On February 20, 1979, All County submitted an Application for Registration and Engineering Design Plans to the Department for the construction and operation of a transfer station to be located at 193 Christie Street, Newark, Essex County, New Jersey (Lot 3, Blox, 2495). On December 18, 1980, All County pled guilty in Newark Municipal Court (Docket No. 94783) to failing to properly secure underground storage tanks and failing to render them inoperable. . . .

190

As of December 1983 these violations were still outstanding in the State of New Jersey.*

A Change in Ownership--More Violations

In December 1982, the Coppolas created a splinter company, All County Resources Management Corporation, located at P.O. Box G, Glenwood, New Jersey. The new company was to handle the septic waste portion of the business exclusively.**

On March 31, 1983 a Solite Facility in Virginia purchased 3,338 gallons of flammable solvents from All County and burned it three days later. Subsequent testing of a sample of the waste by a laboratory hired by Solite indicated that it was heavily contaminated with PCBs. All County was not authorized to handle PCB wastes, Solite was forbidden to burn them.***

On April 30, the Coppolas, who owned two-thirds of the stock in All County Environmental Service Corporation, sold their share of the company to the Mongellis. In return the Coppolas retained all of the assets, accounts, and equipment related to that portion of the business that handled septic wastes. The Mongellis were then the sole owners of the hazardous waste business.****

But in what appeared to be a simultaneous transaction, the Mongellis sold their hazardous waste business to a former employee, James Stroin,***** who had also worked at the notorious Kin-Buc landfill in Edison, New Jersey, the largest chemical landfill in the Northeast. Kin-Buc was shut down in 1977 when toxic chemicals from the site were found to be leaking into the Raritan River,

---

*State of New Jersey, Department of Environmental Protection, Administrative Consent Order, June 6, 1983, pp. 1-3.

**John R. Coppola, Vice President, All County Environmental Service Corporation, Correspondence to Barbara Rinaldi, Division of Regulatory Affairs, New York State Department of Environmental Conservation, December 23, 1982.

***Phone conversations with Martin Harrell, Esq., U.S. Environmental Protection Agency, Philadelphia, July 27, 1984.

****John R. Coppola, Frank G. Coppola, Robert Mongelli, Joseph Mongelli, "Stock Purchase Agreement," April 30, 1983.

*****James Stroin, Robert Mongelli, Joseph Mongelli, "Stock Purchase Agreement," April 27, 1983.

a major drinking water supply.* Shortly thereafter, he was joined by David Rosenberg, who became the vice president and operations manager for All County. Stroin bought the business for $500,000 with a down payment of $50,000. A note for the remainder was due three years later.**

In May, Stroin applied for a New Jersey hazardous waste hauler's permit and indicated that New Jersey wastes would be hauled to Northeast Solite in Mount Marion, and the Norlite Corporation, another industrial kiln, in Cohoes, New York. Stroin, like the Mongellis and Coppolas before him, continued to use Geo-Chem Company of Lowell, Massachusetts as a supplier of flammable solvent wastes.***

On December 22, 1983, only eight months after Stroin purchased All County, the New Jersey DEP issued the company a cease and desist order for failure to apply for a DEP permit within 90 days prior to the change in ownership and the illegal transportation of several shipments of PCB-contaminated waste from Geo-Chem Company to the Edgewater facility. Certain loads were found to contain 3,830 parts per million (ppm) of PCBs. Some of the wastes had been sent to Solite in Virginia and Norlite where they were burned.**** According to the U.S. Environmental Protection Agency,

*All County Environmental Service Corporation, "RCRA Permit Application," November 17, 1983; Gordon Bishop, Sunday Star-Ledger, April 8, 1979, Section 1, p. 18.

**James Stroin, Robert Mongelli, Joseph Mongelli, "Stock Purchase Agreement," April 27, 1983.

***Geochem, Inc., Lowell, Mass., Hazardous Waste Licensee Monthly Operating Report to Commonwealth of Massachusetts, Department of Environmental Quality Engineering, Division of Hazardous Waste, August 25, 1983, September 26, 1983, October 26, 1983.

****State of New Jersey, Department of Environmental Protection, Administrative Consent Order, "In the Matter of All County Environmental Service Corporation," December 22, 1983; Paul R. Kneuer, Executive Vice President, Norlite Corporation, Correspondence to New York State Department of Environmental Conservation, Region IV, Schenectady, November 1, 1983; Phone conversation with Martin Harrell, Esq., U.S. Environmental Protection Agency, Region 3, Philadelphia, July 27, 1984.

Solite incinerated more than 100,000 gallons of the PCB waste.* Stroin and Rosenberg were out of business.

"The RA-MAR Connection"

All County, under the ownership of the Mongellis and Coppolas, had other suspect business associates. One of them was John Coppola's brother, Ralph, who owned RA-MAR Waste Management Corporation, a septic tank cleaning and waste oil collection company. RA-MAR serviced Orange, Rockland and Westchester Counties and had offices in New York and New Jersey.** Like All County, RA-MAR had a history of violating environmental law.

Between September 1979 and June 1981 RA-MAR committed twenty separate violations of New Jersey's hazardous waste laws. The company had used unregistered vehicles to collect and store hazardous wastes; illegally accepted and transported shipments of hazardous wastes and took them to unauthorized facilities.*** One of these facilities was Edgewater Terminals, a waste oil storage facility, located at River Road, Edgewater, next door to All County.**** . . . DEC permit files indicate that in 1981 Ralph Coppola also hauled waste oil to All County's River Road facility.*****

Further proof that the Coppola brothers were in business together appears in the form of a request to DEC by John Coppola, Vice President of All

---

*Phone conversation with Martin Harrell, Esq., U.S. Environmental Protection Agency, Region 3, Philadelphia, July 27, 1984.

**Ralph Coppola, President, RA-MAR Waste Management Corporation, New York State Department of Environmental Conservation, "Application for Septic Tank Cleaner and Industrial Waste Collector Registration," April 15, 1981.

***State of New Jersey, Department of Environmental Protection, Administrative Consent Order, December 22, 1983.

****Ibid.

*****Ralph Coppola, RA-MAR Waste Management Corporation, New York State Department of Environmental Conservation Application, "Waste Transporter Permit," April 15, 1981.

County, to modify All County's permit to add several RA-MAR vehicles to it for work being done at the Suffern Sewage Treatment plant.*

Public documents also provide evidence that link the Coppola brothers and their respective businesses to an incident of illegal toxic waste disposal at a site in West Nyack, New York.

According to Stanley Greenberg, former lieutenant with the Rockland County Sheriff's Department, in 1976 the Sheriff's Department conducted an investigation of a West Nyack dump site where incinerated wastes from the City of Yonkers were being disposed. The dump was actually a construction site for an industrial park and was not authorized to be used for waste disposal. In testimony before the New York State Senate Greenberg stated that subsequent investigations revealed that individuals known to the Yonkers Police Department to be associated with organized crime ran the illegal operation. The Sheriff's Department had trouble resolving the case and asked then Rockland County District Attorney, Kenneth Gribetz, for assistance. Greenberg claimed he refused, but when a local reporter threatened to expose the illegal dumping, Gribetz approached the OCTF and asked the agency to assist in the investigation.**

On a surveillance of the dump site September 27, 1976, Greenberg "observed a large tank truck depositing a clear liquid matter" near the site. Greenberg said he was later told the liquid was used for dust control. It was "surprising," he said "that there was only dust in one spot . . . that's the only place they put the liquid." Greenberg identified the truck as belonging to All County.*** However, an Administrative Consent Order issued to RA-MAR by the NJDEP stated that on the same date RA-MAR had generated and transported 4,000 gallons of oil to the West Nyack site and deposited it on the roadways. Inaccurate manifest forms accompanied the waste and New Jersey noted that New York State law prohibits the use of waste oil on roadways. New

---

*John R. Coppola, All County Environmental Service Corporation, Correspondence to R. Gardineer, New York State Department of Environmental Conservation, White Plains, New York, June 14, 1982.

**New York State, Senate Select Committee on Crime, May 29, 1980, pp. 15-27, 37.

***Ibid., pp. 13-14, 42.

194

Jersey charged RA-MAR with manifest violations and disposal of wastes at an unapproved facility.*

The Noble Oil/Oil Recovery Operation

It is of further interest to note that two of the companies RA-MAR used to dispose of the waste oil collected in the lower Hudson Valley were Noble Oil Company of Vincentown, New Jersey and Oil Recovery of Clayton, New Jersey.** Between May 1983 and January 1984 RA-MAR reported taking 695,000 gallons of waste oil to Noble Oil Company alone. On May 10, 1984, Noble Oil and Oil Recovery were indicted in New Jersey for their alleged central role in a massive operation in which hazardous chemical wastes were mixed with heating oil and then sold to the public. The crimes for which the corporate officers Christopher Grungo (Noble Oil) and Joseph Cucinotta (Oil Recovery), and others were indicted included conspiracy, theft, deceptive business practices and the illegal transportation and disposal of hazardous waste.*** As of this writing a trial date for Noble Oil and Oil Recovery has not yet been scheduled.

The Most Recent Developments

Although All County Environmental Service Corporation is not presently in operation, the Mongellis and Coppolas still operate waste disposal businesses in New York State. Round Lake Sanitation collects garbage in Orange, Ulster and Sullivan Counties.**** Both Round Lake and Tri-State Carting Corporation

---

*State of New Jersey, Department of Environmental Protection, Administrative Consent Order, December 22, 1983, p. 2

**New York State Department of Environmental Conservation, "Waste Transporter Permit," No. JA-042, RA-MAR Waste Management Corporation, June 1, 1983.

***State of New Jersey, Division of Criminal Justice, Press Release and Attachments, May 10, 1984.

****Orange County Department of Public Works, Customer Master List, April 23, 1984; Committee staff telephone survey, April, 1984.

are currently permitted by DEC to transport industrial wastes.[*] I.S.A. of New Jersey is also operating as a garbage hauler in Orange County.[**]

Earlier in this year John Coppola applied for a permit renewal for All County Resource Management.[***] During the course of our investigation, staff from the Committee discovered that on the application for a permit renewal John Coppola had indicated he would collect cesspool sludge, septage and sewage treatment sludge in New York State which the company would haul to themselves. The wastes would be treated and landspread on their site. The address given was P.O. Box G, Glenwood, New Jersey. When the Committee staff questioned the existence of such a disposal facility the Department pulled the renewed permit from the mail and called the company. All County claimed it was an oversight. They did not have a landspreading operation and indicated that the company intended to haul to the same receiving stations they had previously used.[****] Is it coincidence then that on May 1, 1984, Frank and John Coppola submitted a permit application to DEC for yet another company, ECO-TEC Services, Inc., located at P.O. Box G, Glenwood, New Jersey, to operate a large landspreading facility in the Town of Goshen, New York?[*****] The company would collect 3,600 tons of municipal sludge each year from Orange, Sullivan and Westchester Counties and apply it to 570 acres of farmland.[******] The 800 acre site would be located midway between three major waste disposal facilities--the Orange County landfill which the Mongellis

---

[*]New York State Department of Environmental Conservation, "Waste Transporter Permit," September 22, 1983; New York State Department of Environmental Conservation, "Waste Transporter Permit," Tri-State Carting Corporation, September 14, 1983.

[**]Town of Wallkill, "Garbage and Refuse Permit," I.S.A. in New Jersey, 1984.

[***]John Coppola, All County Resource Management, "Application for a Waste Transporter Permit," New York State Department of Environmental Conservation, March 8, 1984.

[****]Ibid.

[*****]Frank Coppola, Secretary, "Application for Approval to Construct a Solid Waste Management Facility," New York State Department of Environmental Conservation, May 1, 1984.

[******]Ibid.

presently use, the Al Turi landfill and the Merion Blue Grass Sod Farm, another landspreading facility which Fine claimed All County used.* All three sites are presently in operation and are included in the Department's inventory of known and suspected hazardous waste disposal sites.**

In May of this year RA-MAR Corporation's permit to haul waste oil to Noble Oil Corporation and Oil Recovery was renewed by DEC.*** And Northeast Solite Corporation in Saugerties continues to burn waste solvents under an agreement with DEC, in spite of mounting pollution problems that have resulted from their activities.****

All of these facts clearly point to the need for significant changes in the solid waste permitting program as well as further investigation of specific corporations and individuals who are chronic violators of the Environmental Conservation Law and who associate with businesses having similar backgrounds. One such change is the development of a permit program to regulate private garbage haulers. Another would be a prohibition on the approval of permits to individuals who simultaneously operate hazardous and solid waste disposal companies. And lastly, a review must be made of the Department's legislative authority and policies regarding the denial and revocation of permits for operators of solid waste disposal facilities.

---

*New York State, Senate Select Committee, July 8, p. 534.

**New York State Department of Environmental Conservation, Inactive Hazardous Waste Disposal Sites in New York State, Annual Report, December 1983, p. C15.

***New York State Department of Environmental Conservation, "Waste Transporter Permit," RA-MAR Waste Management Corporation, May 25, 1984.

****Maurice D. Hinchey, Chairman, New York State Assembly Environmental Conservation Committee, Correspondence to Henry Williams, Commissioner, New York State Department of Environmental Conservation, July 27, 1984.

8

Declaration of Joseph Hauser Before the Permanent Subcommittee on Investigations, April 27, 1983

My name is Joseph Hauser and I make the following statement under penalty of perjury. I will relate my association with various officers of the Hotel Employees and Restaurant Employees International Union and some of their organized crime associates.

Allow me to briefly explain my background. I am currently under the protection of the U.S. Marshals Service following my cooperation with the FBI and Department of Justice since early 1979.

From approximately 1965 to 1974 I operated insurance companies involved in individual life insurance and prepaid health insurance for labor unions in the Los Angeles area. These firms included American Medicare Foundation, National Prepaid Health, Equitable Health, Statewide Insurance Agency, all operating out of Los Angeles, California.

In October 1973 I moved my base of operations to Florida, largely due to an FBI investigation of my activities in Los Angeles. Once in Florida I purchased Farmers National Life Insurance Corporation, Inc., licensed to do business in Florida and five other states including Arizona.

In 1975 two associates of mine succeeded in obtaining a reinsurance contract from Old Security Life Insurance Company of Kansas City, Missouri. This contract allowed Farmers National to go into states where Old Security had a license to sell insurance and write business on their policies. This is known as a "fronting" agreement wherein Old Security was fronting for Farmers National.

Using Old Security as a front I obtained, through bribery and influence peddling, the insurance business of the Laborers, Teamsters and other unions in Arizona, Indiana, Massachusetts, Hawaii, Alabama, Rhode Island, Florida, and many other states.

In late 1975 an associate of mine, John Boden, relocated in California and formed Great Pacific Corporation, a holding company, which in turn purchased Family Provider, a small Arizona based insurance company. With Old Security fronting for Family Provider, I obtained the Teamsters Central States Health and Welfare Fund business amounting to almost $24 million yearly in premiums.

On June 15, 1976 I purchased National American Life Insurance Company, a Louisiana Corporation authorized to sell insurance in most states. This purchase was arranged by Richard Kleindienst of Arizona and Washington, DC, and was financed in part by Carlos Marcello of Louisiana. My associates in these companies were primarily Linda Johnson, John Boden, Mel Wyman, George Herrera and Brian Kavanagh. At one point my companies were doing $180 million a year in premiums.

In March 1977 I was convicted of offering bribes to several Los Angeles area union officials in return for their influence in having various union trust funds award insurance contracts to my firms from 1972 to 1974. In 1979, I pled guilty in Tucson, Arizona, to similar charges.

I was indicted in June of 1978, and after much contemplating and some soul searching, I began cooperating with Special Agent Bill Fleming of the FBI in Los Angeles. I regenerated an insurance business with FBI agents as partners in a government undercover operation known as Brilab. I have testified in federal grand juries as well as federal and state trials in California, Arizona, Florida, Louisiana, Texas and Massachusetts and other states. At least fifteen individuals have been convicted on a variety of charges relating to the mismanagement and corruption of union insurance funds, state insurance contracts and bribery of public officials. Those convicted include union officials, organized crime figures and public officials. All convictions have been directly related to my testimony and the evidence gathered by the FBI during the period of 1974 to February 1980.

Labor Leaders

During the period from 1965 to 1974, the most influential labor union people in the Los Angeles area were Joe Benfatti, deceased associate of organized crime figures, Herman "Blackie" Leavitt, then head of the Los Angeles area locals of the Hotel Workers Union, John Cinquimani of the Building Trades Union, Sig Arowitz, Secretary-Treasurer of the Los Angeles County Federation of Labor and William Robertson, head of a Hotel Workers local in the San Fernando Valley. Robertson succeeded Sig Arowitz as head of the Labor Federation in 1975.

During the period of the late 1960s and early 1970s Arowitz, Robertson and Leavitt spent a great deal of time in my office. Leavitt was an especially frequent visitor during 1972 and 1973 when he was dating my secretary, Miriam Perry, whom he eventually married. At one point, around 1972 or 1973, both

Robertson's son, Bill, Jr., and Leavitt's brother, Julius, were on the payroll of one of my companies.

During the early 1970s Blackie Leavitt and John Cinquimani were involved with Bernard Rappaport, President of American Income Life Insurance Company of Waco, Texas, in arranging union business for Rappaport's company. Cinquimani was hired as a consultant and Leavitt would pinpoint unions and arrange introductions between American Life representatives and the union people. John Cinquimani's daughter Carol worked for Rappaport's company and would funnel payoff money from the company to union people whom she knew at the time. On occasion during this period, payoffs of these funds were made to Leavitt in my office, in addition to other locations such as the Bistro Restaurant in Los Angeles.

To illustrate Mr. Leavitt's influence, I would mention that when attorney Sidney Korshak came from Chicago to Los Angeles, Blackie Leavitt told me he was designated to introduce Korshak to the right people and open all the doors for him. Organized crime leader Tony Accardo, whom I have known for many years as Joe Batters, told me on several occasions, that he had sent Korshak to Los Angeles to represent the mob there. Since then, Mr. Korshak has become well known as a labor consultant in Las Vegas and Los Angeles. I don't need to tell this Subcommittee who Sidney Korshak is.

Payments

From about 1966 to 1973, I paid Blackie Leavitt several thousand dollars in cash. In return for the money, Leavitt introduced me to a number of union officials from various trades, such as the auto workers, in addition to those of the hotel workers union whom he controlled. I would either pay Blackie directly in my office or I would give the money to someone acting as a "bag man" for Leavitt. In either case, I would have Linda Johnson, George Herrera, or someone else in my office go to the bank and cash a check, then give the cash to me and I made the payment directly. Leavitt's introductions helped generate at least 75% of my business. I was given the health and welfare insurance for Hotel Workers locals in Pasadena and San Pedro and obtained membership lists of numerous locals which allowed me to solicit life insurance business through direct mailings. Blackie Leavitt told the locals to give their endorsements to the mailings and in some cases to arrange for dues checkoffs to pay for the premiums. Additionally, through these payoffs to Mr. Leavitt, I had arranged to get all of the Hotel Workers Union business in Los Angeles County but the FBI told the management trustees that I was to be indicted and the deal feel through. Thereafter I moved my operation to Florida.

In addition to the money I paid to Mr. Leavitt, which I previously described, I also made many trips with him to the racetrack and to Las Vegas. Mr. Leavitt was very close to Marge Everett, the owner of Hollywood Park, and he certainly had the run of the place. According to Leavitt, this influence came through Sidney Korshak with whom Mrs. Everett has had contact in the past. Most of the checks I cashed at the track were okayed by Johnny Beverly, head of the Jockey Association at that time.

Our travel to Las Vegas was both business and social. Mr. Leavitt and I usually stayed at the Dunes; however, we received complementary accommodations wherever we went in Vegas. Occasionally others would travel to Las Vegas to pick up money for Blackie from various hotels such as the Dunes. The late Sid Wyman, one of the principle owners of the Dunes, gave Bill Robertson money in my presence and said, "give this to Blackie." I cashed thousands of dollars worth of checks in both places and gave the money to Mr. Leavitt to gamble. I am also aware that Nate and Al's Deli in Beverly Hills, was paying Mr. Leavitt regularly for a "sweetheart" labor contract. Nicky Blair, who owned a place on Sunset of the same name, asked me to help him with Blackie Leavitt. Blair told me, Leavitt had threatened that if he did not pay off, his place would be blown up. I went to Leavitt as requested but there was such a big difference between the amount he demanded and what Nicky would pay there was nothing I could do. Thereafter Nicky Blairs' was blown up.

Mr. Leavitt's influence extended well beyond Los Angeles and into the hierarchy of the Hotel Workers International. Moreover, he had significant organized crime contacts. He was a regional Vice President of the International, and both San Diego and Las Vegas were in his territory. On one occasion I was with Mr. Leavitt in San Diego when we met at Mr. A's restaurant with Joe LiMandri, a member of organized crime and an official of the Hotel Workers San Diego Local. Through Mr. Leavitt I also met organized crime figures Freddy Sicca and Chris Petti. Petti, who operates in San Diego and Los Angeles, is a close associate of Chicago mob figure Tony Spilotro of Las Vegas. Mr. Leavitt wanted me to take care of Petti and Sicca--that is, find a source of income for them.

Al Bramlet, Blackie Leavitt, and the Las Vegas Local

I attended a reception at the Stadium Club in Los Angeles. Also in attendance were Sidney Korshak, Blackie Leavitt and Al Bramlet, then head of the Hotel Workers Local 226 in Las Vegas. During the evening, Mr. Leavitt and Mr. Bramlet became engaged in a heated discussion regarding the Health and Welfare Trust Funds of the Las Vegas Local. Mr. Leavitt told Mr. Bramlet that "Chicago had instructed Hanley" (Ed Hanley, General-President of Hotel

Workers International) to bring Bramlet's funds into the International. The term "Chicago" referred, of course, to Accardo and the mob. Mr. Leavitt said that, "Hanley is up against the wall and wants you (Bramlet) to do it." Mr. Bramlet adamantly refused to agree to a merger and at one point Sidney Korshak said something like, "You know something Mr. Bramlet, I would listen to Mr. Leavitt, he makes a lot of sense." At another point, Mr. Leavitt told Mr. Bramlet not to give him "any shit" about the Las Vegas casino owners as he, Leavitt, had them lined up. Bramlet became very upset, saying that Mr. Leavitt had "screwed" him enough as he was supposed to "get 30%" and was only "getting 5%." I understood Bramlet to mean that he was to get 30% of the money being kicked back in Las Vegas and was only getting 5%. I recall that Mr. Bramlet ripped off the ascot he was wearing and asserted that the funds would only go to the International over his "dead body." Mr. Leavitt responded, "You'll be six feet under the desert if this is not done."

Another time, Mr. Leavitt told Bramlet that he could have Schmoutey elected Secretary-Treasurer of Local 226 in 24 hours and Bramlet would be out. He meant, of course, Ben Schmoutey, then President of the Las Vegas Local. Al Bramlet was murdered in the Las Vegas desert in 1977.

At this time, I would like to point out that, following Mr. Ed Hanley's takeover of the Hotel Workers International, I believe he and Mr. Leavitt, acting at the instruction of Chicago organized crime bosses, undertook steps to get the funds of various locals under International control. They were concerned about how to control the money, what kinds of loans to make which would look good and still allow them to get money under the table. In order to get locals around the country to comply it was important that the International get control of the funds of what was at that time the largest Hotel Workers Local in the country, Las Vegas. It was also Mr. Leavitt's idea to use the International's authority to merge locals and put them into trusteeship to achieve these aims. Mr. Leavitt told me once that "they had to control certain locals because they must have people to answer the phone who would do what they were told." The Laborers Union uses the same tactic, that is, mergers and trusteeship, to control locals. Al Pilotto, an officer of the Laborers International, is also a Chicago organized crime associate of Auippa and Accardo, and the Hotel Workers have used this same technique as the Laborers.

Florida

In 1973 Mel Wyman and I met with several officials of the Hotel Workers International in Minneapolis. The purpose of the meeting was to lay the groundwork for me to get the union insurance business throughout the country over a period of time. Through Mr. Leavitt I met Ed Hanley, General

President, and regional officials, including the late Myra Wolfgang of Detroit and Herbert "Pinky" Schiffman of Miami.

Ed Hanley told me that the people in Chicago had told him about me and that I would be getting a lot of business when I got my national company. Mr. Hanley and Mr. Leavitt were to arrange for me to get the Detroit and Miami business first. After the meeting, which Mel Wyman did not attend, we (Hauser, Hanley, Leavitt and Schiffman) joined Mel at the bar. Mr. Leavitt and I discussed the payoffs, and Mr. Leavitt said that we would do it as he had in the past; he would "take care of Ed and Pinky." Mr. Hanley emphasized that the "Chicago (mob) was involved here" and had to be taken care of. I told him there would be millions in premiums, enough for all. Over the next several months I met with Mr. Hanley and Mr. Leavitt in Los Angeles 4 or 5 more times to discuss the best method of setting up the deal. Mr. Hanley wanted to set up an agency as a front and Bill Robertson's son was mentioned to head the agency. I also met with Myra Wolfgang in Detroit and Pinky Schiffman in Miami regarding their Locals' insurance business.

Expansion

It was during this period that Pinky was in legal trouble in Atlanta (1975). Once, I gave him $1,500 cash, and another time, I had Linda Johnson cash a check for $5,000 which I gave to Pinky. During this same period I had Brian Kavanaugh meet with Florida Administrators who administered the Miami Local's insurance plan. Pinky had told me that Arnold Grossman (head of Florida Administrators) was taking care of him and he had heard from Blackie that I would do better. The bottom line was that we were supposed to take over all the Hotel Worker insurance plans in Florida.

In late 1975 or early 1976, I met with Al Pilotto and Tony Accardo in Chicago to discuss setting up a plan for me to re-insure union dental plans. The way this worked is that if union members went to the union's dental clinic they received 100% coverage. However, if they went to their own dentist the union paid 80% and the member 20%. My company would insure the unions' 80% liability with the union paying the premiums. Around this time, Pilotto and Dan Milano of Consultants and Administrators, a Chicago dental administrator working with Pilotto and the Laborers Union, travelled to Las Vegas to see Al Bramlet to arrange for Consultants and Administrators to get the Las Vegas Hotel Workers business.

In early 1974 I had a meeting with Santos Trafficante, Sal Tricario and John Giardello at Bern's Restaurant in Tampa, Florida, for the purpose of arranging for insurance business for my company.

In the summer of 1975 I met with Trafficante, Bernie Rubin, and George Waugenaux to arrange loans from my company to build a jockey club in Tampa.

At that meeting, Trafficante told me that he would get the Miami hotel trust money into my company. He said that his man to do the job was Hotel Union officer Al Gonzalez from Tampa who handled Miami for him. I told him that when you dealt with the Hotel Workers you had to go through Chicago. Trafficante said no, that Al had the connections and would handle it for him.

During the mid to late 1970s, Louis Ostrer was doing business with the Hotel Workers through his insurance company, Foundation Life Insurance of New Jersey. I believe Mr. Ostrer had been convicted in the early 70s of stock manipulation along with labor racketeer and organized crime figure John Dioguardi, also known as Johnny Dio. Mr. Ostrer's insurance license was revoked by the State of New York. He has since been convicted of other charges relating to corruption of union insurance funds. Of course, Mr. Ostrer was also the subject of hearings held by this Subcommittee in 1977. At one point Ed Hanley told me that Ostrer was on a 50-50 basis with them, that is he was kicking back half of his commission. This conversation occurred at the Carriage House Apartments in Miami. Tony Salerno and Bernie Rubin told me the same thing. Hence, I was pressured to work with Mr. Ostrer in setting up this insurance scheme with the Hotel Workers International. Lou Ostrer told me he was making payments directly to Ed Hanley, Blackie Leavitt and others. I always refused to work with Ostrer.

In late 1979 I had one of my many meetings with Carlos Marcello in New Orleans. We had previously discussed arranging for all of the insurance business of several major International Unions. On this occasion Marcello said he needed 30 more days to complete arrangements. He said "I will get the number one guy (mob leader, Tony Accardo) and travel with you to other cities to write all the insurance business for the Teamsters, Longshoremen, Laborers, and Hotel Workers.

This trip did not occur as I was placed in the custody of the Attorney General before it could be arranged. Here, I would like to again state that during this period I was cooperating fully with the FBI.

The Teamsters

In April of 1976 John Boden and I were trying to arrange to get the Teamsters Central States insurance business through Richard Kleindienst, personal attorney to the Teamster boss, Frank Fitzsimmons. Individually or together, Boden and I met several times with Mr. Kleindienst in Arizona, Washington, DC, and Chicago. At one meeting between Mr. Boden and Mr. Kleindienst in Washington, DC, Mr. Kleindienst asked who would administer the claims. Kleindienst was concerned about administering the claims and writing the add on insurance business which was very lucrative. Mr. Kleindienst strongly urged that we use Allen Dorfman. When Mr. Boden told me of this I told him I didn't want to do business with Mr. Dorfman. I know that Tony Accardo hated Mr. Dorfman though Mr. Dorfman was very close to Joey Aiuppa and Jacky Cerone.

At a later meeting, which I attended, Mr. Kleindienst had a call placed to Allen Dorfman in Chicago and arranged for Dorfman's Amalgamated Insurance Company to handle the claims administration.

I was, thereafter, contacted by Mr. Dorfman and it became clear that, in order to get the Teamster business, I would have to let Mr. Dorfman in on it.

A couple of days after this meeting we reached an agreement in Chicago and the trustees of the Central States Health and Welfare Fund awarded the contract to Old Security. For this I paid Mr. Kleindienst $250,000 in fees. This situation was the subject of a previous Subcommittee hearing in October 1977. I declined to testify at those proceedings; however, my former associate John Boden did testify regarding our meetings with Mr. Kleindienst.

During this period of time, it was arranged for Mr. Dorfman to get a percentage of any individual life insurance business I wrote on the Hotel Workers Union members. I was forced to agree to this because of Mr. Dorfman's close association to Joey Aiuppa of Chicago. Aiuppa and Accardo continue to exert great influence over the union and its President, Ed Hanley.

In closing my prepared remarks, I would like to say that I have had a long history of working in the area of life insurance and prepaid health plans as they relate to labor unions. These unions include the Teamsters, Laborers and Hotel Workers in all geographic areas of this country, with the exception of the Northwest. During this period I have dealt with numerous union officials and public figures, as well as organized crime members at the highest levels.

My statement to you today is that the organized crime element in this country has manipulated and controlled the prepaid health plans, pension plans, as well as life insurance coverage for the majority of the members of these three large International Unions. Based on my experience in this area, it is my personal opinion that organized criminal elements continue to completely dominate this area, giving them ready access to the many millions of dollars involved.

PART THREE

Fighting Back

9

Oversight Inquiry of the Department of Labor's Investigation of the Teamsters Central States Pension Fund

Made by the Permanent Subcommittee on Investigations of the Committee on Governmental Affairs, United States Senate, 1981.

I. Introduction

Background on Hearings on Pension Fund

The Department of Labor began an investigation of the Teamsters Union Central States Pension Fund in late 1975. The Senate Permanent Subcommittee on Investigations examined the Labor Department's inquiry in public hearings held on August 25 and 26 and September 29 and 30, 1980. Thirty-five witnesses testified and 1,049 pages of stenographic testimony were received. Executive session testimony was received as well. . . .

Section 3 of Senate Resolution 361 authorized the subcommittee to investigate "criminal or other improper practices or activities . . . in the field of labor-management relations."

The subcommittee also was authorized to investigate "syndicated or organized crime" which may operate in interstate commerce, and the operations of the Federal Government.

In terms of assets, the Central States pension fund was the 41st largest pension fund in the Nation and the second largest multi-employer trust organized under the Taft-Hartley Act.

Created in February of 1955, the fund--whose full name is Central States, Southeast and Southwest Areas Pension Fund--had about $2.2 billion in assets as of December 31, 1979. Its membership was comprised of about 500,000 active participants and retired pensioners. Employer contributions totaled about

$586 million a year. Pension payments paid out came to about $323 million a year.

Hoffa Disappearance Drew Attention to Fund

Management of the Central States fund was a source of controversy almost from its creation. Critics of the fund's trustees said far too much of the fund's assets were invested in risky real estate ventures.

It was also charged that the trustees were influenced by organized criminals in their investment decisions. Similarly, law enforcement officers said the loans themselves were frequently made to organized criminals or organized crime fronts.

On July 30, 1975, James R. Hoffa, former president of the Teamsters and a felon whose 13-year sentence had been commuted by President Nixon, disappeared. Hoffa was apparently kidnapped. After extensive investigation, law enforcement officials concluded that Hoffa had been murdered. Officials believed that certain organized crime figures had been involved. But insufficient evidence was developed. No one was ever charged. Hoffa's body was never found.

The mysterious disappearance of Jimmy Hoffa, and the nationwide search that followed, resulted in widespread news coverage. Much of the coverage focused on the details of the investigation, on Hoffa's activities the day he was presumably abducted, on the luncheon he was to have attended at the Machus Red Fox Restaurant outside Detroit with two Teamsters leaders with reputed mob ties, Anthony (Tony Pro) Provenzano, and Anthony (Tony Jack) Giacalone.

But also placed under the media spotlight were the allegations of corruption and high level criminal infiltration that had been leveled at the Teamsters Union for many years. With the focus on corruption and mob influence came added attention to the questionable practices of the Central States pension fund. For example, Hoffa's fraudulent use of the Central States pension fund had been one of the crimes that resulted in his going to prison. . . .

The Deming, N. Mex., Loan

The Hoffa case . . . was not the first instance of alleged wrongdoing related to the Teamsters Union and to its Central States fund. News report after news report surfaced in the sixties and in the seventies about corrupt practices in the Central States pension fund.

One such account, based on information from 8,000 pages of trial transcript and extensive interviews, appeared in the <u>Wall Street Journal</u> on July 24, 1975, 6 days before Hoffa disappeared.

The article, written by Jonathan Kwitny, recounted a Federal prosecution that charged seven men with conspiring to defraud the Central States pension fund in connection with more than $4 million in loans made to a company in Deming, N. Mex.

Involved in the case were several reputed organized crime figures with ties to the fund. Also indicted were Albert Matheson and Jack Sheetz, both management representatives on the board of trustees of the Central States pension fund.

The <u>Journal</u> told the story of how the fund poured millions of dollars into a factory in Deming in the form of loans, none of which were repaid and which reportedly benefited the defendants and their associates. It told of the extraordinary efforts Federal authorities had made to prosecute the case, how certain vital evidence had been ruled inadmissible in the trial, and how potential witnesses had been gunned down in gangland style.

The case had examples of how Central States pension fund loans could be diverted and used in ways having nothing to do with their stated purpose.

In bringing the case to trial, the Federal Government hoped . . . that convictions in the Deming, N. Mex., loan case would lead to other indictments and more convictions and, ultimately, that so much public and prosecutorial pressure on the Central States pension fund would result in a house cleaning of the fund and the selection of new, honest leadership.

But, on April 10, 1975, in a Chicago court room, after a 2-month trial and an investment by Federal authorities of millions of dollars and thousands of man-hours, the Federal Government lost the entire case. The defendants were acquitted on all counts.

However, as 1975 wore on, Federal authorities, discouraged by this setback, by their failure to solve the Hoffa case and their continued inability to bring reform to the Central States pension fund, did find something to be optimistic about.

Their optimism was based on approval in 1974 of sweeping and unprecedented pension plan reform legislation. The new law, just then being implemented, would, they hoped, provide the vehicle they needed to end corrupt and questionable practices at the Central States pension fund.

The new pension reform statute, the Employee Retirement Income Security Act of 1974, was known by its acronym, ERISA. The law gave Federal authorities the responsibility to oversee the operations of employee benefit plans and to go to court if there were no other means to rid the fund of mismanagement or corruption.

Equally important, the statute gave the Labor Department unprecedented access to and authority over employee benefit trusts such as the Central States pension fund. It was anticipated that this access to fund operations would be of historic importance to the Justice Department in mounting prosecutions against persons alleged to be guilty of criminal exploitation of pension funds.

Sensitive to the growing public and congressional furor over the Hoffa case and the many more Teamsters scandals, Federal officials planned to use ERISA's investigative provisions for the first time against the Central States pension fund.

At the same time that Jimmy Hoffa's mysterious disappearance was the top news story of the day--the summer of 1975--the Labor Department was preparing for a full-scale investigation of the Central States fund.

A team of experienced attorneys, accountants, auditors, and investigators-- known as the Special Investigations Staff--was being formed at the Labor Department to conduct the inquiry in coordination with prosecutors at the Department of Justice and with the Internal Revenue Service. Federal officials believed that this investigation would succeed where others failed. They based their hopes on new powers given them by the pension reform act, ERISA.

ERISA Was Historic Pension Reform Statute Passed in 1974

Signed into law by President Ford on Labor Day, September 2, 1974, the Employee Retirement Income Security Act, or ERISA, affected 35 million American workers and covered most types of employment benefit plans.

With ERISA, Congress wanted to guarantee that "minimum standards be provided assuring the equitable character of such plans and their financial soundness." Congress found ERISA was needed because there was a lack of information available to employees. There were also inadequate safeguards concerning the operation of employee benefit plans. Employees and their families had, in too many instances, been deprived of their benefits.

. . . The most important provisions of ERISA had to do with fiduciary standards. These standards were established to make certain that those people who conduct a plan's business did so for the exclusive benefit of plan participants.

A fiduciary is a person who occupies a position of trust, one who holds or controls property for the benefit of another person. Regarding employee benefit plans, ERISA defined a fiduciary as anyone who exercised discretionary control or authority over plan management or assets, anyone with discretionary authority or responsibility in the administration of a plan, or anyone who provided investment advice to a plan for compensation or had any authority or responsibility to do so.

According to ERISA, then, a fiduciary was a benefit plan trustee or officer, a director of a plan, a member of a plan's investment committee, and a person who helped select other fiduciaries, or a person who exercised certain discretionary authority with respect to the fund.

ERISA's fiduciary requirements said that . . . a fiduciary . . . must act in the interest of the plan participants and beneficiaries. He must manage the plan assets to minimize the risk of large losses. He must act in accordance with the documents governing the plan.

. . . The fiduciary must act with "the care, skill, prudence, and diligence under the circumstances then prevailing that a prudent man acting in a like capacity and familiar with such matters would use in the conduct of an enterprise of a like character with like aims." This standard has been called ERISA's "prudent man rule." . . .

A fiduciary who violates ERISA's standards is personally liable to make good any losses resulting from his failure to meet his responsibilities and return any profits realized from his actions. . . . Enforcement of fiduciary standards permits both civil and criminal penalties.

Laws Used by Justice Department in Prosecuting Fund Abuse

The Justice Department's interest in the area of employee pension and welfare plans was derived mainly from a number of criminal statutes. These are contained in title 18 of the U.S. Code.

These statutes include 18 U.S.C. 664, which makes it a felony to embezzle or convert the assets of an employee benefit plan; 18 U.S.C. 1954, which makes it a felony for anyone to offer, accept, or solicit anything of value to influence the operations of an employee benefit plan; and 18 U.S.C. 1027, which prohibits the filing of any false documents or statements with an employee benefit plan. The Welfare and Pension Plan Disclosure Act makes it a misdemeanor to willfully violate the reporting and disclosure provisions of that act.

In addition to the specific statutes, many other criminal laws including mail and wire fraud, interstate transportation of stolen and forged securities, and violations of the Federal racketeering statutes may also be applied in the course of investigation into the alleged misuse of benefit plans.

Testifying before the Investigations Subcommittee in 1980, senior Labor Department officials, including Secretary F. Ray Marshall and his Solicitor's Office attorneys, insisted that the Labor Department had very limited responsibility in the criminal area and that responsibility related only to ERISA's reporting and disclosure requirements.

Senator Nunn, who was then chairman of the subcommittee, said that, without the Labor Department diligently carrying out its role in detecting and investigating the alleged influence of organized crime on the fund, no thorough and responsible inquiry of these charges could be conducted.

However, at the 1980 hearing, Labor Department officers disputed that view, saying that since there were no criminal provisions cited in ERISA other than reporting and disclosure, the Department was not required to detect or investigate other possible criminal violations in conducting its inquiry under ERISA.

This conflict between the subcommittee members and senior Labor Department officials was never resolved during the hearings.

Organized Crime Influence Studied

The Department of Labor's first investigation of the Central States pension fund began in 1975 with the creation of the Special Investigations Staff (SIS) whose initial assignment was to make inquiry into the fund.

However, while no actual investigation of the fund took place until SIS got into the picture, the Labor Department did gather information about the fund before 1974 and, to an extent, did monitor the fund's activities.

On January 20, 1975, the Labor Department prepared a study summarizing information on the Central States pension fund's reported ties to organized crime. The study was written at the request of J. Vernon Ballard, the Deputy Administrator of Pension and Welfare Benefit Programs. . . .

The study said the Department had been collecting information on the fund since 1960. The Department had assisted other Federal agencies which were investigating the fund. "Very extensive" investigations of the fund were conducted by U.S. postal inspectors, the FBI and the Internal Revenue Service, the study said.

. . . "This information was made available to the Labor Department and is in our possession." . . .

The study said the lending policy of the fund had been since its creation in 1955 to make "very large real estate loans to high risk ventures." The fund had been criticized for this practice but continued to do it, even though parties to the loan transactions--recipients, brokers, attorneys, accountants--had been identified as being organized criminals or associates of organized criminals, the study said. One estimate, the study said, was that 30 percent of the fund's real estate loans were delinquent.

Information in the Labor Department's files showed eight recipients of fund real estate loans were now bankrupt. These entities were the Beverly Ridge

Estates, Los Angeles, $13 million loan; Kings Castle, Lake Tahoe, Nev., $10 million loan; Seville Hotel, Miami, $1.5 million loan; Henrose Hotel, Detroit, $1.6 million; Truck City, Detroit, $3.5 million; Riverside Hotel, Reno, Nev., $2.7 million; Savannah Inn and Country Club, Savannah, Ga., $2.5 million; and George Horvath of New York, $16.9 million. The study quoted a source as saying that these loans were still carried as loan balances by the fund and were listed as assets. The study pointed out that this list of bankrupt loans did not purport to be the complete aggregate of all the fund's bankrupt loans.

The study said that real estate loans from the fund traditionally had gone to high risk ventures in resort areas. During the late 1950s the loans tended to go to hotels and other ventures in and around Miami Beach. More recently, the study said, many loans were going to entities in and around southern California and Las Vegas. Most prominent of these loans, the study said, were a $50 million loan to the Rancho La Costa Resort and Country Club near San Diego; and a $150 million loan to the Penasquitas Corp., a land development enterprise in San Diego.

In addition, the study said, eight loans were made to hotels, casinos and other developments in Las Vegas--$8 million to the Landmark Hotel, $22 million to Circus Circus, $20 million to Caesar's Palace, $1.5 million to Chris Jo, Inc., $2.4 million to Carousel Casino, $3 million to Aladdin Hotel, $75 million to Argent Corp., representing both the Stardust and the Fremont Hotels, and $6 million to the Dunes.

Morris Shenker, identified by the study as a "well known St. Louis attorney who is a millionaire as a result of his dealings with the pension fund," was reported to own controlling interest in the Penasquitas Corp. and the Dunes.

According to the study, Shenker recently informed the Nevada Gaming Control Board in Las Vegas that the Central States pension fund promised to provide him $17 million. These additional funds were to enable Shenker to take complete ownership of the Dunes, the study said.

The study cited certain major prosecutions of persons who were connected to the Central States pension fund. Investigation revealed that a 10 percent finder's fee was paid on loans made by the fund, the study said.

The first major prosecution discussed by the study had to do with James R. Hoffa . . . .

The second major Federal prosecution cited by the study was that of Allen Dorfman, who was described as an insurance executive and a close friend of James Hoffa. Dorfman was convicted in New York of accepting a kickback on a loan made by the fund to George Horvath. This was the same George Horvath who, representing three corporations, received a $16.9 million loan from the fund for a real estate transaction. The loan was since declared bankrupt, according to the study. Dorfman served as a special consultant to the Central States pension fund until 1974.

The study said Allen Dorfman "was considered the primary mover of pension fund loans." While Hoffa was in prison, the study said, "it was well known that Dorfman carried out the wishes of Hoffa in directing the placement of loans from the fund."

Following his conviction, Dorfman served 1 year in prison. The study said Dorfman was not currently directly associated with the fund but that he still had a say in the fund's lending activities. Alvin Baron, a former assistant to Dorfman in fund matters, was currently in charge of the fund's lending policy, the study said.

A third major prosecution related to the Central States pension fund in the late 1960s, the study said, involved many defendants with organized crime connections. A finder's fee was a central issue in the case, as was a $1 million loan to the Mid City Development Corp. of Detroit.

The case revealed a dispute between organized criminals in Pittsburgh and New York over which faction would receive the finder's fee. Several defendants were acquitted, but two, Sam Berger and James (Jimmy Doyle) Plumeri, were convicted. Plumeri was later slain in a gangland style killing, the study said.

Allen Robert Glick was a mystery man in the pension fund's lending program. . . . Only 32 years old, Glick had come out of nowhere and in 5 years had taken over the Stardust and Fremont Hotels and the Beverly Ridge Estates and controlled property worth more than $100 million, the report said, adding, "Little is known of his background."

Glick and Morris Shenker had become the principal recipients of Central States pension fund loans in recent years, the study said. The study said Shenker was Jimmy Hoffa's attorney in appeals of his convictions . . . and that Shenker represented many other well known defendants.

The study said Morris Shenker became a partner with Irvin J. Kahn several years earlier in land development in San Diego. The fund loaned Shenker and Kahn $150 million for the Penasquitas venture in San Diego, the study said, explaining that Shenker became the sole stockholder in this project when Kahn died.

The study said Shenker was presently spending most of his time planning for the expansion of the Dunes Hotel in Las Vegas, a project which he expected to finance with a $6 million already executed loan from the fund and with an anticipated new loan from the fund of $17 million.

Late in 1974, in proceedings of the Nevada Gaming Control Board, charges were made that Shenker was associated with persons of questionable repute. The study said these associations raised questions about Shenker's suitability to operate a casino in Las Vegas. . . .

The study recommended that investigation of the Central States pension fund by the Labor Department have as its goal the placing of the fund in receivership.

The study said receivership was the only vehicle that would safeguard the funds and insure that its money was managed in such a way as to benefit the Teamsters members and their families. "It is obvious," the study said, "that the persons responsible for [the fund's] administration in the past 15 years have consistently breached their fiduciary responsibilities, and they will continue to do so in the future unless the Federal Government intervenes." . . .

The December 11, 1975, Briefing by James Hutchinson

In late 1975, amid growing reports of widespread corruption in the Teamsters Central States pension fund, the Senate Permanent Subcommittee on Investigations considered beginning an inquiry into the fund.

At the same time, the Senate itself considered a resolution offered by Senator Robert P. Griffin of Michigan to create a select committee to look into the national problem of labor-management racketeering, including allegations of wrongdoing in the Central States pension fund.

Meanwhile, the Department of Labor was mounting what promised to be a full-scale investigation of Central States benefit plans and the benefit plans of other unions. The Labor Department investigation would be the first ever undertaken under the recently passed pension reform act, ERISA, the Employee Retirement Income Security Act.

To discuss what its own course of action should be, to evaluate Senator Griffin's proposal and to receive a briefing on the Labor Department's investigation, the Investigations Subcommittee met in executive session on December 21, 1975. Also invited to attend were Senator Griffin and Senator Harrison Williams of New Jersey, chairman of the Labor and Human Resources Committee. Senator Griffin attended but Senator Williams, who was out of town, could not.

The subcommittee was briefed on the Labor Department investigation by James D. Hutchinson, Administrator of Pension and Welfare Benefit Programs in the Department. Hutchinson had general supervisory and policy authority over pension reform programs in the Labor Department.

Hutchinson's responsibility under ERISA included enforcement authority over the fiduciary standards of the new law. Allegations that the trustees of the Teamsters Central States pension fund had violated their fiduciary trust were his responsibility to look into. . . .

In light of the comprehensive investigation the Labor Department was launching, Hutchinson said, he hoped the subcommittee would take into account the "inherent" problems that could arise if a concurrent Senate inquiry were begun into the same Central States pension fund.

These problems, he said, included delays, the possible granting of immunity to each other's witnesses and conflicts between the government and the legislative branch. . . .

Hutchinson went on to describe how the Labor Department decided to conduct this investigation and what kind of investigation it would be. . . .

Because of ERISA, he said, there were standards of performance that benefit plan fiduciaries had to meet. It was the department's responsibility, he said, to insist that the standards were satisfied.

During the summer of 1975, Hutchinson said, the Labor Department made an analysis of a variety of public charges against the fund. Some of these allegations were long standing, he said, adding that the pre-ERISA statute . . . did not give the department sufficient tools to protect workers' pension plans. . . .

. . . [W]hat ERISA promised, was "a national overall review" of the fund. ERISA offered the Government new tools it did not have before. . . .

Hutchinson said he hoped this provision would enable the Labor Department, for the first time, to seek reform of a pension fund's day-to-day operations when alleged abuses were proven.

In June of 1975, Hutchinson discussed this provision of ERISA with Labor Secretary John T. Dunlop. It would require a major commitment of Department resources to carry out this ERISA provision, Hutchinson said, and he felt the department should either make the commitment or do nothing. . . .

The person selected to be the first Director of SIS was Lawrence Lippe, an attorney with 20 years of experience in Justice Department investigations, having served as an Assistant Chief of the Fraud Section and an Assistant U.S. Attorney for the District of Columbia.

Selecting a staff of auditors, accountants, investigators, and attorneys to serve under Lippe was also a painstaking process, Hutchinson said. The Special Investigations Staff was funded for 20 persons now and 12 to 15 persons actually at work at the moment.

Hutchinson said he could not predict how large the SIS would become. He did say the investigation of the Central States fund could be completed in a matter of months or could last years.

Hutchinson said that during the summer of 1975 the Department gathered from its own files, from the Justice Department and from IRS information related to the Central States pension fund.

Hutchinson sent a directive to the 25 Labor Department field offices asking them to send back information on the fund. This was a massive amount of information. He said the documents piled on top of one another rose 50 feet in the air.

To read and collate this data, he said, the Department assigned six accountants and auditors fulltime and several attorneys from the Solicitor's Office. This task was close to completion. . . .

. . . [T]he Labor Department set out to assure good cooperative work relationships with the Justice Department and the IRS.

Hutchinson, whose previous job was at the Justice Department where he was Assistant Deputy Attorney General, said the Labor Department had formalized its operating procedures with Justice and IRS for the fund investigation. . . .

Hutchinson gave the subcommittee a copy of a December 1, 1975, memorandum of understanding agreed to by Labor and Justice. Signed by Deputy Attorney General Harold Tyler and Labor Secretary Dunlop, the three-page document attested to the creation of an Interdepartmental Policy Committee whose objectives would be to avoid conflicting purposes and duplication as the investigation went forward.*

The memorandum of understanding said responsibility for prosecuting criminal violations would be with the Justice Department. Labor would litigate civil cases. The Interdepartmental Policy Committee would "review such questions as when and where particular proceedings should be initiated and whether in a given case civil or criminal cases should be brought."

The Committee would decide whether civil or criminal proceedings should be initiated in those instances in which both opportunities were available to the Government, the memorandum of understanding said.

The Central States investigating team, currently comprised of Labor Department attorneys and investigators, would be expanded by the addition of Justice Department lawyers. . . .

. . . [T]he SIS Director, Lawrence Lippe, would have operational control of the investigation but that Lippe was to consult with the Justice Department attorneys serving on his staff. . . .

In his briefing of the subcommitttee, Hutchinson discussed how SIS, working within the agreements reached in the memorandum of understanding, would handle evidence of criminal behavior that was developed in the investigation.

Hutchinson said Labor Department officials had assured the Justice Department that when matters of a criminal potential came up, Justice would be

---

*The Labor Department's representatives on the Committee would be Hutchinson and the Department's Solicitor, William J. Kilberg, Representing Justice would be Rex E. Lee, Assistant Attorney General for the Civil Division; Richard L. Thornburgh, Assistant Attorney General for the Criminal Division; and Samuel K. Skinner, U.S. attorney for the Northern District of Illinois, which included Chicago, headquarters of the Central States pension fund.

informed "of those leads and indeed we will probably pursue the investigation to completion, and then refer it to them for litigation."

These words by Hutchinson are emphasized because they have significance as the investigations subcommittee's hearings resumed in 1980, 5 years later. As will be noted later in this report, several Labor Department witnesses, including the Secretary, F. Ray Marshall, and his Associate Solicitor, Monica Gallagher, denied that their department had any responsibility to pursue investigative leads of a criminal nature. . . .

. . . [I]n the subcommittee's 1980 hearings, it was shown that Labor Department investigators were instructed not to alert the Justice Department when the names of organized crime figures were identified with the Central States fund transactions, except in those instances in which the reputed organized crime figures were found to have violated a provision of ERISA. . . .

. . . As will be noted in this report . . . [b]y late 1978, SIS personnel were under instructions to not even discuss the Central States pension fund case with the Justice Department. . . .

When Hutchinson's briefing was completed, he was excused from the hearing room. Senators continued their discussion. There was a consensus that Hutchinson had been an articulate, effective representative of the Labor Department and the feeling that the department's investigation was, at this stage, being carefully and thoroughly planned. . . .

On March 25, 1976, the subcommittee, meeting in executive session, decided against conducting its own investigation of the Teamsters Central States pension fund. The subcommittee felt it would duplicate the work of the Labor Department and might otherwise adversely affect the Department's inquiry. The subcommittee did vote to monitor the progress of the Labor Department's investigation of the pension fund. . . .

SIS Created in Labor Department in December of 1975

The Special Investigations Staff (SIS) was created in the Department of Labor in December of 1975. . . .

From the very start, SIS faced an uphill battle to carry out its mandate. . . . Virtually every procedure, every objective laid down by Hutchinson in his briefing to this subcommittee was thrown out.

The Internal Revenue Service, whose cooperation Hutchinson had called essential and necessary if the inquiry was to succeed, declined to join the Labor Department inquiry. IRS then went off on its own, revoking the Central States pension fund's tax exempt status without notifying SIS beforehand.

The result was disarray, confusion, the loss of valuable investigative time and a clear signal to the pension fund lawyers that the Government was incapable of mounting a concerted investigation. Fund lawyers exploited the Government's lack of organization, converting the fund's apparent weakness--the loss of the tax exemption--into its strength in negotiations with Federal authorities.

Gradually, vital investigative tools were stripped from SIS. Taken from SIS were its ability to conduct planned investigations in the field, its subpoena authority, its independent status as an investigative unit.

Eventually, SIS, which was supposed to work in close harmony with the Justice Department, was under instructions from the Solicitor's Office not to share investigative leads with the Criminal Division of Justice. Inevitably, SIS became an investigative support arm for the Solicitor's Office.

The SIS Director, Lawrence Lippe, resigned in frustration.

The last straw in the misfortune that befell SIS was the appointment in 1977, following Lippe's resignation, of Norman E. Perkins as its chief. During the 2 1/2 years he led SIS, Perkins worked under the impression that the Labor Department had made a secret agreement with the pension fund in which the Department promised it would not investigate certain areas of alleged abuse, including criminal wrongdoing.

Labor Secretary F. Ray Marshall and his senior aides in the Solicitor's office denied that any such agreement existed. Unfortunately, they neglected to tell the man heading up the investigation.

Finally, on May 5, 1980, SIS was abolished.

II. Problems with the Internal Revenue Service

IRS Would Not Coordinate Its Investigation with Labor

. . . GAO [General Accounting Office] found, IRS officials were opposed to Labor's entrance into the general area of the fund investigation and they told the pension fund that the Labor Department would not be a part of IRS's audit. . . .

Hutchinson said that without IRS support, his concept of a unified investigation of the fund was destined to fail. The wisdom of that judgment was seen in the next decision IRS made.

IRS Revoked Fund's Tax Exempt Status

The pension fund enjoyed tax exempt status. On June 25, 1976, IRS revoked that status. IRS took this action without giving advance notice to the Labor Department, the Justice Department or the fund. The revocation was retroactive to February of 1965.

The IRS explanation for its action was that the tax exempt status was revoked because the fund was not operating for the exclusive benefit of plan beneficiaries and the investment policies and practices of the fund were imprudent.

GAO said the IRS revocation surprised the Labor and Justice Departments and fund officials as well. The IRS action, GAO said, "had an immediate and devastating effect" on the fund's financial operations because some of the 16,000 employees withheld their contributions and others threatened to place the money in escrow accounts.

Daniel J. Shannon, who was then executive director of the fund, said that six banks which were handling several hundred million dollars in fund assets began to have doubts about the legality of their investing the fund's money. Shannon said this resulted in a reduced return on investments.

Even IRS recognized that its revocation action could have grave consequences for the fund. GAO said IRS officials knew that had the provisions of the retroactive revocation been fully implemented, the fund's 500,000 participants and beneficiaries could have been required to pay taxes on past returns.

Not only did the revocation come as a surprise to Labor and Justice Department officials, but also they reportedly had both been assured earlier by IRS that no such action would be taken. According to GAO, IRS told the Labor Department in January of 1976 that "there is no way the fund will be disqualified." . . .

IRS tried to cushion the severe consequences of its action. Beginning on July 2, 1976, IRS granted the fund a series of relief measures removing the retroactive features of the revocation.

IRS Entered Separate Negotiations with Fund

Next, IRS, against the wishes of the Labor Department, negotiated with the pension fund a series of actions which the fund trustees would take in managing assets and payments benefits.

The Labor Department protested the IRS's entering into negotiations with the fund. Labor Department officials felt that IRS's acceptance of preliminary or partial reforms could bind the entire Government and jeopardize the Labor Department's investigation and its negotiations with the fund.

Having two separate Government agencies negotiating with the fund was precisely the kind of situation which James Hutchinson, in setting up the investigation, had wished to avoid.

Accordingly, on August 17, 1976, Hutchinson wrote to IRS to say that if the Service accepted proposed reforms by the fund at that time it would undermine the Labor Department inquiry. . . .

In response to Hutchinson, IRS changed its policy. Although a year of hoped-for cooperation had been lost, the Service now agreed to coordinate further actions with the Labor Department.

Lippe Testified on Revocation of Tax Status

Lawrence Lippe, the first Director of SIS, testified that no one had ever given him a satisfactory explanation of why IRS refused to participate in a joint investigation of the pension fund with the Labor Department. . . .

IRS Assistant Commissioner Alvin D. Lurie, explained to him why the Service's policy had changed so abruptly and why the revocation order went in such a short time from an option under consideration to a reality, Lippe said.

Lippe . . . testified that the Assistant Commissioner told him the revocation order came through because of pressure from two points in Washington--Congress and the Internal Revenue Commissioner, Donald Alexander. . . .

The Usery Speech to Teamsters Convention

Former SIS Deputy Director Lester Seidel said he thought the event that triggered the IRS decision to revoke the Central States pension fund tax exemption was the speech that Secretary Usery made at the Aladdin Hotel in Las Vegas before the international convention of the leadership of the Teamsters Union on June 14, 1976. The revocation order was given by IRS 11 days later--on June 25. At this convention, held every 5 years, the Teamsters leaders elected their international president and other executives. In the speech, Usery said:

Let me assure you that even though I don't have a Teamsters card, I belong to this club because I believe in it.

It was Seidel's view that this remark--and other statements Usery made in Las Vegas--spent the patience of Internal Revenue Commissioner Alexander, who personally issued the order to revoke, feeling the Labor Department, under Usery, could not be counted on to approach the Teamsters investigation in a vigorous, objective manner.

Usery's comments ignited a nationwide uproar. Commenting editorially, the New York Times said:

> In fact, the only puzzle in Las Vegas was whatever possessed Secretary of Labor W.J. Usery, Jr., to go to the convention and declare, "I belong to this club because I believe in it," when the Department he heads was conducting an investigation of that very same pension fund.

> . . . IRS officials strenuously denied the idea that the Usery speech caused IRS headquarters to seek immediate revocation of the fund's tax exempt status. . . .

Revocation May Have Been Too Strong a Response

During the 1980 hearing Senator Nunn said the revocation action was such a powerful weapon that IRS was reluctant to use it. It punished not only the fund trustees but the employers and the beneficiaries, both of whom would have lost tax benefits stemming from their participation in the fund, Senator Nunn said, noting:

> It is like going after an infantry platoon with an atomic weapon. Nobody thinks you are going to use it . . . [I]t doesn't have the credibility.

That was why, Senator Nunn said, it would have made more sense to have a less severe tool--such as a written agreement enforceable by a court--that would have given the Government the opportunity to demand compliance with proposed reforms. Then the threat of resorting to "that ultimate sanction"-- revocation--would not have been needed, he said.

Having used the revocation weapon, IRS then found itself in the position of "scrambling around trying to find a way out of it," Senator Nunn said. For that reason, he said, a court-enforced consent decree would have been more effective in bringing about reform of the fund.

Revocation Said to Bring "Worthwhile Changes"

Assistant Commissioner Winborne did not disagree with the assertion that the consent decree approach would have been preferable to revocation.

But he did say that he and his colleagues at IRS thought the revocation weapon "really caused some very worthwhile changes in the fund that had not [previously] been put into effect." . . .

Charles Miriani, the IRS Regional Commissioner in Chicago and, reportedly, the man who made the decision, on his own, to revoke the tax status, recalled the difficult position the pension fund had put IRS in with its poor management of fund assets. . . .

Miriani said that from what he knew of the Labor Department's investigation it would be some time before the Department would have been in a position to take strong action to protect the fund's assets. But the need for action was immediate, Miriani said, asserting, "We needed to do something and to do something quick." Tax status revocation, he said, was the "quickest action" and "it was the only action." . . .

Role of IRS Washington Office Was Discussed

. . . Miriani testified that he had no idea the IRS revocation action would have a negative impact on the Labor Department's investigation. He said he heard that such a negative impact had occurred for the first time in testimony given at the subcommittee hearing. . . .

Miriani's testimony differed from the testimony of witnesses from the General Accounting Office and the Labor Department.

While Miriani said he never thought for a moment the revocation would have an adverse effect on the Labor Department's case, GAO and Labor Department officials testified that the revocation had been especially detrimental. . . .

Disclosure Rules Did Not Stop Dissemination of Information

IRS used the disclosure provisions of the tax code to justify the decision not to tell the Labor Department that it planned to revoke the fund's tax exempt status.

But, Senator Nunn pointed out that in a 1979 subcommittee hearing the IRS maintained in its defense of the disclosure provisions of the Tax Reform Act of 1976 that prior to its enactment there had been "loose dissemination" of tax information and that the new Tax Reform Act of 1976 was needed to tighten such distribution and establish strict procedures on the release of tax information. Thus, IRS claimed that prior to January 1977, the effective date of the 1976 Tax Reform Act, dissemination of information between IRS and other Government agencies was extremely loose. Apparently, in the 1979 hearing concerning the Teamsters investigation IRS had altered its opinion and decided that the pre-1977 disclosure laws were tight enough to even prevent disclosure to the Labor Department of their intent to revoke the tax exempt status of the Teamsters fund.

IRS's refusal to tell the Labor Department that it planned to revoke the fund's tax status showed that IRS was selectively adhering to a strict interpretation of disclosure procedures even before the Tax Reform Act of 1976 was passed, Senator Nunn said.

Labor Department Must Now Concur in Union Trust Revocations

Senator Percy was puzzled as to how the disclosure law could possibly have been construed to prohibit IRS from telling the Labor Department that it intended to revoke the pension fund's tax exemption. Was the IRS actually saying that to have merely notified the Labor Department would have constituted the illegal disclosure of tax information?

That was exactly what IRS was saying, according to Lester Stein, Deputy Chief Counsel of IRS. In the broadest interpretation of the law, which was the interpretation IRS made, to tell the Labor Department of the intention to revoke a tax exemption would have been illegal, Stein said. . . .

Subcommittee chief counsel Marty Steinberg pointed out to the IRS witnesses that the subcommittee had obtained copies of many memoranda in which officials of the Service and the Labor Department discussed their pension fund investigation. . . .

Finally, after imprecise responses, Charles Miriani admitted that IRS had discussed with the Labor Department matters relating to its investigation of the fund and that these discussions took place prior to revocation. . . .

III. Early Stages of SIS Investigation of Fund

Records Were Requested, Not Supoenaed

Along with the problems caused by the IRS go-it-alone attitude and the IRS decision to revoke the pension fund's tax exemption, other significant developments occurred in 1976, the first year of the SIS investigation of the pension fund.

One such development was a policy the department implemented in which it decided that SIS would not subpoena records from the Central States pension fund. Instead, it would request that the fund give them up voluntarily.

ERISA gave the Labor Department the power to use administrative subpoenas to obtain pertinent records. Choosing not to exercise that power, the Department directed SIS to ask the fund for them. For its part, the fund agreed to turn over the desired records upon request. Thus, the investigation came to depend for its success on the cooperation of its target. . . .

SIS Directed To Investigate Real Estate Only

According to GAO, SIS investigators turned up widespread instances of alleged abuse and fiduciary violations in the fund's activities. This information developed from the fund's books and records included alleged breaches of fiduciary trust as described in ERISA.

Records indicated that loans had been made to companies on the verge of bankruptcy. Additional loans were made to borrowers who had been delinquent in the past. Loans were found to have been given to borrowers who used the money to pay interest on other loans from the fund and the fund recorded this return as interest income. SIS discovered the fund using inadequate controls over rental income. . . .

. . . SIS investigators wanted to go ahead with a full scale audit and more inquiry. But SIS's plans were vetoed by the Labor Department. The Department ruled that the inquiry be narrowed to only one area, the fund's real estate mortgage and collateral loans.

The department focused exclusively on real estate because of the large amounts of money involved--close to a billion dollars--and because the single overriding objective the Department had set in the investigation was to "protect and preserve the fund's assets."

GAO was critical of the Labor Department in making this its only objective, saying:

> Labor's approach ignored other areas of alleged abuse and mismanagement of the fund's operations by the former trustees and left unresolved questions of potential civil and criminal violations and alleged mismanagement raised by its own investigators.

. . .

SIS Did Not Receive Full Staff Complement

It was the view of the General Accounting Office that SIS was never given sufficient employee strength. The original concept of SIS required a staff complement of 45. That was the required number the Labor Department requested in budget proposals submitted to the Office of Management and Budget and to Congress. In August 1976, SIS was authorized 45 positions.

SIS never came near its authorized hire of 45. Its permanent staff never numbered more than 28. . . .

Security was very questionable in the conference room. Teamsters fund employees could walk in and out of the room at their leisure. Locks on the SIS files were easy to pry open. What security the locked files provided was compromised when someone left the keys on the cabinets overnight. . . .

IV. SIS Was Ordered To Stop Third Party Investigation

Third Party Investigation Planned by SIS

In 1976, the fund's investment totaled about $1.4 billion. Of this amount, $902 million was real estate and collateral loans, consisting of 500 loans made to 300 borrowers. SIS set out to examine 82 of these loans, with a total value of $518 million. The overwhelming majority of the loaned funds--$425 million of the $518 million--went to seven entities, which were largely controlled by Morris Shenker, Allen Robert Glick, and Alvin Malnik. Law enforcement officials believe all three have organized crime connections.

SIS found that on many loans the trustees had not followed basic safeguards that a prudent lender would have. The trustees approved loans without knowing fundamental information about the borrower. Then, once the loans were made, the trustees did not monitor them. Nor did the trustees exercise rights over the borrowers as vested in the fund by the terms of the loan contracts.

SIS spent about 1 year reviewing the 82 loans from documents made available to them at the fund offices in Chicago. But this was only the first step in what SIS hoped would be a thorough review of the loans. What remained to be done was what investigators believed was an equally important aspect of the review of the loans--third party investigation.

Third party investigation is that phase in any case when investigators move beyond the original records. For example, there is a limit to what can be learned from studying the contract of a given loan, reading the minutes of the trustees meeting when they approved the loan and interviewing trustees and fund officials about their recollections of why the loan was made. The next step is to go into the field and interview the borrower and other persons who have knowledge of the loan and the project which the loan financed and obtain records about their operations. That is third party investigation.

It is important to note that third party investigation is essential in the preparation for both civil as well as criminal cases.

According to GAO, Lawrence Lippe, the SIS Director, was ready late in 1976 to send his men into the field to begin third party investigations. . . .

. . . Especially productive was the inquiry into the Morris Shenker grouping of loans that demonstrated the highly questionable $40 million loan commitment the pension fund had made to Shenker on behalf of the Dunes Hotel and Casino in Las Vegas. . . .

Third Party Investigation Stopped

. . . But third party investigation by SIS was stopped by the Solicitor's Office and other senior Labor Department officials. Their decision was made in December 1976 and was frequently reasserted from then on. In December 1976 it became Department policy to have SIS prepare exclusively for the filing of a civil suit against the fund's trustees. Preparation for the civil suit eclipsed all other SIS activity.

Secretary Marshall defended this policy in his 1980 appearance before the subcommittee. His primary concern, he said, was to preserve and protect the fund's assets. Senator Nunn pointed out that in the proper preparation for civil cases third party investigation was also required.

Reviewing SIS files and records in the Solicitor's Office of the Labor Department, GAO accumulated documentation revealing how the Department's new civil litigative strategy had completely cut off Lippe's hoped-for third party investigation.

SIS and Solicitor's Office files showed that Lippe prepared a list of 80 third parties he wanted interviewed and who were to give sworn depositions and were to be subpoenaed to produce records in connection with 19 targeted loans. But, GAO said, only 14 of the 80 third parties actually gave depositions or were subpoenaed.

GAO said many of the depositions and subpoenas were dated in September and October 1977. By this time the civil litigative strategy was in full force and SIS operations were redirected to work in support of the civil case and under the supervision of the Solicitor's Office.

By that time, SIS's original mission was canceled. Morale was sinking at SIS. Lippe's deputy, Lester Seidel, quit in September. Lippe resigned in October. Serious disputes and bureaucratic infighting broke out within SIS and between SIS and the Solicitor's Office.

The demise of the third party investigation was the end of SIS as originally organized. It also signaled trouble ahead in the Labor Department's ability to assure the public and the Congress that it was capable of conducting a thorough investigation of the Teamsters Central States pension fund. . . .

In July 1977, Labor Secretary Marshall testified before the investigations subcommittee. He said that the department's investigation of the pension fund was shifting from a review of fund records to a search for evidence in the possession of third parties.

In the 1980 hearings, evidence was developed that clearly demonstrated that third party investigation was not allowed to go forward, that third party inquiry had actually been cut short even before Marshall's July 1977 appearance before the subcommittee. . . .

Both Civil and Criminal Cases Require Third Party Inquiry

In the fall of 1976, SIS, under Director Lawrence Lippe, was embarking on its planned third party investigation, according to Lippe's Deputy, Lester Seidel. . . .

Seidel said the service of the subpoenas . . . was essential to successful inquiry, whether it was leading to civil or criminal cases. To demonstrate this point, he cited an investigation SIS wanted to make of a loan of some $20 million from the pension fund to Argent Corp. Representing Argent was Allen Robert Glick, who wanted the money for improvements to the Stardust and Fremont hotel-casinos in Las Vegas.

To borrow this money, the borrower needed about 10 percent of the principal, Seidel said. A corporation called G&H, which was to supervise the general contractor, was paid 10 percent of the construction loan. Seidel said the G&H Corp. was a corporation in name only and didn't do anything to earn its fees. . . .

Altogether, the Stardust-Fremont loan raised more questions than it answered and, Seidel said, third party investigation was called for quickly. Of additional significance was information SIS had indicating that Allen Robert Glick, a reputed front for crime syndicates, was actually representing a Chicago organized criminal who wished to conceal his ownership of several Las Vegas properties, . . .

Seidel said that third party investigation into the Stardust-Fremont loan was called for whether the end result of the inquiry was civil or criminal. It was his view that what mattered was that the investigation be conducted, the third parties deposed, subpoenas served and vital documentation obtained. Once the third party investigation was completed, it could then be decided what use to make of the information.

However, third party investigation on the Stardust-Fremont casinos loan was called off, just as other third party investigations into the other loan groups were sidetracked, Seidel said. . . .

. . . Monica Gallagher and Steven Sacher, representing the Solicitor's Office, "had assumed control of any potential litigation" and would control all further investigation. Ryan said it was clear that SIS would no longer be allowed to do anything of consequence without the permission of the Solicitor's Office.

Lawrence Lippe . . . testified as to how and when he was ordered to halt third party investigations.

The orders were from Steven J. Sacher, the associate solicitor, and William J. Chadwick, the administrator of pension and welfare benefit programs.

Lippe said Sacher and Chadwick met with Lester Seidel and him in mid-December 1976 and gave them the word. SIS was to abandon third party investigations and devote itself exclusively to supporting the Solicitor's Office. . . .

Chadwick, who, as successor to James D. Hutchinson, was Lippe's boss, and Steven Sacher listened while the SIS Director protested their directions. . . .

SIS personnel learned of the changes in how they were to proceed from the Solicitor's Office, and frequently, the information came to them from Monica Gallagher, an attorney who became associate solicitor in November 1977 and who took over operational control of SIS that year.

There were sharp differences between Monica Gallagher and SIS as to how best to conduct the pension fund investigation. . . .

Mrs. Gallagher's intention was to create the illusion of a criminal investigation, an exercise with high visibility, something that could be cited as evidence that the Labor Department was making progress in developing information of a criminal nature. . . .

Lloyd F. Ryan, Jr., an attorney in the SIS organization, was with Lawrence Lippe in the February 1977 meeting . . . when Monica Gallagher put forward her plan to obtain depositions from persons whose names she selected from the minutes of the trustee's meetings.

Ryan's recollection of the meeting was that Monica Gallagher and [another] . . . convened it for the purpose of fashioning a response to demands from Congress that the Teamsters Central States fund investigation make more progress. Ryan said Gallagher did most of the talking. "She recommended that in response to congressional interest, we should put on a quick, high visibility show to get Congress off our back," . . . Ryan added, "I understood the full substance of her remarks to advocate that the Department of Labor put on a false show of activity for the sole purpose of deceiving Congress concerning the progress of the Central States pension fund investigation." . . .

Following the February meeting, the next conference was held the afternoon of Wednesday, April 13, 1977. Attending were Monica Gallagher; Thomas J. Bauch, a consultant to the Labor Department; and four SIS employees, Lawrence Lippe, the director; Lester Seidel, his deputy; Lloyd F. Ryan, Jr., an attorney; and Salvatore A. Barbatano, an attorney. . . .

Barbatano's memorandum indicated that Monica Gallagher announced at the meeting that the . . . Labor Department was to take no further action on investigative leads of a criminal nature. These leads should be referred to the Justice Department, Gallagher was quoted as saying. Gallagher said SIS was not to be involved in joint Labor-Justice investigation . . .

It was Mrs. Gallagher's intention . . . to draw up a list of persons associated with the pension fund and have them interviewed in sworn depositions taken by SIS. The depositions would be referred to the Justice Department, as evidence that the Labor Department had fulfilled its obligation to come up with information of a criminal nature and send it to Federal prosecutors.

Monica Gallagher presented the SIS men with the names of 81 persons. She wanted depositions taken from these subjects, Barbatano recalled . . . and she wanted this action taken without any preliminary investigation. . . .

In his affidavit, Barbatano recalled . . . the impact of Monica Gallagher's instructions on the SIS inquiry. . . .

> The practical effect of this decision by the Department of Labor was the cessation of the Central States fund investigation. During the remaining 2 1/2 months of my employment with SIS, there was, to my knowledge, no meaningful investigative effort conducted by anyone on behalf of the Department of Labor with respect to the Central States pension fund.

Barbatano's affidavit said the dispute resulted in "the complete frustration and subversion of the investigation of the Teamsters Central States pension fund. This bureaucratic wrangling has done an enormous disservice to the government and the public. It has, in effect, perpetuated the looting and irreparable depletion of a $2 billion pension fund. There are many victims of the scenario; but those suffering the greatest injustice are the Teamsters Union members who will be deprived of pension benefits because the Labor Department failed in its mission." . . .

Edward F. Shevlin, an SIS investigator, testified that he learned of Monica Gallagher's decision to obtain sworn depositions from 81 persons as an alternative to conducting the third party investigations in the spring of 1977. Shevlin said Gallagher wanted to begin a 60 to 90 day "high visibility investigation. . . . "

Shevlin said he warned Lawrence Lippe that if SIS carried out Gallagher's directive it would ruin hopes that in the future a procedurally sound investigation by the Justice Department might succeed.

A meeting was held on May 4, 1977. . . .

Shevlin said the SIS people told Mrs. Gallagher that SIS did not have sufficient information and substantive data on many of the 81 subjects. . . . Mrs. Gallagher did not agree. It was her view that many of the persons SIS planned to obtain depositions from were familiar figures already under investigation. Shevlin said Mrs. Gallagher claimed to have come up with her list of 81 names in about 3 hours' time.

One of the persons on Gallagher's list was Richard Kleindienst, the former Attorney General. Here is what Shevlin recalled Monica Gallagher said about how to handle the Kleindienst deposition:

She said that she would ask him how much money he offered as a bribe in connection with a certain loan. [Lester] Seidel pointed out that the loan she had reference to had never been disbursed. She commented she would ask him [Kleindienst] if he thought the loan would have been approved if he, Kleindienst, offered more bribe money. It was incredulous. I could hardly believe my ears. I never heard anything quite so professionally irresponsible concerning an approach to a witness.

. . .

The "High Visibility Road Show" Allegation

One of her major concerns about the subcommittee's investigation, Monica Gallagher testified, was the frequency with which witnesses had taken out of context remarks she had made and completely misconstrued her intent.

Mrs. Gallagher said this had happened to her comments about cooperation with the Justice Department. And, she said, it happened again in statements she had made about the so-called high visibility road show investigative effort allegedly created to appease Congress.

It was "totally wrong and misleading" to say--as witnesses from SIS said-- that she had tried to set up a high profile investigation to deceive Congress into thinking the Labor Department was making criminal inquiry, Gallagher testified.

What actually happened, she said, was that, in the spring of 1977, when the holdover trustees had agreed to resign and an independent assets manager was taking over investments, Secretary Marshall wanted to consider new directions for the investigation.

Gallagher said the "department's highest officials" had concluded that SIS lacked an "overall investigative plan" and was, therefore, ill-prepared to make the kind of examination needed regarding loans the pension fund had made.

Lawrence Lippe was told to come up with alternative proposals as to how the SIS investigation could be redirected, Gallagher said. Lippe either did not make any proposals or his proposals were unsatisfactory, Gallagher said. In any event, she said, other proposals were invited.

A meeting was held attended by Steven Sacher, Eamon Kelly and herself, Gallagher said. Sacher, the Associate Solicitor, was her boss. Kelly was a consultant to the Labor Department who worked directly for Secretary Marshall on matters related to the Teamsters Central States investigation.

At this meeting, Gallagher said, it was decided that the department needed to quickly "survey and categorize the other asset management activities so as to identify those meriting further immediate attention."

One approach to making such an assessment, Gallagher said, was to take administrative depositions from persons not associated with the fund but who would have firsthand knowledge about fund loans.

Gallagher was given the assignment of preparing a list of persons who, in giving sworn depositions, could make "some better informed judgments" about which loans warranted investigation, she said. She prepared such a list. It had 81 names on it. . . .

Background on How List of 81 Names Was Conceived

Monica Gallagher expressed no doubts about her strategy to have SIS obtain depositions from 81 persons whose names she had culled from the minutes of the trustees' meetings. She reportedly selected the names after one reading of the minutes. Lippe and other SIS personnel objected, saying they should not have been directed to interview these 81 persons without the opportunity to do more investigation.

Senator Nunn asked Gallagher if she still thought her idea was a good one. She replied, "I am not an investigator. If I had been running this investigation from the outset, I would have tried to become an investigator. . . ."

Mrs. Gallagher, who, before joining the Labor Department, was an attorney in the Civil Rights Division of the Justice Department, an instructor at the Georgetown University Law Center and a counsel for the pension fund of the United Mine Workers, went on to say, ". . . I am not certain that it would have been a total waste of time to inquire from persons who were in a position to know what they knew about this plan's loan transactions. It was something that was never done. So I don't think we can assess whether it would have worked well or badly."

Then Gallagher added, "Certainly, if the investigative staff had been totally prepared and had examined all the loan files and had been ready to take these depositions with full preparation by that time, that would have been a far better situation. It doesn't take an investigator to know that."

In stating that SIS was not prepared to conduct investigation of targeted loans, Mrs. Gallagher failed to point out that SIS Director Lippe had already targeted numerous transactions and had prepared subpoenas which were to be served in the opening round of the third party investigative strategy, a strategy which was stopped by Steven J. Sacher, who preceded Mrs. Gallagher as Associate Solicitor, and by William Chadwick, whose job was Administrator of Pension and Welfare Benefit Programs. . . .

What Mrs. Gallagher Had in Mind with Kleindienst Deposition

Monica Gallagher did not categorically deny telling SIS that former U.S. Attorney Richard Kleindienst should be asked, if, in a hypothetical situation, he would have offered a bribe.

Asked about the Kleindienst matter, Mrs. Gallagher replied this way:
That conversation--the report of that conversation has just enough truth in it that I think the only way to deal with it is to describe it and it may look worse rather than better. But in the course of trying to advance these dozens of arguments about why the program that Mr. [Eamon] Kelly and the Secretary [Marshall] wanted to have initiated couldn't be initiated, one of the arguments made was that they [SIS] couldn't possibly think of anything to ask these people such as, for example, what would we ask somebody like Mr. Kleindienst?

And I think I would have said to that something like ask him what he knows about this loan application. You understand, Mr. Senator, that Mr. Kleindienst had represented a prospective borrower with respect to the fund as well as being involved in a number of other fund transactions, it turns out. So some of them, opposed to the project, would say, "Well, but the loan wasn't made. How could we ask him about the loan?"

I would say something like, "Well, ask him if it would have been made, if there had been a kickback involved."

It was one of those conversations of frustration, Mr. Senator. It was my attempt to say I am sure if you put your heart into this effort, you could find a way to make it a productive effort on the part of the Department of Labor to figure out what is happening in this plan's asset portfolio.

Senator Nunn pointed out to Mrs. Gallagher that surely she would want some evidence, some background, something more than a hunch, before asking a former Attorney General to respond to a hypothetical question based on the premise that he would give a bribe.

Senator Nunn put it this way:

> Would you think without any more evidence than that that a former Attorney General of the United States would be willing to answer that kind of question and give you meaningful information, [a question like] "Would the loan have been made if you gave him a bribe?" There is no background, no evidence, no nothing.

Mrs. Gallagher replied:

> We are aware, Mr. Senator, that in at least one case, one of the prospective borrowers from the fund was told that if he made a kickback he would get the loan. I am not saying that is what happened in Mr. Kleindienst's case. I don't have any idea whether that happened in Mr. Kleindienst's case. I don't have any idea whether that happened in any other case, but I am saying if you asked witnesses what happened, under compulsory process, some of them may tell you what happened. And that would put us ahead of the game in our investigative efforts from where we were.

Senator Nunn said her reply suggested "sort of a strange investigative technique." . . .

As for the idea itself--that of obtaining the 81 depositions--it wasn't hers anyway, Gallagher said, asserting that it was one of several possible approaches that she proposed to Eamon Kelly, who, as a Labor Department consultant, was reporting directly to Secretary Marshall on pension fund matters. "Mr. Kelly chose that approach," Gallagher said. "I was the messenger who apparently got all the 'miscredit' for this being my plan." . . .

V. Government Failed to Attain Enforceable Agreement

Consent Decree Discussed at Spickerman Deposition

SIS and the Labor Department generally objected to the IRS decision to revoke the pension fund's tax exempt status in June of 1976. Critics of IRS said the revocation was ill-timed, that it was done hastily and without proper preparation and that it left the Government with no leverage in future negotiations. It was alleged that once the ultimate weapon, the revocation order, was handed down, the Government was under pressure to restore the tax exemption.

However, despite its shortcomings, the revocation order did have the effect of impressing upon the fund that the Government was serious in its efforts to bring about reform. And, once IRS agreed to forgo its go-it-alone attitude and join forces with the Labor Department, negotiations between fund lawyers and the Government began to progress.

During 1976, SIS formed a strategy that was aimed at having the fund enter into some kind of an enforceable agreement, a binding contract under which the fund would agree to carry out certain specified reforms in its operations. One such enforceable agreement would have been a court-enforced consent decree. . . .

. . . [I]n the summer of 1976, a consent decree was being pursued by SIS.

In a court-enforced consent decree, the fund, without admitting or denying guilt, would have agreed to implement a series of reforms put forward by the Government. A consent decree would have prescribed the manner in which the trustees could manage existing assets and make investments.

It is important to note that the entering into a consent decree would have in no way jeopardized or hindered the ongoing investigation of the fund by SIS.

Lester B. Seidel, Deputy Director and Special Counsel in SIS, testified that . . . in July of 1976 . . . a very real possibility [existed] that the consent decree approach would succeed. . . .

Seidel said . . . that the fund was willing to accept a consent decree. The key to the consent decree strategy, Seidel said, was the Labor Department's insistence that the agreement entail a commitment from the fund, something the fund could not renege on later. "What we were essentially looking for is an agreement which had teeth in it," Seidel said, "What I mean by teeth is something that is enforceable." "We were unwavering in our position," he said.

The consent decree continued to be discussed between SIS and the fund lawyers and, as late in the investigation as September 20, 1976, Seidel was convinced that the consent decree was a realistic goal. . . . .

It was made very clear to the fund attorneys that a consent decree had only to do with asset management procedures--and that, consent decree or no, the SIS investigation would continue . . .

Among the provisions of the proposed consent decree, Seidel said, was SIS's insistence that the jurisdiction be under the U.S. District Court in Washington, DC. Fund attorneys wanted venue to be in Chicago.

Seidel said SIS believed venue should be in the Nation's Capital because the investigation of the pension fund was a national case with nationwide implications. Equally important, he said, was the likelihood that the Labor Department could demand strict adherence to the terms of the consent decree if the affected court were in Washington.

Venue was a crucial consideration, to Seidel's point of view, because it was the court that ultimately would enforce the new management asset procedures. . . .

By late September, Seidel said, the consent decree seemed more and more likely. But pension fund lawyers . . . came up with a counter proposal. . . .

. . . The idea was a mass resignation of the trustees and a restructuring of the board. . . .

. . . Ultimately, the mass resignation action was only that--a resignation of trustees. In fact, Seidel said, "a certain fear" was current among senior Labor Department officials who were concerned that the trustees would resign anyway, thereby taking away an "attractive remedy from us and we won't get any type of enforceable agreement."

Moreover, as indicated earlier in this report, Seidel felt an adequate procedure had already been established to remove trustees from the board. The technique was perfected by Lawrence Lippe and Seidel when SIS took a sworn deposition from trustee William Presser.

William Presser refused to answer certain questions about his conduct on the board of trustees. Upon being questioned about his fiduciary duties, he invoked the fifth amendment. SIS demanded he resign, saying, in effect, the Constitution did not give a fiduciary the right not to testify because of self-incrimination when the questions had to do with his conduct as a fiduciary.

It was Lester Seidel's view that SIS could go about the task of testing other trustees on the same fifth amendment principle and, ultimately, remove them from the board systematically. . . . The trustees knew what was coming and quickly offered to resign en masse, thereby hoping to win concessions from the Labor Department for an action they were going to take anyway.

The strategy worked. The Labor Department went along, abandoning the consent decree, which was the one binding commitment the fund did not want to be saddled with. Consent decrees are written, they are specific and they are enforceable. But even in agreeing to the mass resignation, the Labor Department did not force all the trustees off the board. Only 11 trustees resigned, 12 counting William Presser, who had resigned earlier. That left four of the most influential trustees still on the board.

Still serving and representing the labor side were Frank E. Fitzsimmons, president of the Teamsters International, hand picked for the job by Jimmy Hoffa before he went to prison; and Roy Lee Williams, an international vice president of the Teamsters and the most powerful Teamsters officer in Kansas City. Continuing to represent employers on the board were Andrew G. Massa, of the Motor Carriers Employers Conference, Central States; and John F. Spickerman, Sr., of the Southeastern Area Motor Carriers Labor Relations Association.

If the mass resignation was an effective tactic for persuading the Labor Department to drop the consent decree strategy, the pension fund's leaving the four powerful trustees--Fitzsimmons, Williams, Massa, Spickerman--on the board was even more ingenious. Now it became a major focus of Labor Department policy to do something to force the four "holdover" trustees to resign.

As will be noted in more detail in this report, the Department spent the next 6 months trying to force the holdovers to step down. When finally they did, it was only after long difficult negotiations. The negotiations themselves were tainted by a rumor that would not die.

The rumor was that the Labor Department, under its new Secretary, F. Ray Marshall, had entered into a secret agreement with the pension fund. The alleged agreement, known as the "phantom agreement," was that Fitzsimmons, Williams and the others agreed to resign only after they had extracted a pledge from Marshall that all future investigation of the pension fund would be limited, and that one of the self-imposed constraints on the Department would be that SIS would investigate nothing at the fund, or in connection with the fund, that might result in criminal prosecution. It was also agreed that the fund would turn over management of its assets to an independent investment firm for 5 years.

Marshall denied he or his aides ever agreed to any secret accord. But there was an unfortunate gap in communication at the Labor Department. Norman Perkins, the man Marshall put in charge of SIS, believed there had been a so-called phantom agreement. He ran SIS accordingly.

The subcommittee could never establish for certain whether or not there was a phantom agreement. But the subcommittee did establish that certain areas of inquiry were not pursued including no further criminal investigation by SIS and that no information developed by SIS formed the substance of any criminal prosecutions by the Justice Department.

In addition, the fifth amendment approach to removing trustees from the board as envisioned by Lester Seidel was not tested again. But one of the most prominent of the former trustees, Roy Lee Williams, did turn out to be another fifth amendment witness. . . .

VI. Labor Department Policy Inadequate

Marshall Wanted to Avoid Litigation

A new President of the United States, Jimmy Carter, was sworn in on January 20, 1977. His Secretary of Labor, F. Ray Marshall, after reviewing the pension fund case, felt that long and bitter litigation was likely.

Wishing to avoid that, Marshall directed that his Department work with the fund's attorneys in achieving desired reforms without litigation. It was

Marshall's policy that the Labor Department's main responsibility was the "protection and preservation of the fund's assets." All other considerations paled in comparison. Marshall's phrase, "protection of fund assets," was used repeatedly to answer charges about the Department's shortcomings in the investigation.

Labor and IRS drafted the Government's demands that the fund would have to meet before the tax-exempt status would be restored. The fund would have to persuade the four holdover trustees--Fitzsimmons, Williams, Massa, Spickerman--to resign and the board would have to be restructured so that neutral professionals would outnumber the union and employer representatives.

Next, the fund was informed that the Government was prepared to go to court to remove the four holdover trustees and to take the new trustees out of the day-to-day management of the fund's assets. The Government said it was also ready to initiate court action to force the fund to comply with ERISA and with IRS rules on tax exemptions.

The Government's demands were put forward on February 16, 1977. The next week, the fund agreed to comply with ERISA. But the fund proposed that the trustees would continue to manage noninvestment affairs but that investment authority would be turned over to a committee of independent, neutral professionals.

By that time the Government had backed down from most of its original demands, even though Government officials felt that these were the minimum acceptable standards. Negotiations continued into April of 1977. Fitzsimmons, Williams, Massa, and Spickerman resigned. On April 27, IRS restored the fund's tax exemption. However, eight conditions would have to be met by the fund. If they were not, the exemption would be revoked again. . . .

In an April 26, 1977, letter to the pension fund, the Internal Revenue Service spelled out eight conditions the Government was requiring for the fund to qualify as a tax-exempt trust.

The first condition was that the trustees amend the fund's trust agreement so that the fund would conform to standards set forth in the Internal Revenue Code and in ERISA.

Second, the fund had to have in operation by the end of 1977 a data base management system that would insure that union members who had participated in the fund at some point since its inception in 1955 would receive "credited service" commensurate with the extent of benefits due them. . . .

The last condition was that the fund's assets be turned over to an independent, outside investment firm of established reputation for integrity.

In its letter, IRS also required the fund to allow the Service to have access to fund records and documents. The letter did not stipulate such ready access for the Labor Department, although the Labor Department was apparently under the impression that its access to records was insured by its informal agreement with the fund. . . .

According to the General Accounting Office, after the fund agreed to comply with the Government's eight conditions, the Labor Department said it would end that portion of its investigation that focused on the fund's asset management procedures.

In May of 1977, the Labor Department ended its onsite investigation in fund offices in Chicago. . . .

SIS was now working exclusively in preparation for the civil action which the Department of Labor planned to bring against former trustees of the fund. In this role, SIS was to become an investigative support arm for the Solicitor's Office in the Labor Department. . . .

The fund asked for restoration of its tax-exempt status on September 20, 1976. To win restoration of its status, the fund would now have to show that its plan was amended to conform with ERISA and that it had safeguards to protect the fund assets and properly pay benefits to pensioners. . . .

Of all the agreements that were reached . . . only one of them was in the form of a written contract. That was the agreement between the Equitable Life Assurance Society and the pension fund.

The Government had promoted the idea of the fund turning its assets over to an independent manager. But neither the Labor Department nor IRS nor any other Government component was a party to the contract itself.

Under the terms of the contract with the independent asset managers, the trustees agreed to turn over management of most of the pension fund's investment assets to Equitable and other outside investment firms for a period of five years. This was an enforceable contract. It expires in 1982.

All other agreements were between the fund and the Federal Government. And all of them were strictly oral agreements. Nothing was committed to writing in the form of enforceable contracts. The most prominent written documents were a press release announcing the accords and a letter from IRS listing eight conditions for requalification. . . .

Trustees' Spirit of Cooperation Did Not Last Long

Once their tax exemption was restored, the trustees became even less enthusiastic about cooperating with the Government. They stopped giving SIS access to records. They tried to compromise the two principal independent firms managing investments. They stopped reporting on progress they were supposed to be making in living up to the eight conditions. And they gave the appearance of opening up the fund to renewed influence of former trustees.

In the fall of 1977, some 4 months after IRS restored the fund's tax exemption, the trustees refused to provide records which SIS requested. In March of 1978, the trustees formally notified the Labor Department that the era of voluntary cooperation had officially ended.

March of 1978, 6 months after the fund's investment authority was taken over by the Equitable Life Assurance Society of the United States and the Victor Palmieri Co., the trustees passed a series of resolutions aimed at compromising the independence of the investment managers. The resolutions said the trustees could fire Equitable and the Palmieri Co. for cause without the approval of the Secretary of Labor; and that the board of trustees had to be given at least 30 days' notice before the managers could sell assets worth more than $10,000. The Labor Department informed the trustees that neither resolution was enforceable.

Next, the trustees set up their own staff of real estate analysts to make independent inspections of all assets under the management of the Palmieri Co. In addition, $72.7 million to $100.5 million in real estate assets were actually managed by these same fund analysts.

Then the trustees tried to reduce the Palmieri Co.'s management fees. The Labor Department informed the trustees that the Palmieri fees were reasonable, that they had to be paid and that under any circumstances neither Equitable nor the Palmieri firm could be fired without the approval of the Secretary of Labor.
. . .

IRS Assistant Commissioner S.A. Winborne also noted that the pension fund's spirit of cooperation "began to deteriorate" in 1979. The fund sent a letter to IRS barring the Service from conducting further audits at fund offices on August 24, 1979. Winborne said this prohibition "was a serious limitation on our ability to monitor the fund." . . .

It was apparent . . . that, without recourse to an enforceable agreement, the Government's only option was to begin a new investigation. In 1980, both IRS and the Labor Department began new investigations of the Central States pension fund.

Five of Eight Conditions Still Not Met

IRS Regional Commissioner Charles Miriani provided the subcommittee with an IRS summary of the degree to which the fund failed to comply with the eight conditions it had promised to meet to gain restoration of its tax exempt status.
. . .

When it became apparent that the fund was not living up to the eight conditions, the IRS studied the situation, but took no enforcement action to compel compliance.

As of August of 1980, no action of any kind had been brought against the Central States pension fund for its having failed to comply fully with the eight conditions of requalification. . . .

Roy Williams Linked to Organized Crime

Roy Lee Williams, president of the over-the-road truck drivers, Teamsters Local 41 in Kansas City, MO, and a vice president of the Teamsters International, had frequently been mentioned as the man most likely to succeed the former Teamsters president, Frank Fitzsimmons, who died on May 6, 1981.

Williams, secretary-treasurer and director of the 700,000 member Central Conference of Teamsters, had also directed the 20,000 member Teamsters Joint Council 56, making him the undisputed chief of Kansas City's largest union for the last 25 years.

In addition, Williams served as a labor representative on the board of trustees of the Central States pension fund from 1955 to 1977. Williams was one of the four "holdover" trustees who were forced to resign in April of 1977 under pressure from the Labor Department. The original trustees resigned in 1976 due to Labor Department actions at that time.

In leaving his position on the board of trustees of the pension fund, Williams retained his other Teamsters posts in Kansas City and with the international.

Williams had brushes with the law. Three Federal grand juries indicted him. But he was never convicted.

In 1962, Williams was charged with conspiracy with six fellow Teamsters officials to steal union funds by inflating expenses. He was acquitted. Four subordinates were convicted.

In 1972, Williams was charged with embezzling from the union, allegedly by paying himself a $16,000 bonus without proper authorization from the union. He was acquitted.

In 1974, Williams was indicted on a charge of fabricating minutes of a union meeting authorizing a dues increase for local 41. The Government said the meeting never occurred. The case was dismissed.

A Government memorandum, which has been authenticated by the Department of Justice, identified Roy Lee Williams as being controlled by Kansas City's reputed mob leader, Nicholas Civella.

The memorandum, portions of which were reprinted in the June 6, 1978, hearing record of the Oversight Subcommittee of the House Ways and Means Committee, was verified as being "substantially the same in content as a memorandum written at Justice [Department] at least 7 years ago."

This authentication was given the House Subcommittee on July 14, 1978, by David Margolis, Deputy Chief of the Organized Crime and Racketeering Section of the Criminal Division of the Justice Department. The Department of Justice never located the original report, according to Margolis.

The memorandum said that in 1961 the Organized Crime and Racketeering Section was investigating reported thefts of Teamsters Union funds by Teamsters officers.

During the investigation, it was learned that Roy Lee Williams and Sam Ancona were associated with Nick Civella.

The memorandum said that Ancona, former president of Teamsters Local 951 was Nick Civella's representative at the Teamsters hall.

Roy Williams, the memorandum said, "was under the complete domination of Civella." It added, "Williams will not act contrary to the wishes of Civella apparently because of both self-interest and fear." . . .

The subcommittee staff learned that Roy Lee Williams, Allen Dorfman and certain organized crime figures met on several occasions in 1979 and 1980 in Kansas City and Chicago. The purpose of these meetings was to fashion a strategy for enabling crime syndicate bosses like Civella in Kansas City and Aiuppa in Chicago to reassert their influence upon the Central States pension fund.

The subcommittee staff learned that one such meeting was held on April 23, 1979, in the home of Philip Simone, who lived near Nick Civella in Kansas City. Simone a terminal manager for a trucking line, is a relative of Carl "Cork" Civella. . . .

No Criminal Violations Cited by IRS

IRS began its investigation of the Central States pension fund in 1968. Senator Nunn asked IRS witnesses how many criminal convictions had resulted from that investigation in that 12-year period.

At the hearings, no IRS witness could recall how many successful tax cases resulted from the Service's pension fund investigation.

Following the hearings, IRS searched its files and reported to the subcommittee that one criminal conviction had been obtained in connection with the fund investigation since 1968. Alvin Baron, who had been a fund official, was convicted of solicitation of a bribe, filing a false income tax return and five counts relating to a scheme to defraud by wire. . . .

Failure of Inquiry Was Loss of Historical Opportunity

Opportunity lost is the most apt way to characterize the failed Labor Department investigation. Lost was the opportunity to put the new pension reform statute, ERISA, to good use, to utilize ERISA to bring about lasting reform of the fund.

Lost was the opportunity to assure that the fund would be run by trustees and officials whose primary interest was the welfare of union members and fund beneficiaries. Lost was the opportunity to take to court, in civil proceedings or criminal, borrowers and other third parties who had profited from questionable loans and investments.

Lost was the opportunity to bring to justice some of the Nation's most notorious organized criminals. An opportunity of such historical significance does not come along often. . . .

10

Government's Memorandum of Law in Support of Its Motion for Preliminary Relief

United States District Court, Southern District of New York, United States of America, Plaintiff, against International Brotherhood of Teamsters, Chauffeurs, Warehousemen and Helps of America, AFL-CIO, et al., Defendants. Rudolph W. Giuliani, United States Attorney for the Southern District of New York, Attorney for Plaintiff, 1988.

Preliminary Statement

Plaintiff United States of America (hereinafter, the "Government") submits this memorandum of law in support of its motion for preliminary relief, pursuant to the civil remedies provisions of the Racketeer Influenced and Corrupt Organizations ("RICO") statute, 18 U.S.C. §1964.

In a recent series of successful criminal and civil prosecutions, the Government has shown that La Cosa Nostra has gained control over the International Brotherhood of Teamsters, Chauffeurs, Warehousemen and Helpers of America, AFL-CIO (hereinafter, the "IBT," the "Teamsters International Union" or the "Teamsters"), through a pattern of racketeering activity and now uses the IBT and many of its affiliated entities to engage in racketeering activity. Indeed, that control is so pervasive that for decades IBT's leadership has permitted La Cosa Nostra figures to dominate and corrupt important Teamsters Locals, Joint Councils and Benefit Funds.

Since approximately 1970, the Government has successfully prosecuted well over 300 persons associated with the Teamsters (including many union officials) for Teamsters-related crimes (e.g., extortion through threats of union problems, embezzlement of union funds, illegal labor payoffs).* . . . During that same

---

*Several of those successful prosecutions have resulted in convictions of IBT General Executive Board members for crimes involving abuses of their union

(continued...)

245

period, however, the IBT's General Executive Board has rarely taken disciplinary action against, or even investigated, corrupt Teamsters officials or subordinate entities. . . . This inaction is particular outrageous, given the affirmative obligation of these officers under federal law and the IBT's Constitution to prevent union corruption. . . .

This deplorable situation will undoubtedly continue unless this Court grants immediate relief. Indeed, only last month, a federal jury in this district convicted La Cosa Nostra kingpin Anthony "Fat Tony" Salerno and others of

*(...continued)

offices. For example, defendant Maurice Schurr, who is currently an IBT Vice President, was recently convicted of receiving illegal labor payments from Teamsters employers, see United States v. Schurr, 775 F.2d 549 (3d Cir. 1985), aff'd on rehearing, 794 F.2d 903 (3d Cir. 1986); defendant Salvatore Provenzano, who only recently resigned his IBT Vice Presidency, was convicted of various criminal offenses and enjoined from further union associations in connection with IBT Local 560 in New Jersey, see United States v. Marcus, 83 Cr. 104 (D. N.J.), aff'd mem. sub. nom. United States v. Provenzano, 770 F.2d 1077 (3d Cir. 1985); United States v. Local 560, 780 F.2d 267 (3d Cir. 1985), cert. denied, 476 U.S. 1140 (1986); and former IBT President Roy Williams was convicted, along with Chicago La Cosa Nostra figure Joseph Lombardo, of conspiring to bribe a U.S. Senator with realty owned by the Teamsters Central States Pension Fund to influence his actions on trucking deregulation legislation, see United States v. Williams, 737 F.2d 594 (7th Cir. 1984) cert. denied, 470 U.S. 1003 (1985). Williams was under indictment for that offense at the time he was elected IBT President in 1981, and he only resigned as union head after his 1983 conviction. Moreover, his successor, defendant Jackie Presser, is currently under federal indictment, along with defendant Harold Friedman (a current IBT Vice President and convicted felon), for arranging a "ghost" employee scheme involving Teamsters Local 507 in Cleveland, Ohio. See United States v. Presser, Cr. No. 86-114 (N.D. Ohio). Four of the last five IBT Presidents have faced federal felony charges, with three of them (David Beck, James Hoffa and Williams) having resigned their union posts as a result of their convictions and the fourth (Presser) still retaining his office while awaiting trial; and six of the 18 current IBT General Executive Board members have criminal records. See Mastro Dec. Exs. AL, AS-AW, BE. Indeed, almost 50 percent of the persons who have served on the IBT General Executive Board since 1970 have been either convicted, indicted or otherwise publicly cited for improper activity before or during their tenures in office; and 10 of the 18 current IBT General Executive Board members fall within this category. See Mastro Dec., Ex. BE.

criminal RICO offenses involving illegal labor payments to union officials representing Teamsters Local 282 in New York City and Teamsters Local 560 in New Jersey. See United States v. Salerno, 86 Cr. 245 (MJL) (S.D.N.Y.) (hereinafter, "the Genovese Family trial"). . . . That criminal trial also included extensive evidence of La Costa Nostra figures' prominent role in picking the last two Teamsters Presidents (Roy L. Williams and defendant Jackie Presser).*

In the face of these convictions and this evidence, however, the IBT's leadership has publicly announced that it plans to do nothing whatsoever. . . . Immediately after the jury verdict in the Genovese Family case, the IBT issued a press release, which read in part: "General President Presser, General Secretary-Treasurer Weldon L. Mathis, and the entire General Executive Board are gratified by the jury's verdict, feel vindicated by its action, and are comforted by the fact that after over one year of testimony this jury was able to accurately ferret out the truth." . . . The release made no mention of the fact that the jury convicted La Cosa Nostra figures of making illegal labor payments to officials of IBT Locals 282 and 560. Indeed, the IBT leadership has responded to this proof of corruption by recently appointing to International Union office one of the very Local officers proven in the Genovese Family trial to have been the recipient of an illegal labor payment.**

---

*While the jury there acquitted defendant Salerno and two others in wire fraud charges relating to their role in the Williams and Presser elections, that criminal verdict has no collateral consequences here because of the Government's lesser burden of proof in civil cases . . . ("preponderance of the evidence" standard applies in civil RICO actions, rather than "beyond a reasonable doubt" standard applicable in criminal cases). In this civil action, the Government alleges that La Cosa Nostra figures took steps to insure that Williams and Presser got elected. . . . The evidence supporting those allegations includes the prior sworn testimony of Williams and Cleveland La Cosa Nostra chieftain Angelo Lonardo, as well as recorded conversations in which Genovese Family Boss Anthony Salerno and Kansas City Family Boss Nicholas Civella each describe their support of Presser and Williams, respectively. The Government now submits that evidence for the Court's consideration in connection with this application for preliminary relief. . . .

**Edward Halloran, an associate of the Genovese Family of La Cosa Nostra, was convicted in the Genovese Family trial of having made an illegal labor payment to Teamsters Local 282 President Robert Sasso. Incredibly, Sasso was recently appointed to two high union offices, including the post of International Representative. . . .

248

It comes as no surprise, then, that the President's Commission on Organized Crime recently described the IBT as the union "Most Controlled" by organized crime. See Organized Crime Commission Report to the President and Attorney General, THE EDGE: Organized Crime, Business and Labor Unions at 89 (March 1986) (hereinafter, "President's Commission Report"). . . .

Because the IBT leadership has so flagrantly abdicated its responsibility to root out union corruption, the Government now seeks immediate relief to have the Court appoint a temporary court liaison officer to prevent racketeering activity within the IBT and to review certain actions of the IBT's General Executive Board during the pendency of this litigation.* . . . The Government

---

*More specifically, as preliminary relief, the Government asks that the powers of the court liaison officer include the following:

(i) To discharge those duties of the IBT General President and/or General Executive Board under the Teamsters International Union Constitution (including Articles VI and XIX thereof) and Title 29 of the United States Code which relate to the disciplining of corrupt or dishonest officers, agents, employees or members of the Teamsters International Union, its affiliated Locals or other subordinate bodies and, where necessary to prevent corruption, the appointment of temporary trustees to run the affairs of any such subordinate bodies; provided, however, that in the exercise of those duties, the court liaison officer may petition the Court to be relieved from any provision of the Teamsters International Union Constitution that impedes or prevents the court liaison officer from disciplining corrupt or dishonest officers, agents, employees or members of the Teamsters International Union;

(ii) to review the proposed actions of the General Executive Board insofar as they relate to expenditures of union funds, appointments to union office, or changes in the International Union Constitution or bylaws, and to petition the Court for an order restraining any such proposed action when the court liaison officer deems it necessary to protect the rights of members of the Teamsters International Union, consistent with the provisions of Title 29 of the United States Code and the Constitution of the Teamsters International Union.

As permanent relief, the Government requests that the Court bar IBT General Executive Board members and La Cosa Nostra figures found to be racketeers from participating in union affairs. The Government also requests that the Court appoint a trustee for the International Union to ensure free and

(continued...)

also seeks to enjoin the IBT's current officers from interfering in any way with the court liaison officer's activities. Finally, the Government seeks to enjoin La Cosa Nostra figures from participating in union affairs.

The prosecutions which form the backdrop for this action graphically illustrate La Cosa Nostra's pattern of involvement with the IBT's affairs. By establishing control over select union officials—including the IBT's highest ranking officers, individuals with access to union benefit funds, and officers of large IBT Locals—La Cosa Nostra has effectively infiltrated and used the IBT to engage in racketeering activity on a nationwide scale.

As is clear from the evidence submitted in support of this motion, the IBT leadership has made a devil's pact with La Cosa Nostra. La Cosa Nostra figures have insured the elections of the IBT's top officers, including the union's last two Presidents. In return, union officers have allowed La Cosa Nostra ready access to union funds and jobs and free reign over certain IBT Locals, which La Cosa Nostra figures have used as instrumentalities to extort monies from employers. Thus, the IBT's leaders get their union offices, and La Cosa Nostra figures get their money—all to the detriment of union members, victimized businesses and the general public.

The preliminary relief now sought by the Government addresses this "screaming national scandal." . . . The defendants' continuing racketeering activity has devastating consequences for the union's membership, affected businesses and the public. It is to protect these victims that the Government now requests immediate relief.

I. Statement of Facts

A. La Cosa Nostra: A Nationwide Criminal Organization

The existence of La Cosa Nostra—a nationwide criminal organization consisting of various crime "Families"—can no longer be credibly disputed. In recent RICO prosecutions, the Government has repeatedly proven the existence

---

*(...continued)
fair elections of new IBT officers and to discharge, as the trustee deems necessary, any of the duties and responsibilities of the IBT General Executive Board (other than negotiating and entering into collective bargaining agreements or participating in the affairs of any IBT political action committee) until such time as free and fair elections of new union officers can be held.

of La Cosa Nostra through electronic surveillance evidence and the testimony of several La Cosa Nostra insiders. . . ."

---

*The Government has already demonstrated the existence of specific La Cosa Nostra Families in the following cases:

(a) Genovese Family (New York)
  (i)   United States v. Salerno, et al., 85 Cr. 139 (S.D.N.Y.) (RO)
  (ii)   United States v. Salerno, et al., 86 Cr. 245 (S.D.N.Y.) (MJL)

(b) Gambino Family (New York)
  (i)   United States v. Salerno, et al., 85 Cr. 139 (S.D.N.Y.) (RO)
  (ii)   United States v. Gallo, et al., 86 Cr. 452 (E.D.N.Y.) (JBW)

(c) Colombo Family (New York)
  (i)   United States v. Persico, et al., 84 Cr. 809 (S.D.N.Y.) (JFK), aff'd in relevant part, 832 F.2d 705 (2d Cir. 1987), cert. denied, 56 U.S.L.W. 3805 (U.S. may 24, 1988)
  (ii)   United States v. Local 6A, et al., 86 Civ. 4819 (S.D.N.Y.) (VLB)
  (iii) United States v. Salerno, et al., 85 Cr. 139 (S.D.N.Y.) (RO)

(d) Luchese Family (New York)
  (i)   United States v. Santoro, et al., 85 Cr. 100 (E.D.N.Y.) (CPS)
  (ii)   United States V. Salerno, et al., 85 Cr. 139 (S.D.N.Y.) (RO)

(e) Bonanno Family (New York)
  (i)   United States v. Rastelli, et al., 85 Cr. 354 (E.D.N.Y.) (CPS)
  (ii)   United States V. Ruggiero, et al., 81 Cr. 803 (S.D.N.Y.) (RWS), aff'd in pertinent part, 726 F.2d 913 (2d Cir. 1984)
  (iii) United States v. Salerno, et al., 85 Cr. 139 (S.D.N.Y.) (RO)

(f) Philadelphia Family
  (i)   United States v. Salerno, et al., 85 Cr. 139 (S.D.N.Y.) (RO)
  (ii)   United States v. Riccobene, et al., 709 F.2d 214 (3rd Cir.), cert. denied, 104 S.Ct. 157 (1983).

(g) Cleveland Family
  (i)   United States v. Gallo, et al., 82 Cr. 119 (N.D. Ohio), aff'd in pertinent part, 763 F2d. 1504 (6th Cir. 1985)

(continued...)

*(...continued)
- (ii)   United States v. DeLuna, et al., 83 Cr. 00124 (W.D. Mo.), aff'd sub nom. United States v. Cerone, 830 F.2d 938 (8th Cir. 1987), cert. denied, 56 U.S.L.W. 3789 (U.S. May 17, 1988)
- (iii)   United States v. Salerno, et al., 85 Cr. 139 (S.D.N.Y.) (RO)
- (iv)   United States v. Sinito, et al., 82 Cr. 119 (N.D. Ohio), aff'd, 714 F.2d 143 (6th Cir. 1983), related to 723 F.2d 1250 (6th Cir. 1983)
- (v)   United States v. Licavoli, et al., 79 Cr. 103 (N.D. Ohio), aff'd, 725 F.2d 1040 (6th Cir. 1984)

(h) Chicago Family
- (i)   United States v. DeLuna, et al., 83 Cr. 00124 (W.D. Mo), aff'd sub nom. United States v. Cerone, 830 F.2d 938 (8th Cir. 1987), cert. denied, 56 U.S.L.W. 3789 (U.S. May 17, 1988)
- (ii)   United States v. Dorfman, et al., 81 Cr. 269 (N.D. Ill.), aff'd sub nom. United States v. Williams, 737 F.2d 594 (7th Cir. 1984), cert. denied, 470 U.S. 1003 (1985)
- (iii)   United States v. Salerno, et al., 85 Cr. 139 (S.D.N.Y.) (RO)
- (iv)   United States v. Salerno, et al., 86 Cr. 245 (S.D.N.Y.) (MJL)

(i) Milwaukee Family
- (i)   United States v. Balistrieri, et al., 81 Cr. 152 (E.D. Wis.)
- (ii)   United States v. DeLuna, et al., 83 Cr. 00124 (W.D. Mo.), aff'd sub nom. United States v. Cerone, 830 F.2d 938 (8th Cir. 1987), cert. denied, 56 U.S.L.W. 3789 (U.S. May 17, 1988)

(j) Kansas City Family
- (i)   United States v. Civella, et al., 84 Cr. 00032 (W.D. Mo.)
- (ii)   United States v. DeLuna, et al., 83 Cr. 00124 (W.D. Mo.) aff'd sub nom., United States v. Cerone, 830 F.2d 938 (8th Cir. 1987), cert. denied, 56 U.S.L.W. 3789 (U.S. may 17, 1988)
- (iii)   United States v. Salerno, et al., 85 Cr. 139 (S.D.N.Y.) (RO)
- (iv)   United States v. Salerno, et al., 86 Cr. 245 (S.D.N.Y.) (MJL)

(continued...)

252

Just last year, the Government proved the existence of a ruling council or "Commission" of La Cosa Nostra Families in its successful prosecution of the Bosses of New York's La Cosa Nostra Families (including defendants Anthony Salerno, Boss of the Genovese Family, Anthony Corallo, Boss of the Luchese Family, and Carmine Persico, Boss of the Colombo Family) for criminal RICO offenses predicated upon acts of labor racketeering, extortion and murder.
. . .

Judges presiding at . . . prosecutions of Teamsters officials and La Cosa Nostra figures have expressly recognized the existence of La Cosa Nostra as a nationwide criminal enterprise. For example, in the trial of former Teamsters President Roy Williams and defendant Joseph Lombardo (a prominent Chicago La Cosa Nostra figure), both of whom were convicted of conspiracy to commit bribery, United States District Judge Prentice H. Marshall of the Northern District of Illinois stated:

I am convinced, clearly, unequivocally and beyond a reasonable doubt that a structured organization exists, that it is broken down geographically and that various cities have their various bosses. I am convinced that, as the Congress has said, there is a domestic criminal cartel.

. . .

Moreover in ordering one of the Teamsters' largest Locals (Local 560) put into trusteeship under the civil RICO statute, United States District Judge Harold Ackerman of the District of New Jersey vividly described La Cosa Nostra's domination of that IBT Local:

John L. Lewis, former president of the Congress of Industrial Organizations and the United Mine Workers once said that "Labor, like Israel, has many sorrows."
A careful review of the evidence in this unprecedented case reveals the verity of that observation.

---

*(...continued)
(k) Los Angeles Family
　　(i)　　United States v. Brooklier, 74 Cr. 1801 (C.D. Cal.), aff'd, 685 F.2d 1208 (9th Cir. 1982).
　　(ii)　　United States v. Persico, et al., 84 Cr. 809 (S.D.N.Y.) (JFK), aff'd in relevant part, 832 F.2d 705 (2d Cir. 1987), cert. denied, 56 U.S.L.W. 3789 (U.S. May 17, 1988).

It is not a pretty story. Beneath the relatively sterile language of a dry legal opinion is a harrowing tale of how evil men, sponsored by and part of organized criminal elements, infiltrated and ultimately captured Local 560 of the International Brotherhood of Teamsters, one of the largest local unions in the largest union in this country.

This group of gangsters, aided and abetted by their relatives and sycophants, engaged in a multifaceted orgy of criminal activity. For those that enthusiastically followed these arrogant mobsters in their morally debated activity there were material rewards. For those who accepted the side benefits of this perverted interpretation of business unionism, see J. Hutchinson, The Imperfect Union, p. 371 (1970), there was presumably the rationalization of "I've got mine, why shouldn't he get his." For those who attempted to fight, the message was clear. Murder and other forms of intimidation would be utilized to insure silence. To get along, one had to go along, or else.

. . .

In addition, in affirming criminal convictions involving several members of the Los Angeles Family of La Cosa Nostra, the United States Court of Appeals for the Ninth Circuit wrote: "Appellants are members of La Cosa Nostra, a secret national organization engaged in a wide range of racketeering activities, including murder, extortion, gambling, and loansharking." United States v. Brooklier, 685 F.2d 1208, 1213 (9th Cir. 1982). . . .

The IBT: The Labor Union "Most Controlled" by La Cosa Nostra

The President's Commission on Organized Crime (hereinafter, "President's Commission"), chaired by Judge Irving Kaufman of the United States Court of Appeals for the Second Circuit, recently . . . concluded that:

> The leaders of the nation's largest union, the International Brotherhood of Teamsters (IBT), have been firmly under the influence of organized crime since the 1950s. Although many of the hundreds of IBT locals and joint councils operating throughout the country are not criminally infiltrated, organized crime influences at least 38 of the largest locals and a joint council in Chicago, Cleveland, New Jersey, New York, Philadelphia, St. Louis, and other major cities. Former Teamster president Roy L. Williams told the Commission, "every big [Teamsters] local union . . . had some connection with organized crime." These locals operate in the nation's major business and economic centers and include the majority of the union's 1.6 million members. They are the foundation of organized crime's union-wide influence.

. . .

La Cosa Nostra exerts influence over the IBT at the union's highest levels. The President's Commission found that "[f]or decades, organized crime has

254

exercised substantial influence over the International Union, primarily through the office of the president."* . . .

Because the IBT plays a critical role in transporting the nation's goods, control of the union gives La Cosa Nostra power to intimidate, extort and make money from legitimate businesses which need those goods to function. IBT members drive the trucks and operate the warehouses that move and store "[a]lmost everything Americans eat, drink or use at home or on the job . . ." S. Brill, The Teamsters at 3 (Pocket Books 1978). "Control of the truckers thus provides leverage over thousands of businesses dependent on Teamster's deliveries." President's Commission Report at 91. . . .

La Cosa Nostra profits from its control over the Teamsters in many ways. For example, La Cosa Nostra figures have been able to extort monies from employers in exchange for "labor peace." . . . Under threats of work stoppages and other pressure applied through La Cosa Nostra-controlled Teamsters entities, businesses have succumbed to extortion. These businesses have, in turn, often received "sweetheart" deals and other concessions from the union. La Cosa Nostra's infiltration of the marketplace has thus given corrupted businesses a competitive edge over legitimate businesses. In addition, La Cosa Nostra figures have helped themselves to the IBT's substantial assets, which include vast funds from employee benefit plans. . . . By controlling fund managers and trustees, La Cosa Nostra figures have plundered literally millions of dollars for use in speculative real estate and other ventures. Similarly, La Cosa Nostra figures have been able to secure lucrative service contracts with the Teamsters and to place associates and relatives in "no-show" Teamsters jobs. . . . La Cosa Nostra figures have even used Teamsters' assets to bribe public officials in an effort to protect La Cosa Nostra interests. . . . For example, in 1983, then IBT General President Roy Williams, defendant Joseph Lombardo (a prominent Chicago La Cosa Nostra figure) and others were convicted of conspiring to bribe former U.S. Senator Howard Cannon with property owned by the Teamsters Central States Pension Fund. See United States v. Williams, 737 F.2d 594 (7th Cir. 1984), cert. denied, 470 U.S. 1003 (1985). . . .

La Cosa Nostra's Control Over the IBT: Selection of IBT Presidents
La Cosa Nostra keeps a firm grip over the IBT by controlling the union's top leadership. Indeed, La Cosa Nostra bosses actually supported and took steps to insure the elections of the last two IBT Presidents. As electronic surveillance

---

*Indeed, four of the last five Teamsters Presidents have faced federal felony charges. Three of them (David Beck, James Hoffa and Roy L. Williams) were convicted of felonies, and one (defendant Jackie Presser) is about to stand trial on federal felony charges.

evidence and witness testimony have substantiated, . . . La Cosa Nostra defendants Anthony Salerno, Milton Rockman and John Tronolone, together with other La Cosa Nostra figures (including defendants Joseph John Aiuppa and John Phillip Cerone), backed Roy Williams and Jackie Presser as the last two IBT Presidents.

Angelo Lonardo, former Underboss of the Cleveland Family, has testified that La Cosa Nostra figures supported Roy Williams for the position of IBT President in 1981. Lonardo vividly recounted a series of meetings among La Cosa Nostra figures to discuss Williams's selection. Lonardo testified that Kansas City Family Boss Nicholas Civella, who was backing Williams for the job, sent Lonardo to meet with other La Cosa Nostra bosses to solicit their support for Williams. Lonardo first met in Chicago with defendants Joseph John Aiuppa and John Phillip Cerone, . . . who agreed to support Williams. Thereafter, Lonardo went to New York and met with defendant Anthony Salerno . . . and other La Cosa Nostra figures in an effort to get Salerno's approval for Williams's candidacy. The meeting took place at Salerno's hangout, the Palma Boy Social Club on East 116th Street in Manhattan. Lonardo related the substance of that meeting:

> Q. What, if anything, did you tell Salerno at this meeting?
> A. That we had been to Chicago and we talked to them [Aiuppa and Cerone]. That we knew that Fitzsimmons was dying. Fitzsimmons was head of the Teamsters Union at the time.
> Q. Head of the national union?
> A. National Teamsters Union, yes. And Nick Civella [Boss of the Kansas City Family] was recommending Roy Williams for the job, when and if Fitzsimmons would pass away. And he thought it would be a good idea to get ready with delegates for Roy Williams.
> Q. And what was Anthony Salerno's response to this statement that you made to him?
> A. He said was Chicago satisfied with Roy. We said yes. He says: Well, okay, we'll go along.

. . . Lonardo also described how Salerno "lined up" support for Williams.

> Q. Did Salerno tell you he would line up delegates?
> A. He says he would get ahold of Sammy Provenzano and talk to him to start lining up the delegates.
> Q. Do you know what position if any Sammy Provenzano had with the Teamsters?
> A. International Vice president.

. . .

With the backing of these powerful La Cosa Nostra figures, Williams became the IBT's President in 1981, even though at the time of his election Williams was under federal indictment (along with defendant Joseph Lombardo, a notorious Chicago La Cosa Nostra figure) for conspiracy to bribe a public official, wire fraud and other offenses for his role in the Senator Cannon bribery scandal. Within two years, Williams and Lombardo had been convicted of those offenses, and Williams was forced to step down as Teamsters President. See United States v. Dorfman, et al., 81 Cr. 269 (N.D. Ill.), aff'd sub nom. United States v. Williams, 737 F.2d 594 (7th Cir. 1984), cert. denied, 470 U.S. 1003 (1985) . . .

Lonardo has also vividly described how, when Williams's corrupt tenure was about to end, La Cosa Nostra Bosses again colluded about the IBT's Presidency. The same La Cosa Nostra leaders who lined up IBT support to elect Williams used the same means to make defendant Jackie Presser the union's current President. Presser had the backing of Lonardo and other Cleveland Family representatives, who then convinced the Chicago Family Bosses (defendants Aiuppa and Cerone) to support Presser's candidacy.* Once again, Lonardo went to New York and met with defendant Salerno and others to obtain Salerno's support for Presser. Lonardo related the substance of that meeting:

Q. And can you tell us what your discussion was with Salerno on this occasion?

A. We had told him that we had been to Chicago and talked about Jackie Presser running for the president of the Teamsters Union if something should happen to Roy Williams. And we thought we should start getting ready with the delegates.

Q. And what, if anything, was Salerno's response?

A. He says that he would go along with Presser.

---

*Lonardo testified that the Chicago Family Bosses (Aiuppa and Cerone) originally preferred candidates other than Presser:

Q. Who did they have?

A. Ray Schlessinger [sic], Anderson from San Francisco, Morgan from Florida and they mentioned another fellow by the name of Peters.

Q. Did they describe their relationship with the people you just mentioned?

Q. Yes, that they were very close with them and they could control them.

. . . Defendants Joseph Morgan and Donald Peters are current IBT Vice Presidents. Ray Schoessling was, until recently, the IBT's Secretary-Treasurer; and M.E. Anderson was, until recently, an IBT Vice President.

Q. And do you know whether Jackie Presser became the president of the International Brotherhood of Teamsters?
A. After Roy Williams got convicted, yes, he did.

. . . Lonardo added that his Cleveland Family associate, defendant Milton Rockman, "would control" Presser. Rockman told Presser that he "could thank Chicago and New York and Angelo" for his new post as IBT President. Id at 1840.

Lonardo explained La Cosa Nostra's objectives in controlling IBT Presidents Roy Williams and Jackie Presser:

Q. Mr. Lonardo, what was the purpose for controlling Williams and Presser?
A. (Lonardo): So you could get favors done from him.
Q. What sort of favors, sir?
A. Well, if you wanted somebody appointed to the union, like a business agent, get charters.
Q. What sort of charters?
A. For membership
Q. For union charters?
A. Union charter, yes.
Q. What else?
A. Vending and skimming.
Q. Anything else?
A. To get favors from the central states pension fund.*

---

*Lonardo further testified that one such favor occurred when defendant Jackie Presser appointed defendant and current IBT Vice President Harold Friedman to high Teamsters office at the urging of Cleveland Family associate Milton Rockman.

Q. Do you know an individual by the name of Harold Friedman?
A. Yes, I do.
Q. And what if any job did he obtain with the union?
A. Well, he got to be vice-president and joined council 41 underneath Jackie Presser.
Q. And did you have any conversations with Milton Rockman about Harold Friedman?
A. Well, he was going to recommend Harold Friedman, but Jackie Presser already had appointed him and Jackie told Maishe, he says, "I knew you were to recommend Harold for that job, that's why I put him in."

(continued...)

258

. . .

Lonardo's sworn testimony is corroborated by court-authorized electronic surveillance of conversations in which defendant Anthony Salerno . . . and his criminal confederates regularly discussed Jackie Presser and IBT affairs. . . .

For example, in a series of intercepted conversations on June 6, 1984, Salerno told La Cosa Nostra confederates that "I had Presser" elevated to higher Teamsters office, over the objections of "them guys in Chicago"--an apparent reference to the Chicago Family Bosses who originally opposed Presser's elevation to the Teamsters Presidency.* . . . Salerno then recounted how he once got his personal attorney, Roy Cohn, to convince a Cleveland newspaper to run a retraction of a story describing Presser as a government informant. . . . Of Presser, Salerno said, "Here I am, sticking up for the fucking guy," and, "All I ever did with this guy favors." . . . One of Salerno's crime family associates added about Presser, "You know, he knows things about so many people." . . .

Further evidence of Salerno's control over the selection of the IBT's President is found in a conversation intercepted on November 27, 1984. There, Salerno commented on the presidential aspirations of defendant Joseph "Joe T" Trerotola, who is currently the IBT's first Vice President. Salerno said that "Joe T. would like" to have "Jackie Presser's job." . . . Salerno added, however, that "Twice I voted him down," and "We ought to fuck him." . . . Salerno had the following conversation with defendant John Tronolone (a prominent Cleveland La Cosa Nostra figure):

> SALERNO: Now the other day I picked up the newspapers from Vegas. And ah, the Teamsters are getting rid of all their mortgages, all their, all their land, whatever they got to pay for the commercials (UI).**

---

*(...continued)
Q. And how do you know that, sir?
A. Maishe told me.

*In those same conversations, Salerno anticipated the reaction of the Chicago Family Bosses to a news report "that Jack Presser is a stool pigeon for the Government." . . . Salerno said: "I think these fuckin' Chicago guys are going to knock my brains in." Salerno told his crime family associates that he supported Presser because "I knew his old man"--former IBT Vice President William Presser--"like I know you."

**"(UI)" means that portion of the conversation was unintelligible.

TRONOLONE: Send for Maishe again. Tell him to come in, tell him to get that fuckin' (UI) cocksuckers (UI).

SALERNO: In other words, then other guys are all making money.

TRONOLONE: They sure are, aren't they? And I told him. I said, "This is a fucking shame," I says, "What went through wasn't that good. They went through a lot for us," I says, "and they ain't making nothing," I says. "And you just sit there, all you're doing is just, he didn't do anything," I says.

SALERNO: You see where this Joe T. would like his job.

TRONOLONE: Oh, I wondered why he used to go out with Jackie.

SALERNO: 'Cause if anything happens to Jackie Presser, he's next. He's the First Vice President. So he's in line for that job. Jackie Presser's job.

TRONOLONE: Uh hum.

SALERNO: Twice I voted him down.

TRONOLONE: That's why he wanted Schoessling's job [as IBT Secretary-Treasurer].

SALERNO: We ought to fuck him.

. . . Thus, in this conversation Salerno again confirmed La Cosa Nostra's prominent role in the selection of IBT Presidents.

These intercepted conversations also confirm Salerno's influence in filling vacancies in other top IBT posts. For example, in a May 9, 1984, conversation, Salerno was asked to select the successor to IBT Secretary-Treasurer Ray Schoessling, who was planning to resign. Prominent Cleveland La Cosa Nostra figure John Tronolone put it bluntly to Salerno: "You're going to name whoever you want to for [Schoessling's] job." . . .

The Teamsters' election process facilitates La Cosa Nostra control. IBT officers are elected at conventions held every five years--the maximum period permitted under the Landrum-Griffin Act. See IBT Const., Art. III, Sec. 1. . . . Delegates to the convention are selected almost exclusively from among Local union officers and business agents. See IBT Const., Art III, Sec. 5. Moreover, when the IBT Presidency is vacated during the five-year period between conventions (as occurred in 1981 when Frank Fitzsimmons died in office and in 1983 when Roy Williams was convicted while in office), the General Executive Board selects the new President, giving him the crucial advantage of incumbency at the next convention. See IBT Const., Art. VI, Sec. 8. Similarly, Vice Presidential vacancies are filled by appointment of the President, with the approval of a majority of the General Executive Board. See IBT Const., Art. VI, Sec. 1(a). Of the 16 current IBT Vice Presidents, 13 first came to office through this appointment procedure, and the three remaining Vice Presidents ran with the incumbent slate at conventions at which the IBT's General Executive Board was expanded to create new Vice Presidential slots for them. Thus, La Cosa Nostra's influence over the top IBT leadership and the officers of many major Local unions allows La Cosa Nostra to control the

Teamsters electoral process and install International Union officers without ever subjecting them to vote by the full membership. . . .

D. Racketeering Activity Conducted Through the IBT

The Government's successful prosecutions of Teamsters officials and La Cosa Nostra figures have exposed rampant labor racketeering, extortion, embezzlement, bribery and other corrupt activities conducted by La Cosa Nostra through its instrument, the IBT. In recent years, the Government has successfully prosecuted literally hundreds of defendants associated with the Teamsters, many as IBT officers, agents or employees. . . . Those prosecuted have included many of the Teamsters' highest-ranking officers. Among the IBT General Executive Board members who have been convicted of Teamsters-related crimes are: defendant Maurice Schurr,* who, incredibly, remains an International Union Vice President to this day; defendant Salvatore Provenzano, who, until recently, was an International Union Vice President; defendant Anthony Provenzano, who, like his brother Salvatore, was also an International Union Vice President; and former IBT Presidents James Hoffa and Roy Williams. . . . In addition, three of the last five Teamsters Presidents (David Beck, James Hoffa and Roy Williams) have been convicted of federal felony offenses,** and current IBT President Jackie Presser awaits trial on

---

*After being convicted of conspiracy (18 U.S.C. §371) and receiving illegal payments as a union official from an employer (29 U.S.C. §186), Schurr was sentenced in 1984 to a six-month term of incarceration for conspiracy and a two-year suspended sentence and term of probation for receipt of payments by a union official, with the term of probation to begin after Schurr's release from incarceration. In addition to the probation and incarceration, Schurr was fined $10,000. On November 3, 1986, Schurr reported to Allenwood Federal Prison Camp in Montgomery, Pennsylvania, to serve his prison term. That same year, Schurr was reelected an International Union Vice President, along with all of the other incumbent IBT General Executive Board members, who ran with and supported Schurr for reelection.

**David Beck, who served as IBT President from 1952 to 1958, was convicted of federal income tax and labor offenses. James Hoffa, who served as IBT President from 1958 to 1971, was convicted of obstruction of justice and, in a separate case, of mail fraud, wire fraud and conspiracy involving a scheme to defraud the Teamsters Central States Pension Fund. See Hoffa v. United States, 385 U.S. 293 (1966); Hoffa v. United States, 436 F.2d 1243 (7th Cir. 1970), cert. denied, 400 U.S. 1000 91971). Roy Williams, who served as IBT

(continued...)

federal felony charges for labor racketeering involving Teamsters Local 507 in Cleveland, Ohio. See United States v. Presser, 86 Cr. 114 (N.D. Ohio). . . .

1. Extortion of Businesses Through the IBT

In several recent cases the Government has obtained convictions against IBT officials and La Cosa Nostra figures for their involvement in labor extortion schemes. Proof amassed by federal and state prosecutors has revealed labor racketeering in the air freight, waste carting, construction, moving and trucking industries. The evidence in these criminal cases shows how La Cosa Nostra Families, operating through IBT Locals, use these unions to threaten businesses and to extort money.

For example, in two recent criminal RICO trials in this district, United States v. Salerno, 85 Cr. 139 (RO), and United States v. Salerno, 86 Cr. 245 (MJL), the Government showed that the Commission of La Cosa Nostra and the Genovese Family punished recalcitrant concrete contractors by threatening that IBT Local 282 and other unions would disrupt ongoing work unless those businesses met the extortionate demands of La Cosa Nostra. . . . Members of IBT Local 282 transport ready-mix concrete and other construction materials to job sites. . . .

Federal juries have also convicted La Cosa Nostra figures of using other IBT Locals in schemes to maintain La Cosa Nostra cartels in particular industries. In United States v. Rastelli, 85 Cr. 00354 (E.D.N.Y.), a jury found that defendant Philip Rastelli, Boss of the Bonanno Family, controlled "the officials and affairs of Teamsters Local 814." . . . Defendant Rastelli and others (including all of IBT Local 814's top officers) were found to have threatened a number of moving and storage companies with labor disruption through IBT Local 814 in order to operate a bid-rigging and market division scheme. The Bonanno Family had interests in certain moving companies in the New York metropolitan area and used the threat of labor problems created by IBT Local 814 to prevent other companies from competing with the criminally-controlled companies.*

**(...continued)
President from 1981 to 1983, was convicted of conspiracy to bribe a public official and other offenses. See United States v. Williams, 737 F.2d 594 (7th Cir. 1984). cert. denied, 470 U.S. 1003 (1985).

*In related civil RICO action brought by the Government, Teamsters Local 814 has been put under the supervision of a court-appointed trustee. See United
(continued...)

In another example of La Cosa Nostra corruption of the Teamsters, Luchese Family defendant Frank Manzo and others (including a local Teamsters official) were convicted of criminal RICO charges stemming from a labor peace scheme operated at John F. Kennedy International Airport through IBT Locals 295 and 851.* See United States v. Santoro, 85 Cr. 100 (E.D.N.Y.). . . .

Finally, high-ranking IBT officials have themselves used their IBT positions to threaten employers and to extort money in exchange for labor peace. For example, in 1984, defendant Maurice Schurr, a current IBT Vice President, was convicted of selling labor peace to employers of IBT Local 929 labor in Philadelphia, Pennsylvania. See United States v. Schurr, 775 F.2d at 551-52. . . .

2. Benefit Fund Abuse

La Cosa Nostra figures have used their control over the IBT to secure loans for the purchase and construction of Las Vegas casinos. Successful criminal prosecutions of cash skimming operations at the casinos have exposed these improper loans and La Cosa Nostra's easy access to Teamsters benefit funds.

For example, in United States v. DeLuna, et al., 83 Cr. 124 (W.D. Mo.), . . . defendants Joseph John Aiuppa, John Phillip Cerone, Joseph Lombardo, Frank Balistrieri, Carl DeLuna, Carl Civella, Milton Rockman and other La Cosa Nostra figures were convicted of criminal offenses in connection with the unlawful skimming of more than $2 million from Las Vegas casinos, including the Stardust and Fremont Hotels. . . . The purchase and construction of these casinos were funded by a $62.5-million loan from the Teamsters Central States Pension Fund.** The skimming operation represented the combined efforts of

---

*(...continued)

States v. Bonanno Organized Crime Family, 87 Civ. 2974 (ILG) (E.D.N.Y.). . . .

*Manzo pleaded guilty to criminal RICO charges. Co-defendant Frank Calise, the President of Teamster Local 295, pleaded guilty to a criminal RICO charge as well. Co-defendant Harry Davidoff, the Vice President of Teamsters Local 851, was convicted after trial of criminal RICO and extortion charges. However, Davidoff's conviction was reversed on appeal on the ground that the district court erred in denying Davidoff's request for a bill of particulars. See United States v. Davidoff, No. 86-1523 (2d Cir. April 20, 1988).

**. . . Two other cases involved related schemes. . . . La Cosa Nostra associates were convicted of unlawfully skimming profits from the Las Vegas Tropicana Casino. The evidence there also showed that the defendants were

(continued...)

the Milwaukee, Chicago, Cleveland and Kansas City Families, which shared the skim money. The evidence in the case showed La Cosa Nostra's domination of the Teamsters Central States Pension Fund and the complicity of several prominent IBT officials in facilitating this skimming scheme. . . .

The Teamsters Central States Pension Fund has repeatedly been the victim of its supposed fiduciaries and service providers. Allen Dorfman, the asset manager of the Pension Fund, was convicted of receiving kickbacks in connection with a Pension Fund loan.* See United States v. Dorfman, 470 F.2d 246 (2d Cir. 1972), cert. dismissed, 411 U.S. 923 (1973). Dorfman's successor, Alvin Baron, was also convicted of accepting kickbacks in connection with a Pension Fund Loan. See United States v. Baron, 602 F.2d 1248 (7th Cir.), cert, denied, 444 U.S. 967 (1979). See also United States v. Webbe, 558 F. Supp. 55 (D. Nev. 1983), aff'd, 755 F.2d 1387 (9th Cir. 1985) (fund employee convicted of failing to report kickbacks received in connection with Central States Pension Fund loan to Aladdin Casino). In Donovan v. Fitzsimmons, 78 Civ. 342 (N.D. Ill.), the Secretary of Labor brought suit to protect the Central States Pension Fund from fiduciary breaches. Pursuant to a consent decree entered in 1982, an Independent Special Counsel was appointed to oversee the operations of the Central States Pension Fund.**

---

*(...continued)
able to insure that uncooperative casino owners did not receive loans from the Teamsters Central States Pension Fund. Similarly, in United States v. Goldfarb, 643 F.2d 422 (6th Cir.), cert. denied, 454 U.S. 827 (1981), the defendants were convicted of crimes involving the maintenance of a hidden interest in the Las Vegas Aladdin Casino through a loan from the Teamsters Central States Pension Fund.

*In 1983, Dorfman was gunned down in a parking lot in Lincolnwood, Illinois. . . . Dorfman's murder took place one month after a federal jury found him guilty, along with then IBT President Roy Williams, Chicago La Cosa Nostra figure Joseph Lombardo and others, of conspiring to bribe Senator Howard Cannon. . . .

**In that same case, on November 10, 1987, United States District Judge James B. Moran of the Northern District of Illinois entered a consent decree requiring former trustees of the Central States Pension Fund (including defendants Jackie Presser, Robert Holmes, Joseph Morgan and Donald Peters, former IBT President Roy Williams, and the estate of former IBT President Frank Fitzsimmons) to pay $175,000 to the Fund out of their personal assets and requiring their fiduciary liability insurer to pay $3.85 million to the Fund.

The Teamsters Central States Health and Welfare Fund has also been the victim of extensive abuse. Even after his 1972 felony conviction, Allen Dorfman remained under contract to provide services to the Health and Welfare Fund. In United States v. O'Malley, 84 Cr. 825 (N.D. Ill.), a Health and Welfare Fund Trustee was convicted of soliciting kickbacks from Dorfman. . . .

3. Extortion and Fraud of the IBT Membership

A primary victim of this racketeering activity has been the union membership itself. La Cosa Nostra's open and notorious domination of many Teamsters operations (such as Local 560) has forced union members to live in fear and to forego the rights guaranteed them under the Labor-Management Reporting and Disclosure Act (hereinafter, "LMRDA") and other federal labor laws. . . .

(a) Violence and Intimidation. The Government has proven in several recent prosecutions that union members' rights have been systematically abused, betrayed and extorted. The proof in those cases has established that, in exchange for employer payoffs, La Cosa Nostra figures and the Teamsters officials whom they control eagerly sell out the union membership's rights. Moreover, La Cosa Nostra maintains control over the union membership and curbs protest through a campaign of intimidation and violence. Indeed, in its complaint in this action, the Government cites more than a dozen murders of Teamsters dissidents or persons prepared to testify about Teamsters corruption. . . .

In United States v. Local 560, . . . the court granted the Government's request to put IBT Local 560 into trusteeship because that Local had been captured and controlled by the Provenzano faction of the Genovese Family. . . . The evidence showed that the Provenzanos and their cohorts conducted a campaign of violence, murder and threats of physical and economic injury against Local 560 members in order to bludgeon them into submission and to extinguish all challenges to the Provenzanos. For example, in April 1961, defendant Anthony Provenzano recruited two men to kill Anthony Castellitto, a Local 560 member who opposed Provenzano's union leadership. On June 6, 1961, Castellitto was murdered. Anthony Provenzano was later sentenced to life imprisonment for his part in the murder of Castellitto.* See People of New York v. Provenzano, 79 a.D.2d 811, 435 N.Y.S.2d 369 (3d Dep't 1980).

---

*A similar incident occurred in May 1963 when Walter Glockner, another Local 560 member who opposed the Provenzanos, was murdered the morning following a dispute with defendant Salvatore Provenzano. . . .

Discussing the Castellitto murder, United States District Judge Harold Ackerman wrote in 1984:

[T]he disappearance [of Castellitto] generated a perception among the membership that anyone who represented an actual or potential threat to the Provenzano Group's dominance and control over Local 560 ran the risk of physical injury. The nature and intensity of that perception has been such that it survives to the present day.

. . . Having cowed union members into abandoning control over the affairs of their own Local, the Provenzano group used IBT Local 560 for its own purposes--embezzling money, appointing convicted criminals to official union jobs and extorting money from employers. . . .

The Government proved a . . . sell-out of union members' rights in United States v. Boffa, et al., 80 Cr. 36 (D. Del.), aff'd in pertinent part, 688 F.2d 919 (3d Cir. 1982). cert. denied, 460 U.S. 1022 (1983), and United States v. Sheeran, 80 Cr. 36 (D. Del.), aff'd in pertinent part, 699 F.2d 112 (3d Cir.), cert. denied, 461 U.S. 931 (1983). Defendant Eugene Boffa, an associate of the Bufalino Family, and defendant Frank Sheeran, then President of the IBT Local 326 in Wilmington, Delaware, were convicted of inducing trucking companies to fire Teamsters members and hire workers from Boffa's labor-leasing service. . . . Boffa bought Sheeran's cooperation by giving him payoffs and by selling him a Lincoln Continental at below market price. As a result of these labor switches, Teamsters members lost jobs and benefits due them under collective bargaining agreements. La Cosa Nostra thus deprived the IBT membership of union jobs and benefits by bribing corrupt local union officials. . . .*

IBT officials . . . have approved the direct use of such violence to maintain their power. For example, in October 1983, an organized dissident group known as Teamsters for a Democratic Union ("TDU") met in Michigan to air its grievances against the union's current leadership. The TDU meeting was literally overrun by another Teamsters group, the Brotherhood of Loyal Americans and Strong Teamster ("BLAST"), which supported the incumbent IBT leadership. BLAST members violently disrupted the TDU meeting and had to be forcibly restrained by law enforcement authorities. National Labor Relations Board records show that the BLAST participants in the raid included approximately 20 officers of IBT local unions. . . . After that disgraceful

---

*Subsequent investigative efforts have disclosed the national scope of Boffa's labor-leasing scheme, which involved Teamsters Locals throughout the country. . . .

incident, current IBT President Jackie Presser praised the BLAST participants in comments to union officials in Cleveland, Ohio. Presser said:

> I know all about the BLAST program taking place in Michigan. I must have gotten a hundred calls. I know exactly what happened there. I was pleased to see that there are Teamsters who want to stop all of that crap. . . . The thing that affected me the most about last Sunday in Detroit, Michigan, was that there were a lot of guys there, I got the pictures of who was there. . . . [Y]ou know who was in the front line of a real wild fight with state highway patrolmen and police there? The Secretary/Treasurer of our Joint Council, Bill Evans, who's had two heart attacks. . . . Bill, I want to tell you, you're a hell of a guy to take it on yourself. I would have been there, but I'm not you. . . . I'm going to tell you something. We should be doing more of that. I'm going to tell you, I'm not going to let up on these people.

. . .

. . . [E]vidence of the use of violence against IBT members comes from the testimony of . . . henchmen who served La Cosa Nostra. Charles Allen, a self-confessed killer and "strong arm" man who worked for IBT and La Cosa Nostra figures such as defendants Frank Sheeran and Anthony Provenzano, has graphically described his role in maintaining mob control over the IBT membership. In 1982 testimony before the Senate Permanent Subcommittee on Investigations, Allen explained his relationship with Sheeran (then president of Teamsters Local 326 in Wilmington, Delaware) and other labor officials:

> SEN. RUDMAN: What was your job, your responsibility, what were you supposed to do? What was your job?
> MR. ALLEN: I actually did anything I was told to do, from murder to selling drugs, from extortion to beating up people, hijacking, whatever they told me to do, I did.
> SEN. RUDMAN: And as a matter of fact, by your testimony, you would do what was asked of you?
> MR. ALLEN: Yes.
> SEN. RUDMAN: So that if it looked like some legitimate union or a person were going to move into the leadership position in the union and you were told to go down and make sure they were discouraged or something like that, you would do that?
> MR. ALLEN: Yes.
> SEN. RUDMAN: Including beating up people?
> MR. ALLEN: Yes.
> SEN RUDMAN: Including murdering people?
> MR. ALLEN: Yes, sir.
> SEN. ROTH: How were they able to assert this influence? Why didn't anybody run against their chosen candidates?

MR. ALLEN: Take Frank Sheeran in Delaware. When anybody was going to run against him, myself and a few other guys would go down and give them a lot of trouble, if not beat the hell out of them, and we discouraged them. At union meetings, we would go there and not let anybody talk except for Sheeran, and we let everybody know we were with Frank Sheeran and if anybody was against him, they would get hurt.

SEN. ROTH: So there was the threat of physical violence, if you ran against the candidates chosen by the "family?"

MR. ALLEN: That is true.

. . . Allen also made this pointed observation during his testimony:

SEN ROTH: . . . [T]he historical record shows that once organized crime takes over a union, it never withdraws, that it is able to maintain its influence indefinitely. Is this true, in your personal observation?

MR. ALLEN: That is the absolute truth, yes, sir.

SEN. ROTH: What can be done by the law enforcement officials or Congress to change this? Do you have any recommendation or recommendations?

MR. ALLEN: Probably not a damn thing, Senator. See, money is a hell of a thing. Once they see that money coming in, it is hard to put down, believe me.

. . .

La Cosa Nostra's threats of violence and intimidation reach the Teamsters' highest levels. Former IBT President Roy Williams has testified that both of his two immediate predecessors, James Hoffa and Frank Fitzsimmons, lived in fear of La Cosa Nostra figures, especially from the Detroit Family. . . . Moreover, Williams has admitted that "I was controlled by Nick" Civella, the Kansas City Family Boss, "[a]nd when he threatened me, why, that's when I became his boy." . . . In addition, defendant Jackie Presser, the IBT's current President, once described that office as an "electric chair" and a "death chair." . . . Presser added:

[I]f you're totally honest and if you try to clean up the union like you say I should, and you try to do it fast enough and without making accommodations so the government won't get you, the other guys--the hoods--will get you. . . . So that's a death chair either way.

. . .

(c) *Failure to Remedy IBT Corruption.* Many current or former Teamsters International Union officers have already been convicted or indicted for crimes related to their union activities. . . .

Indeed, since approximately 1970, the Government has convicted more than 300 persons associated with the Teamsters (including many union officials) for Teamsters-related crimes. . . . Those convicted criminals include several other current International Union officials, including International Representatives Rolland McMaster (convicted of receiving illegal labor payments from an employer, . . . Charles "Chuckie" O'Brien (convicted of receiving illegal labor payments from an employee and making false statements on a loan application), . . . and George Vitale (convicted of receiving illegal labor payments from a Teamsters employer and embezzlement of union funds). . . .

Just as telling as these overt acts of corruption has been the IBT leadership's reaction--or lack thereof--to this deplorable situation. In response to the rampant corruption within the IBT, the Teamsters' General Executive Board members have literally done nothing, despite their affirmative obligation under federal law and the IBT's Constitution to rid the union of corruption. The IBT Constitution expressly grants the President and the General Executive Board authority to expel corrupt members and to impose trusteeships on corrupted Local unions or other subordinate bodies. As a matter of law, an adverse inference can be drawn from the union leadership's failure to act in the fact of this persistent pattern of illegal conduct affecting the IBT. As the Third Circuit explained in the Local 560 case, "if an individual fails to act when he has an affirmative duty to do so, negative inferences concerning his intent can be drawn from this inaction." . . . Indeed, because of the "elevated duty of care owed to union members by their officers," the Local 560 court drew just such a negative inference from the inaction of the Teamsters officials there and ruled that those officials had "aided and abetted" acts of racketeering. . . .

(d) *Appointing Persons with Criminal Records to Union Office and Associating with Known Criminals.* Neither indictments nor convictions have deterred the current IBT leadership from supporting persons with criminal records for prominent union offices and from associating with criminals who do not hold official union positions. Indeed, more than 35 persons who hold or have held International Union office since 1970 have been convicted, indicted or otherwise publicly cited for improper activity before and/or during their tenures in office. . . . Those individuals include 25 current International Union officials, 10 of the 18 current General Executive Board members . . . three former IBT Presidents . . . and three former IBT Vice Presidents. . . . Indeed, almost 50 percent of the persons who have served on the IBT General Executive Board since 1970 fall within this category. . . .

Appointments to IBT office of persons with criminal records is a common occurrence. For example, in or about 1983, defendant Jackie Presser appointed defendant Harold Friedman, a Cleveland Teamsters official who had previously been convicted of a felony offense, to fill a vacancy as a Vice President on the International Union's General Executive Board. Similarly, in or about 1985,

Presser appointed defendant Theodore Cozza, who also has a felony record, to fill another vacancy as a Vice President on the International Union's General Executive Board.

The evidence of racketeering activity presented in the Government's successful prosecutions and before the President's Commission on Organized Crime chronicles notorious associations between the IBT leadership and La Cosa Nostra figures. Kansas City Boss Nicholas Civella's payoffs to former IBT President Roy Williams are a matter of public record, admitted by Williams himself. . . . Moreover, the Government has already proven the Bonanno Family's control over IBT Local 814, the Genovese Family's capture of IBT Local 560, the Luchese Family's control over IBT Locals 295 and 851, the Bufalino Family's domination of IBT Local 326, and Genovese Family infiltration of IBT Local 282. . . . The extent of La Cosa Nostra's influence over the IBT is further illustrated by the substantial evidence of defendant Salerno's role, together with other La Cosa Nostra chieftains, in installing Williams and defendant Presser as the IBT's last two Presidents. . . .

The IBT leadership's support of criminals for union office and association with La Cosa Nostra figures serves to extort the membership's rights. As the Third Circuit observed in United States v. Local 560, the open association of Teamsters leaders with La Cosa Nostra figures undoubtedly coerced the members from exercising "their right to democratic participation in the affairs of the union." 780 F.2d at 286. The Local 560 court further found "the repeated appointments to union office . . . of known or reputed criminals" to be evidence of extortion of the membership's LMRDA rights in violation of the Hobbs Act. . . .

The evidence already assembled by the Government goes far beyond isolated instances of Teamsters corruption. The numerous investigations, and the resulting successful prosecutions of IBT officials and La Cosa Nostra figures, vividly document the existence and operations of a national criminal cartel. The Teamsters Union has served as a principal instrument of La Cosa Nostra's infiltration into widely dispersed sectors of the national economy. La Cosa Nostra's control over IBT labor and access to IBT funds enable La Cosa Nostra to commit extortion, embezzlement, bribery, fraud and other acts of racketeering. The Government now asks this Court to use RICO's broad remedial provisions to end La Cosa Nostra's tyranny over the IBT, and to bar corrupt individuals from the union.

II. Argument

The Government is Entitled Under 18 U.S.C. §1964(b) to the Preliminary Relief Sought in This Motion

. . .

The preliminary relief now sought by the Government is narrowly drawn to address the immediate and pressing problem of Teamsters corruption fostered by La Cosa Nostra and unremedied by the IBT leadership. More specifically, the Government now seeks: (i) the appointment of a temporary court liaison officer to prevent racketeering activity within the IBT and to review certain actions of the IBT's General Executive Board during the pendency of this litigation; (ii) preliminary injunctions barring current IBT officers from engaging in racketeering and from interfering in any way with the court liaison officer's duties; and (iii) preliminary injunctions barring La Cosa Nostra figures from participating in union affairs.

A. The RICO Statute Empowers the Court to Grant Sweeping Equitable Relief to Protect the Public Interest

1. The Statute and Its History
The RICO statute prohibits the following activities:

(b) It shall be unlawful for any person through a pattern of racketeering activity or through collection of an unlawful debt to acquire or maintain, directly or indirectly, any interest in or control of any enterprise which is engaged in, or the activities of which affect, interstate or foreign commerce.

(c) It shall be unlawful for any person employed by or associated with any enterprise engaged in, or the activities of which affect, interstate or foreign commerce, to conduct or participate, directly or indirectly, in the conduct of such enterprise's affairs through a pattern of racketeering activity or collection of unlawful debt.

(d) It shall be unlawful for any person to conspire to violate any of the provisions of subsections (a), (b), or (c) of this section.

. . . A "'pattern of racketeering activity' requires at least two acts of racketeering activity."* . . .

In this case, the Government presents four separate claims for RICO relief. First, the Government alleges that the defendants have acquired and maintained control of the IBT through a pattern of racketeering activity. . . . Second, the Government alleges that, having gained control over the IBT, the defendants have participated in the conduct of the IBT's affairs through a pattern of racketeering activity. . . . Finally, the Government alleges that the defendants have conspired to violate each of those two provisions. . . .

The RICO statute's civil remedies provisions expressly state that a defendant's RICO convictions have collateral estoppel effect in a subsequent civil RICO action:

> A final judgment or decree rendered in favor of the United States in any criminal proceeding brought by the United States under [RICO] shall stop the defendant from denying the essential allegations of the criminal offense in any subsequent civil proceeding brought by the United States.

. . . In this action, the La Cosa Nostra defendants cannot deny the essential allegations of their RICO violations because they have already been convicted of RICO and other offenses relating to the Teamsters. In light of those

---

*"Racketeering activity," as defined in Section 1961 of the RICO statute, includes the following crimes:

> (a) any act or threat involving murder, kidnapping, gambling, arson, robbery, bribery, extortion, or dealing in narcotic or other dangerous drugs, which is chargeable under State law and punishable by imprisonment for more than one year; (b) any act which is indictable under any of the following provisions of Title 18, United States Code: Section 201 (relating to bribery), . . . section 664 (relating to embezzlement from pension and welfare funds), . . . section 1341 (relating to mail fraud), section 1343 (relating to wire fraud), . . . section 1503 (relating to obstruction of justice), . . . section 1951 (relating to interference with commerce, robbery, or extortion), section 1952 (relating to racketeering), . . . section 1954 (relating to unlawful welfare fund payments), . . . (c) any act which is indictable under title 29, United States Code, section 186 (dealing with restrictions on payments and loans to labor organizations) or section 501(c) (relating to embezzlement from union funds) . . .

convictions (and the factual findings they embody), this Court must now decide what equitable relief to impose . . . to protect the union membership, affected businesses and the public from continued racketeering involving the Teamsters.

The civil RICO statute provides for an extremely broad range of equitable remedies to prevent and restrain violations. . . .

(a) The district courts of the United States shall have jurisdiction to prevent and restrain violations of section 1962 of this chapter by issuing appropriate orders, including, but not limited to: ordering any person to divest himself of any interest, direct or indirect, in any enterprise; imposing reasonable restrictions on the future activities or investments of any person, including, but not limited to, prohibiting any person from engaging in the same type of endeavor as the enterprise engaged in, the activities of which affect interstate or foreign commerce; or ordering dissolution or reorganization of any enterprise, making due provisions for the rights of innocent persons.

(b) The Attorney General may institute proceedings under this section. . . . Pending final determination thereof, the court may at any time enter such restraining orders or prohibitions, or take such other actions, including the acceptance of satisfactory performance bonds, as it shall deem proper.

. . . [T]hus, 18 U.S.C. §1964(b) expressly authorizes a court to employ before final judgment such remedies "as it shall deem proper" to protect the public interest.

The "RICO statute was intended to provide new weapons of unprecedented scope for an assault upon organized crime and its economic roots." . . . Indeed, in discussing the RICO statute, Senator Hruska, one of the bill's sponsors, emphasized that RICO was aimed at "striking a mortal blow against the property interests of organized crime." . . .

The Senate Judiciary Committee's Report on the RICO statute specifically addressed the problem of La Cosa Nostra's influence over labor unions in several industries, including the trucking business:

Closely paralleling its takeover of legitimate business, organized crime has moved into legitimate unions. Control of labor supply through control of unions . . . provides the opportunity for theft from union funds, extortion through the threat of economic pressure, and the profit to be gained from the manipulation of welfare and pension funds and insurance contracts. Trucking, construction, and waterfront entrepreneurs have been persuaded for labor peace to countenance gambling, loan sharking and pilferage. As the takeover of organized crime cannot be tolerated in legitimate business, so, too, it cannot be tolerated here.

. . .
The legislative history further clarifies the breadth of the civil remedies available under RICO:

> Where an organization is acquired or run by defined racketeering methods, then the persons involved can be legally separated from the organization, either by the criminal law approach . . . or through a <u>civil law approach of equitable relief broad enough to do all that is necessary to free the channels of commerce from all illicit activity.</u>

. . . The Senate Report added that:

> [T]hrough a remedy such as the prohibition of engaging in the same kind of activity in the future, the criminal element will not only be removed from an area of activity, they will also be prohibited from using the know how acquired to start the same type of business or other organization again under a different name.

. . .
The breadth of RICO's civil remedies is also evident when RICO and the Organized Crime Control Act of 1970 are read as a whole. The statute provides that "[t]he provisions of this title shall be liberally construed to effectuate its remedial purposes," Pub. L. 91-452, §904(a), 84 Stat. 947--a directive which is apparently unique in the entire body of substantive federal criminal law. . . . Moreover, in its statement of findings and purpose for the Organized Crime Control Act, Congress declared:

> It is the purpose of this Act to seek the eradication of organized crime in the United States . . . by providing enhanced sanctions and new remedies to deal with the unlawful activities of those engaged in organized crime.

. . . The Supreme Court has repeatedly recognized the significance of this statement of findings and purpose in holding that RICO is to be broadly applied and liberally construed. . . . Indeed, the Supreme Court has expressly held that "if Congress' liberal-construction mandate is to be applied anywhere, it is in §1964 [the civil remedies section], where RICO's remedial purposes are most evident." . . .

2. Standard for Granting This Equitable Relief

Where, as here, the Government seeks an injunction pursuant to federal statute, the court's role is to effectuate the legislative intent through vigilant enforcement of the statute. As the United States Court of Appeals in this Circuit has explained:

[T]he function of a court in deciding whether to issue an injunction authorized by a statute of the United States to enforce and implement Congressional policy is a different one from that of the court when weighing claims of two private "litigants." . . . [T]he legislative goals are the framework within which the court operates in deciding whether to grant injunctive relief.

. . . Other courts have similarly recognized that injunctions must be issued if necessary to effectuate the legislative intent. . . .

The standard for issuance of a preliminary injunction sought by the Government in a civil RICO action was squarely addressed by this Court in United States v. Ianniello, 646 F.Supp. 1289 (S.D.N.Y. 1986), aff'd, 824 F.2d 203 (2d Cir. 1987). In granting the Government's motion for appointment of a receiver pendente lite for a restaurant controlled by racketeers, Judge Haight found the Government's demonstration of likely success on the merits a sufficient basis for granting the requested relief. No further showing was necessary because the civil RICO statute authorizes entry of equitable relief "'without any requirement of a showing of irreparable injury other than that injury to the public which Congress found to be inherent in the conduct made unlawful by section 1962.'" . . .

The standard applied in the Ianniello case is similar to that followed when the Government acts under other statutes, such as the antitrust laws,* which expressly authorize equitable relief to protect the public interest. In such cases the primary consideration for issuance of a preliminary injunction sought by the Government is "whether the Government has shown a reasonable likelihood of success on the merits." . . .

Congress specifically intended RICO to provide the courts with "the full panoply of civil remedies . . . now available in the antitrust area." S.Rep. No. 91-617 at 81. Congress did not, however, want the courts to impose the same restrictions on civil RICO suits that have developed under the antitrust laws. . . . Indeed, the civil RICO statute authorizes remedies broader than those that the antitrust laws allow so that courts can deal effectively with organized crime. . . .

3. Specific Equitable Remedies Available Under the RICO Statute

In seven leading civil RICO cases brought by the Government, courts have emphasized the breadth of both the preliminary and permanent equitable relief available under 18 U.S.C. §1964. See United States v. Ianniello, 824 F.2d 203

---

*The Clayton Act, like RICO, expressly allows the Government to obtain both preliminary and permanent injunctive relief to prevent violations of the act's substantive provisions. . . .

(2d Cir. 1987); United States v. Local 560, International Brotherhood of Teamsters, 780 F.2d 267 (3d Cir. 1985), . . . United States v. Cappetto, 502 F.2d 1351 (7th Cir. 1974), . . . United States v. Local 6A, Cement & Concrete Workers, 663 F. Supp. 192 (S.D.N.Y. 1986); United States v. Local 359, United Seafood Workers, Smoked Fish & Cannery Union, 87 Civ. 7351 (TPG) (S.D.N.Y.); United States v. The Bonanno Organized Crime Family of La Cosa Nostra, 87 Civ. 2974 (ILG) (E.D.N.Y.); United States v. Local 30, United Slate, Tile and Composition Roofers, 87 Civ. 7718 (LB) (E./D. Pa.).

. . . RICO's civil remedies are broad enough to authorize both the preliminary relief and the permanent injunctions which the Government seeks in this action. Because the Court indisputably has this authority, the Court need only determine at this point whether it has an adequate factual basis to grant the preliminary relief sought by the Government and whether such relief is appropriate. Under the facts of this case, the preliminary relief sought by the Government is not only proper but also necessary to prevent future illegal conduct affecting the IBT. . . .

The Government comes before this Court having convicted members of the ruling Commission of La Cosa Nostra, bosses of numerous La Cosa Nostra Families, other La Cosa Nostra figures and high-ranking Teamsters officials of RICO violations and other crimes relating to the Teamsters. There is absolutely no reason to believe that the unlawful conduct of these defendants has ceased or will diminish in any way without prompt and effective injunctive relief from this Court. Under these circumstances, the Court should appoint a temporary court liaison officer to prevent racketeering activity within the IBT during the pendency of this action, enjoin the IBT's current officers from engaging in racketeering and from interfering with the court liaison officer, and enjoin the La Cosa Nostra defendants from any participation in the affairs of the IBT or any other labor organization during the pendency of this action.

Conclusion

For the foregoing reasons, this Court should grant the Government's motion for preliminary relief in all respects.

About the Book and Editor

Members of organized crime syndicates have gained control of key businesses and trade unions through their strategic positions as arbiters of labor-management conflicts and as dispensers of illegal credit. They are managing important sectors of the contemporary marketplace, engaging in activities far more significant than the vice enterprises usually associated with criminal activity.

Difficult to access for scholarly study, organized crime is best documented in judicial findings and in legislative reports from criminal investigations and public hearings. In this book, Alan Block has assembled a rich cross section of these reports. Taken together, they illustrate how organized crime has infiltrated important industries and taken control of union pension and welfare funds. Designed for students of criminology, sociology, and deviance, the book provides a comprehensive overview of the business of crime in America today.

Alan A. Block is professor of administration of justice at The Pennsylvania State University.

Index

288